Inside the Treasure House

Inside the Treasure House

A TIME IN TIBET

CATRIONA BASS

LONDON
VICTOR GOLLANCZ LTD
1990

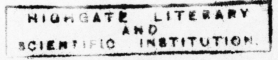

First published in Great Britain 1990
by Victor Gollancz Ltd
14 Henrietta Street, London WC2E 8QJ

British Library Cataloguing in Publication Data
Bass, Catriona
 Inside the treasure house.
 1. Tibet. Social life
 I. Title
 951.5058

ISBN 0-575-04390-3

Photoset in Great Britain by
Rowland Phototypesetting Ltd, Bury St Edmunds, Suffolk
and printed by St Edmundsbury Press Ltd,
Bury St Edmunds, Suffolk
Illustrations printed by BAS Printers Ltd,
Over Wallop, Hants

CONTENTS

ILLUSTRATIONS

Monlam. Monks announcing the start of a ceremony with the echoing call of the conch

Facing page 128

Awaiting the Panchen Lama's appearance on the roof of the Jokhang
The Panchen Lama appears

Facing page 129

Yerpa Valley with the prayer, *Om Mani Padme Hum*, embossed across its slopes

Facing page 160

Yerpa. Heads of Buddhas rescued from the rubble and placed on a mound of earth
A nomad with her child

Facing page 161

A picnic tent
The author and Rosemary preparing for a picnic
A school bus near Samye

The original Tibetan regions of Amdo and Kham have been partly absorbed into the neighbouring Central Chinese provinces of Yunnan, Sichuan and Qinghai.

Author's route

ACKNOWLEDGEMENTS

The friends, family and advisers who have been involved in this book cannot help knowing how I have depended on their support – and exploited it at times.

PREFACE

I am not a good traveller. I get bad-tempered tracing the surface of an unknown country. It is true that some of my most exhilarating moments in Tibet were spent on journeys, but my book is not about travelling. It is about living in Lhasa.

"Write about us," several friends said when I left Tibet at the end of 1986. My book is about them, and me. Those particular friends had no political motive in urging me to write. At the time their lives were better than they could remember. After two decades in which they had been unable to do anything except focus on immediate animal survival, the Chinese government was making reforms. They could travel more freely, political control had been relaxed, and there was more religious freedom than they had known for twenty years. Although many people expressed anger at continuing inequities, these friends were cautiously optimistic.

If I had written this preface then, it might have reflected some of their optimism. They hoped that 1985 and 1986 would mark the beginning of a new era.

Nine months later police were shooting people in Lhasa. October 1987. *Violence flares in Tibet. Demonstrators chant pro-independence slogans. Six feared dead as protesters burn police station. Troops round up rebels.* It was the newspapers' standard fare. But for the first time in my life, people I knew were involved. I had no idea who might have taken part, who might have been imprisoned, tortured, or killed even. And I had no way of finding out. I could only imagine their terror – a terror which I knew Chinese friends would be feeling too.

"Write about us." I had been writing about them, but as the months passed, as Tibet fell prey to the clichés of the press, and then was dropped altogether, they became my main reason for writing. I thought of the tendency which all nations have to reduce others to a handful of adjectives. It was this, I was convinced, that was partly responsible for the enmity within Tibet, and for the indifference of many people outside.

As a foreigner without complete command of Tibetan or Chinese, there are certainly things of which I was unaware. But my experiences will at least give a glimpse of the people behind the images of desperation, violence and death.

PROLOGUE

Nyalam, Tibet. 20th October 1985

Shadows of giants are leaping at each other across the ornate beams. Like me they are confused by the swaying light-bulb – and keep dissolving.

Four Tibetan traders have entered. From my burrow of quilts I watch as they unload their bags at the far end of the room. Foxes are strewn across the bed, legs splayed, bodies rigid with cold or rudimentary curing. Over one side droops a bouquet of tails; over the other jut snouts.

Still swinging from the blast of their entrance, the light is glazed with breath and smoke. The men are smaller than their shadows. They have settled in a circle on a bed by the wall, legs crossed inside sheepskin robes, turquoise strung through their ear-lobes, burly plaits piled on their heads with amber rings and tassels of silk. Teeth which glint gold.

As hunks of meat are downed with tea, the scene flows into ceremonial drunkenness. An old man takes from his bosom a bowl made of wood with a lining of beaten silver. He smiles as another man fills it with *chang*, and his cheeks draw into a bow of wrinkles. Tracing a finger over this cloudy spirit, he tosses droplets into the air above his head, three times, in offering to the gods. Three times he sips and proffers the bowl to be refilled. Then serenaded drunkenly, hauntingly, melodiously, he downs the spirit in one.

October 1989: When I hear the word Tibet now, it resonates with the lives of friends, the lives of ordinary people in a repressive society. Yet occasionally the word can still catch me unawares. It plays a conjuring trick with my imagination, making it leap backwards through accretions of experience to this other Tibet, the embodiment of my childhood preconceptions.

A year before I went to Lhasa I was teaching in Wuhan in the Central Chinese province of Hubei. There my childhood image was challenged by the Chinese view of the place. The two images were irreconcilable. One was swathed in the romance of western nostalgia, the other in centuries of contempt. Tibet held no mystery for my students. Xizang, the Western Treasure House: Tibet's name in Chinese, was a Siberia to which the less favoured students were terrified of being sent. The Treasure House: it sounded romantic. But its treasure was Tibet's potential for agricultural production, and the rich mineral deposits beneath the soil. Tibetans were dirty and primitive, the students warned my colleague, Rosemary, and me. And they were hostile to outsiders.

When the *lingdao*, the leaders of the university where we were teaching, heard that we had written to the Tibetan authorities about working in Lhasa, they sent a delegation to our room to urge us not to go. They were genuinely concerned for our safety.

We ignored their advice. We'd signed contracts to teach at a truck factory in Shiyan in the north of Hubei Province and were planning to travel back through Tibet after a few months in England.

But until that night with the traders, we had found nothing to justify either Chinese or western preconceptions. Until that moment, Tibet had seemed neither primitive nor exotic: just filled with the frustrations of modern China.

"No permits for Tibet." The iron gate of the Chinese Embassy in Kathmandu shut. Again.

"Forget it!" An Australian who had joined us walked off. For two days we had been trying to get inside.

Rosemary burst out laughing. "Tea break?" she suggested, unwrapping a packet of Indian biscuits and squatting on her haunches in the dust. This was why we got on so well, I suppose. We shared a streak of perversity, or naïvety perhaps, which seemed, as it did now, to prevent us from accepting reality. Rosemary could persuade anyone that there was sense in the most hare-brained schemes. I thought of the first time I met her, a slight, almost child-like figure charming the phalanx of officials at Moscow airport into giving me a temporary visa. Having arrived together for a three-month Russian course, I had been locked up to await repatriation. My visa, for a reason I couldn't explain, was lying on the dining-room table in Oxford.

It was the element of surprise that worked. Rosemary gave the impression that she was shy: barriers would fall and suddenly people would find themselves carried away by her extraordinary enthusiasm.

Someone suggested to me that if she looked gloomy she would bear a resemblance to Virginia Woolf, but gloom was rare and the similarity hard to find.

In Moscow she had negotiated for two days to prevent them from sending me back to England. It was to be good preparation for Wuhan where bureaucratic wrangles required the skill of a game of chess. It was now four months since we'd left Wuhan, and we thought we were proficient. Nothing could exceed the days we'd spent negotiating train tickets, and permits for forbidden regions. Or so we imagined.

"You're wasting your time!" the Australian shouted back, kicking the ground as he turned the corner and sending a cloud of chickens into the air.

"I'm sure he thought we had some deal with the Embassy," I said.

Rosemary was looking at our truck factory contracts. We'd received a message in Kathmandu that the *lingdao* had cancelled them: they had decided we should renegotiate when we reached Shiyan. "I did tell him that we could be sitting around here for days and end up with nothing."

And so we could. The Chinese authorities, having barred the world from Tibet for more than thirty years, were dismantling the barricades with extreme caution. Although they had allowed tours to visit since 1983, only now were foreigners being trusted to enter alone. Lhasa was open. But everyone had to fly in by plane from Chengdu in Central China.

It made our letters to the Tibetan authorities requesting permission to teach in Lhasa seem absurd. If westerners couldn't travel around Tibet, they certainly couldn't live there. Anyway, the authorities had replied politely, Tibet University was under construction.

"We need a new strategy," I said as even a tourist's glimpse of Lhasa was beginning to slip beyond our reach.

A steely-haired woman in shorts and climbing boots was banging on the Embassy gate. "Permit for Tibet?" came a beguiling voice from inside. The woman's face lit up in surprise.

"Yes."

"No permits for Tibet." The gate shut.

We had been convinced that we would persuade a diplomat in Nepal to let us go overland. The previous year we met someone who had sneaked to Lhasa across the Changthang plateau in the north, but nobody on this side seemed to have got beyond the border. Our only chance was to use our Chinese contracts. Tibet – primitive place – we weren't interested at all. We simply had to get to our students in China, and we couldn't afford to fly.

The steely-haired woman had disappeared; several others came and went. Plucking up our courage and our best Chinese we knocked again.

"Permits for Tibet?"

"*Bu shi*," No, we chorused, hoping to impress. "*Wuomen shi laoshi zai Zhongguo.*"

"Teachers in China?" The gateman looked dubious. He had seen us before.

We continued talking in Chinese. He, with one hand on the gate, answered in English. I felt the *No permits for Tibet* hovering in his throat; his hand was twitching on the gate. Then suddenly there was an official walking across the yard behind him.

"*Wuomen shi laoshi zai Zhongguo*," I repeated, looking past the gateman and bringing a note of desperation into my voice. "*Qing gei women bang man.*" Please help us.

The official, amused by our Chinese, took a step towards us. It was all we needed. With eyes fixed on him we walked through. The gateman turned as we passed. "You speak good Chinese," he smiled: we were no longer his responsibility.

Inside the Embassy, in the room for Foreign Friends, the plastic armchairs were like the ones we had had in Wuhan. So was the cork picture of the Yellow Crane Pavilion.

Mr Lin, whose fine, rather sensitive face made him look younger than he could possibly be, introduced himself, poured us tea, and launched the conversation in the conventional way.

We had been taught the art by a Chinese friend in Wuhan. At first ask many nice questions, she would advise before we went into meetings with the *lingdao*. Only later tell them the problems. So we explained how I had got the post of English teacher at the university in Wuhan.

It was September 1984. The telephone was ringing in my parents' home.

"It's Rosemary here." A voice crackled down a distant line.

"Rosemary?" We hadn't seen each other since the Russian course eighteen months before and, at first, I couldn't think who Rosemary was.

"Would you like a job in China?" The university where she was working needed another English teacher.

Nyalam Village, on the road from the border

Pilgrims picnicking after visiting Tashilhunpo
Monastery in Shigatse

Above: The Potala Palace through the pinnacles of the Jokhang Temple

Left: Burning fragrant juniper before the Jokhang

Opposite: On the Barkhor, the pilgrim path and market street which surrounds the Jokhang

I wanted time to think. I had just left university and, having made other plans, was drifting towards the lethal security of a job in London. But Rosemary had taken five days to get through. I had the length of the call to decide: not long because the university was paying.

"Yes," I shouted raising my voice above the other conversations down the line.

We told Mr Lin how much we were looking forward to going back to China. We showed him our contracts which he read in both Chinese and English. Then we launched into our story, scattering slogans about China's radiant future, our responsibility towards our students, and impressing on him our shortage of money.

"So, you see, we need your help." Rosemary smiled.

Mr Lin laughed. "Please drink some tea." He wafted a hand towards our mugs and, half-lifting the lid of his own, took a gulp through the steam.

"We are stranded here with no way of getting to China." My voice sounded earnest.

Mr Lin set his mug down. "You should fly to China."

I caught Rosemary's face in the glass of the cork picture, and wanted to laugh. The conversation was going to follow traditional lines.

"But we don't have the money to fly to China."

"There are flights to Hong Kong."

"Yes, we know but we don't have enough money to fly."

"You could fly from Pakistan."

"But we can't afford to fly."

"You should borrow some money."

"From whom?"

"From other foreigners."

"We don't know any other foreigners."

"From England."

"We don't have any money in England."

Mr Lin looked perplexed. "So what do you want to do?"

I held my breath, turned to Rosemary, blew nonchalantly across the surface of my tea. "Go through Tibet."

Mr Lin frowned slightly, then smiled. "Ah yes you can take a China Travel Service 3-day tour to Lhasa." He sat back in his chair, evidently pleased with this idea. "Lhasa, hmmm. We call it Sun City," he mused. "Foreigners like it."

A tour, we had discovered on our first day in Kathmandu, cost more than the money we had brought for a year. Rosemary shook her

Opposite: The Potala with Lhasa at its feet

head: more expensive than the flight to Hong Kong. Then, fly to Hong Kong.

The argument, like so many of our bureaucratic battles in Wuhan, had its own logic and a kind of spurious reasoning. We were back at the chess-game where every piece we took from the board was ceremoniously returned. We began to play Mr Lin by his own rules. We began returning our chessmen too, repeating our story and our plea for help, countering suggestions with the same suggestions. We were all cheating, we knew we were all cheating; politely earnest, we continued the game.

I tried flights to Lhasa: I knew there weren't any. Mr Lin thought for a while. "Next year."

"Then we must travel by road to Lhasa, and fly from there to Chengdu."

Silence.

Mr Lin was smiling in alarm. I think he had begun to regret ever having rescued us from the gateman.

He tried to look firm. "I'm sorry, that is impossible. Foreigners cannot travel alone in Tibet."

"But we are used to travelling alone."

"No, it is impossible."

The argument spun off in another spiral of non-sequiturs. Mr Lin began telling us of the dangers of Tibet: the poor hotels, the poor vehicles, the poor roads, the poor climate, the landslides. Yes, we knew, we knew, but we had no money, and we needed to get to China and . . .

Suddenly Mr Lin got up and stood looking at us from the middle of the room. I began to feel guilty. His smile, I noticed, was hovering around his face as if uncertain of its appropriateness. But it fixed itself and broadened; there was a hint of smugness about it now.

"I must help you," he said. "I must telex for permission for you to go through Tibet." He allowed the words to fall slowly, reeking benevolence.

Rosemary jumped up. He took a step backwards as though afraid that she might throw her arms around him. "Please come back in two weeks."

Two weeks! No, surely not. We would have to be at the truck factory in Shiyan in two weeks. We began again.

Mr Lin kept smiling, kept adding hot-water to our mugs. I don't know why he didn't lose his temper or simply send us away. He showed none of the exasperation which was rising in me. In the fourth hour he stood up again. "Excuse me, I have something to do." He disappeared.

"Now what?" Rosemary gulped her tea, the leaves had stewed and sunk to the bottom. Were we going to be defeated? Should we cut our losses and simply enjoy the time we had left in Kathmandu?

The compound was silent. It was the hour of *xiuxi*, the after-lunch nap that China allows to all but officials in Peking. Lawns sprawled through a humid haze of bougainvillaea. But there was no sign of Mr Lin. Would he come back? Perhaps he'd gone for a *xiuxi* too. A black limousine rolled down the drive, its solitary passenger blurred to a stereotype behind silk curtains. "He's escaping," Rosemary said, peering in as it slid through the gates.

By the time two men eventually emerged from the Embassy building, it seemed as though hours had passed. They were ambling so slowly down the drive, that it was a while before we recognised Mr Lin. But the smile was hovering again. What did it mean? He turned off into the gateman's lodge. Was our audience over?

"Mr Lin!" The earnestness of my voice was genuine this time.

He looked back over his shoulder. "The Leader says you must go."

After all that. We couldn't go now. "Where is the Leader?" We were ready to confront him.

"No," he said unperturbed by our loss of composure. "You must go to Tibet."

The trials which Mr Lin promised for our journey to Lhasa proved to have at least an element of truth. For three days we climbed by truck and bus, viewing the barren splendour of Tibet through an icy fog of altitude sickness.

We were unprepared. We had read about blinding headaches and insomnia but thought it only affected the unfit, and we were fit. We had imagined the cold in the balmy evenings of Kathmandu: an intoxicating frosty brightness. At 17,000 feet in the back of a truck it felt as though the ice was driving splinters under our nails. More than anything else, I, at least, was unprepared for the grandeur of Tibet.

Although I knew Tibet was the size of western Europe, my imagination had always insisted on a snow kingdom huddled in the peaks around Everest. For three days I grappled with terrifying, exhilarating space. We were travelling, for a time, through a sky gorged with stars. Then it was the morning of the second day and we were poised on top of a pass. There was nothing above us. Peaks lay frozen across a dawn, far below.

Through the glassy light of afternoon the road ran on indefinitely, bringing the mountains on the horizon beguilingly close. Hours passed; it brought them no closer. And by sunset we seemed to have been petrified in the surrounding sand and rock.

The men who had shared our dormitory in Nyalam on the first night travelled with us for a while. They left at the bottom of a pass, their foxes wrapped round their heads as if against snow.

There was no snow. There was nothing to give even the illusion of growth in this spectacular wilderness. It was hard to imagine how it had fostered life at all. But it was harder to imagine, as we stood in the glittering courtyard of Shigatse's Tashilhunpo monastery the following day, how it had created so rich a culture.

In the frescoed *tsokhang*, the ceremonial hall of the main temple, gilt shadows of Buddhas moved through a glow of candleflames from chalices of butter. In a long enfilade of chapels behind, solitary elders sat curved in prayer. The colours were subdued, yet gorgeously rich. Emerging as we had from two days of desert we were perhaps more susceptible to the monastery's richness. And susceptible, too, to the contrast. Stark mountains rose behind the gold roofs as we walked outside. Perhaps it was this starkness which had borne Tibetans to these pinnacles of spirituality and culture.

Shigatse is Tibet's second town, and seat of Tibet's second spiritual leader, the Panchen Lama. In three years' time he would die here, proclaiming that the cost to Tibet of China's forty-year presence, far outweighed its gains. But the Panchen Lama, or Panchen Rinpoche as he is known in Tibet, was a controversial figure. Just how controversial, we would only discover when we reached Lhasa – the Dalai Lama's seat – and found an historical rivalry continuing between the followers of the two lamas. To many Lhasa people, Panchen Rinpoche was a *go niba*, a two-headed one: a collaborator. To Shigatse people, even his marriage to a Chinese woman was malicious rumour. The Dalai Lama, however, was revered by all, although we did meet a few people who said he had abandoned a sinking ship when he fled to India in 1959.

Outside, a group of pilgrims had gathered. Telling their prayer-beads, turning prayer-wheels, chanting prayers, they passed the waiting hours. Panchen Rinpoche was on a rare visit from his residence in Peking.

Suddenly from the monastery gates a motorcade shot out. Keeping close ranks, police outriders hooted wildly, as they swerved to avoid pilgrims prostrating themselves in the road. Not knowing which jeep concealed the Lama, people bowed frantically at all the jeeps. The motorcade fled round the bend streaming with white silk *katags*, their ceremonial prayer scarves.

Somewhat bemused, we walked back to the bus station dormitory where we were spending the night.

"The whole scene was so odd," Rosemary said. "The monastery, the dust road, a handful of herdsmen, and then this battery of jeeps and police motorcycles roaring through." It seemed strange to us that the Panchen Lama should need military protection from a group of pilgrims. We still had a lot to learn about the authorities' attitude to religious gatherings.

The following day two Chinese officials returning to Lhasa gave us a lift in their Japanese Land-Cruiser. Like Mr Lin they couldn't understand why we were in Tibet. Why were we not going to the famous places in China: the Terracotta Warriors, the Stone Forest in Kunming, the mountains of Guilin? They hadn't been to these places themselves, but they spoke with an exile's longing of the glories of a distant home.

We passed the fortress in Gyantse where the British had once established a military garrison; the stereo was turned up loud playing *Jiu Gan Tang Mai Wu*, Empty Bottles for Sale, last year's number one in the Chinese charts. Conversation continued in a desultory fashion; the shores of Lake Yamdrok slipped through the dark. Long before we anticipated, we were over the Gamba la pass, over the Tsangpo, an adolescent Brahmaputra, and entering the Lhasa valley on the first tarred road.

We slid through the brightly lit boulevards of Chinese suburbia. All around us, high-walled compounds, characterless blocks and broad lines of streets stood out with the same desolate symmetry. Despite the miles and mountain ranges separating Tibet from Central China, it seemed to me as we neared the centre, that Lhasa had nothing to distinguish it from Wuhan, Chengdu, Xian or Peking. Even the shadows cast by the street lamps looked the same.

Then out of the sky above the town, the Potala emerged. It loomed over us, darker than the night. Clusters of lamp-lit windows were gleaming from its towering expanse of stone. As it tapered into the heavens with the surrounding mountains, it drew my imagination with it, making promises beyond the concrete and corrugated iron, beyond the brightly lit streets, suggesting that, in the darkness, secrets of a different Lhasa still lay concealed.

Chapter 1

LHASA

"*Piu!*" Monkey. The crowd giggles, pulling the hairs on my arm in disbelief and taking turns to compare their own amber skin with mine. Lhamo laughs. "The Tibetans are descended from a monkey," she says. "He married an ogress at the beginning of history. But no Tibetan would look like a monkey now." I catch Rosemary's eye through the broad faces of the crowd and find myself giggling too, half in embarrassment at their apparent scorn.

The market is filled with pilgrims, nomads from distant mountains who flood Lhasa at the end of the autumn harvest: swashbuckling Khampas from the peaks of Kham, their tresses braided round their heads with tassels of silk, jewelled knives in the folds of their coats; Amdowan women with the family's jewels entwined in their plaits. Sheepskin coats trail their sleeves to the ground, bosoms bulge with tea bowls, trinkets to sell, religious texts: all kept in the pouch that forms above the belt, safely next to the skin.

As we emerge Lhamo says, "It isn't really scorn. The monkey was an incarnation of Chenresig, the Buddha of Compassion."

"I see," Rosemary teases. "So we may not be as highly evolved as Tibetans, but at least we show traces of sanctity."

We woke on our first morning in Lhasa to the hum of prayer. Lhamo, in the woollen tabard of the Kongpo people, was eyeing us as she braided silk tassels into her hair. She had arrived in the night at the Tibetan-run hotel where the Chinese officials had left us. Lhamo thought we needed help, although she too was alone and younger than us, but she would be staying with her relatives, as soon as she could find their house.

"You don't speak much Tibetan," she had said when we told her that we were used to travelling without our family. "I can help you buy food and translate for you." We had to communicate with Lhamo in Chinese as our Tibetan was still limited to what we had learned from a Tibetan in Nepal.

Unlike most of the country people in Lhasa, Lhamo was not on pilgrimage; she was trying to get a passport from the Gong An Ju, the Public Security Bureau. She wanted to visit India where most of her family had been living since they escaped from Tibet before the Cultural Revolution. Although her application would take months to process, with relatives abroad, her chances of getting a passport were good.

At nine-thirty the market is just beginning. Most people ignore Lhasa's official dawn, the bureaucratic figment of Peking's imagination which takes place in ice and darkness two hours before sunrise. Xinjiang Muslims from China's far west are laying out heaps of dried apricots. They glisten deliciously but at three *yuan* a *jing*, a sparse Chinese pound, Lhamo scorns them. Villagers sell plump jars of yoghurt and milk from plastic jerry-cans.

"Woma si, woma si." A boy darts out from behind the milk and catches hold of my jacket.

"*Sho si*," a woman calls. "Take the jar, you can bring it back tomorrow." She thrusts the yoghurt into Rosemary's hand. "*Shimbu shibu shi du*." It's delicious.

Lhamo takes the jar and turns it upside down, anticipating our horror with a sly grin.

"If it's fresh it won't fall out," she says, putting it into my bag.

In the next alley the crowd is stuck. People are forcing their way through a storm of bicycle bells; others turn their prayer-wheels and wait. A line of meat traders, squatting inside their yak carcasses, watch the throng dispassionately as they test the keenness of their blades on pieces of bone. Dogs with matted dreadlocks are sniffing at yak heads beneath the tables.

Light-headed and heavy-limbed we amble on to the Barkhor, which surrounds the main temple. The air, distilled through twelve and a half thousand feet, gives an exhilarating sharpness to everything. From shadows rimed with ice we pass into patches of sunlight where the heat burns red patches on children's cheeks.

"But Lhasa's climate is mild," Lhamo is surprised at us and demonstrates with great swoops through the air, the daily temperature variation on the Changthang plateau. There, she says, the temperature soars like an eagle to the twenties during the afternoon, plummeting with the sun to depths of minus fifty in winter.

"I feel like Lhamo's eagle myself!" I say to Rosemary whose fair skin is already glazed with a Tibetan ruddiness. But she has been less affected by the altitude than I have. From heights of exhilaration I still swoop into blinding headaches; even at night my mind wages battles for oxygen, swirling with dreams of psychedelic vividness. Lhamo is not encouraging about how long the effects of the altitude will last; the briefest conversation leaves us panting for breath.

"Some Chinese never get used to it," she says, her laughter bristling with scorn as we rest by two women selling walnuts and hot potatoes.

Both old and wrinkled, they sit on the most tempestuous corner of the Barkhor. Here the twang of Amdo dance music clashes with Hong Kong disco. Jangling shouts of Chinese hawkers and chattering soldiers compete with the trill of two child beggars intoning their prayers from inside a cardboard box. Beneath them drones the incantation of a youth whose bare back is crazed by the cold. Crouching with his face in the dust, his hands cupped above his head, he begs in rhythm with his chant. From the open doors of Nepalese shops comes the sickly sweetness of Nepalese incense which hangs beneath the juniper smoke billowing from a Tibetan offertory burner outside. But the two women seem oblivious of this pandemonium of cultures. They sit at the edge of the road competing with each other in generosity.

"*Chik, nyi, sum, shi* . . ." The walnut woman counts out fifty walnuts for us, then giggling toothlessly tips the rest of her basket into our bag. The potato woman pats her quilted nest of boiled potatoes, making small puffs of steam escape through the folds. We don't need any, but they are irresistible. We stand unprotesting as she burrows inside to find the largest and saltiest of them, talking continuously, to us incomprehensibly, and smiling through small bulging spectacles, attached behind her ears with lengths of twisted metal.

Khampas ogle as we wander on. Lhamo has a classical Tibetan beauty with high cheekbones, broad smile and slender height. But she is not going to marry, she is adamant about that. She wants to become a nun.

"You should be careful of the Khampas," she warns as we pass a group of them, hands up each others' sleeves, bargaining over furs in a tactile morse code. They are Tibet's warriors and still inspire fear in Tibetans from other regions.

"Are you shy?" Rosemary asks noticing that she is blushing.

"Not of the men!" Lhamo is embarrassed about her traditional Tibetan clothes, it transpires. "I feel stupid," she says, eyeing Lhasa girls in the high heels and narrow trousers that are the dictate of Chinese fashion. Although the authorities now encourage ethnic costume, it was attacked as being the dress of reactionaries for so long that only the old and people from rural areas now wear it. Even Lhamo has tucked her hair into a khaki cap of the People's Liberation Army.

A crowd has gathered around the Khampas. Bulging into door-ways, spilling into courtyards, it expands as people are drawn by the prospect of a spectacle. Lhamo makes for the middle and burrows her way through to the front.

A bicycle collision. Egg, dribbling down the spokes of one bike, oozes into an expanding pool. A Chinese man is shouting at one of the Khampas. His bike is scratched. It belongs to a friend. Some people should look where they are going. The men pick up their bikes and still muttering, pedal off in opposite directions. Lhamo turns to the other onlookers:

"It was the Chinese man's fault. . . ." "No, if the Khampa hadn't. . . ." "He wasn't looking. . . ." "No respect. . . ." "Poor man . . . and it wasn't his bike. . . ."

People are still joining; the cyclists forgotten, the crowd is now entertaining itself.

"Come on, this will go on for hours," Lhamo says, dragging us away, "but it is very interesting isn't it?"

She giggles. "I suppose I wouldn't be a very good nun. You see, I love to know everything that's going on. I think maybe a nun's life is too boring. Maybe I can't sit alone and pray all day." Her eyes sparkle. *"Om mani padme hum, Om mani padme hum, Om mani padme hum . . ."* she drones with playful piety as we return to our hotel, the Banak Shol.

Lhasa is built on concentric circles of pilgrim paths. With wooden "gloves", leather aprons and white dusted foreheads, the devout circumambulate the town in body-lengths of prostrations. The outer path, the Linkhor, encompasses the whole town and takes a week of 11,000 prostrations to complete. Pilgrims still defiantly stretch them-selves out along the original route, across truck-laden roads, between high walls of Chinese work-units, past rock-sculpted Buddhas, under strings of prayer-flags which no longer join the Potala to the Tibetan Medical College, but to a television mast that stands in its ruins on Chakpori hill.

The Barkhor encircles the Jokhang temple, Tibet's holiest shrine, and has traditionally accommodated the trading community of Nepa-lis, Indians, Chinese, Bhutanese, Sikkimese and Tibetans. Now only the Nepalis have returned from abroad. Increasing numbers of stalls are being taken by Chinese settlers. But for Tibetans the Barkhor is essentially a pilgrim path; Chinese soldiers, who saunter against the clockwise religious flow, recall the past when everyone was forced to profane religious buildings by walking anti-clockwise.

At the heart of Lhasa is the Sharkhor, the smallest pilgrim path. This lies within the Jokhang Temple which was built in the seventh century by King Songtsen Gambo for his Nepalese and Chinese wives. Inevitably, these days, greater prominence is given to the Chinese princess, Wen Cheng.

"All the Tibetan people love Wen Cheng and all their folk songs sing her praises."

"Wen Cheng brought China's superior knowledge to Tibet and the Tibetan people were very grateful."

It was from Chinese living in Lhasa that we heard these eulogies; most of them knew little more about Tibetan history. For them, Wen Cheng's marriage to Songtsen Gambo marked the beginning of Tibet's dependence on China. It was proof that Tibet had always been part of The Motherland.

The Jokhang was badly damaged during the suppression of the Lhasa uprising in 1959. And throughout the Cultural Revolution it was used by the army. Even after the soldiers had moved out in the late Seventies, the authorities continued to offend the Tibetan population by appointing a Muslim as its leader. The year before we arrived, however, the Muslim had been replaced and the temple, partly restored, began functioning again.

One day towards the end of our third week in Lhasa I was sitting on the new Jokhang square with a Danish tourist. We were talking about the link between the restoration of the monasteries and tourism. Here, historic buildings and winding alleys had been swept away a few months before; replaced by baubled lamps and concrete flowerbeds to give the view of the temple more grandeur. The Dane was dismissive.

"Religion in Tibet is just a showcase to dupe the passing tourist," he said and delivered a diatribe on how all the lamas of any value escaped with the Dalai Lama in 1959. Instinctively, I felt angry. It wasn't the first time I had come across the attitude that the only *authentic* Tibetans now lived outside. Anyone inside Tibet was either a collaborator, or had been completely corrupted by the Chinese. As he talked I looked towards the temple. Tibetans of all ages were prostrating themselves before its wooden gates. The flagstones were once more polished to smooth sheen as thousands came to perform this public act of devotion. One thing was certain: tourist attraction or not, for these people the Jokhang was still the most sacred place in Tibet. Nothing, it seemed, could diminish its importance.

Inside, pilgrims shuffled round the dimly lit halls, touching each shrine with their foreheads and, where the crush of people would allow, prostrating themselves at its feet. They carried with them offerings of *tsampa* (milled barley), money, jars of butter to replenish the flickering lamps. Everywhere, monks were trimming wicks, retrieving those that had sunk into the melted butter. The air was dark and warm with the smell of incense, butter vapour, sheepskin.

Carried by the crowd, I wandered from chapel to chapel. Near a two-storey image of Palden Lhamo, the Dalai Lama's protective deity, a woman nudged my arm. She looked old. Her face was dry and leathery, her hair grey. But in her coat – a *chuba* with its commodious pouch above the belt – she carried a baby.

"We call this the sleeping statue," she said, in a confidential tone. I look at her puzzled "Sleeping?" The god's eyes were wide open.

"Yes, the Red Guards attacked it in the Cultural Revolution. The spirit of Palden Lhamo has left the image and won't return."

Despite the god's absence the woman pressed her forehead against Palden Lhamo's robes blackened by the grease and dirt of previous foreheads. Determined that her baby too should acquire merit in this way, she pulled him from her bosom and banged his head against the Buddha's knee. He wailed, and continued to wail as his mother bundled him back inside her *chuba* and moved on into the gloom of another chapel.

In the sunlight outside, the tide of worshippers had risen. Everywhere, except where dogs had claimed the warm flagstones, people were prostrating themselves. Hands clasped above their heads, moving slowly downwards, they knelt, then slid forwards stretching out their length on the ground. Some had been there since early morning, bowing and unfolding like waves before the gates of the temple.

The new streets cut through Lhasa like knives, slicing up the old medieval town. But it was not long before we discovered, between the drab grid of Beijing Road, Liberation Street, Happiness Road, the middle ages still flourishing in their chaotic fashion. Streets wound at will, leading us astray through frozen mud and darkened puddles, past wooden gateways with their clutter of cloistered courtyards. Here and there people sat moulding the earth into images of deities, spinning yarn with sticks, rolling yak dung into patties for fuel, preparing offerings to place before the gods. Chanted prayer mingled with conversation, providing the rhythm for their work. They would break off to watch a passer by, to give instructions to a child, then begin again. Religion is not confined to temples and specific ceremonies. It is tempered by life, interwoven with it and so it seems to raise daily routine above drudgery.

In everything, even in the Lhasa architecture, the earthy and the ethereal affect and condition each other. From the humblest dwelling to the expanse of façades and pinnacles that is the Potala, Tibetan houses follow the same pattern. Rooted in the earth at the broad base, they draw the eye up their tapering, fort-like walls to the roofs, where prayer-flags float in colours of the elements sending their prayers on the wind to the gods.

For the first few weeks, we were immersed in the Tibetan part of Lhasa, visiting temples, wandering round the Barkhor, browsing through the market. I began to see in everything, even the Tibetans themselves, with their spontaneous humour and natural refinement, this combination of earthy and ethereal. I began to share the Tibetan belief that heaven meets earth at the peaks of its mountains.

Chapter 2

LETTERS OF INTRODUCTION

———————

The letter of refusal from Tibet University which we had we received in Wuhan the previous year had banished from our minds all thoughts of working in Tibet. As we left England, the lure of the emerald hills, the red mud and mists of Shiyan was strong. But after three weeks in Tibet my vision of the place had become distorted. The mists became the nagging damp of winter, the factory loomed large with its workers uniformed like the myriad other inhabitants of the city. And the wrangle we were anticipating over the renegotiation of our contracts with the leaders at the truck factory seemed an enormous obstacle. The desire to stay in Tibet was becoming obsessive.

Lhamo thought we were mad to embark on the process of trying to get jobs. Westerners hadn't been allowed to live in Lhasa since the arrival of the Chinese. Was it worth forgoing Tibet's vibrant skies to spend days in bald concrete buildings for what might simply be a rehearsal of our Shiyan battle?

The opinions of the Chinese we met should have dissuaded us. "Oh no, Lhasa is very backward. You couldn't live here," a Canton English teacher told us. "Life is too primitive. It is not suitable for foreigners." Everyone had suggestions of more comfortable places in China. For several days we wandered round the monasteries, un-decided, remembering the fruitless forays behind China's red tape that we had made in the past. But then we heard that there was, after all, a westerner teaching at the university.

"Yes, Mr Morse is American," a young woman told us when we eventually found the English Department. "But he was born in China. He is like a Chinese." He had arrived a few weeks before, the teacher explained, adding quickly that they didn't need any more teachers.

"You should try the Tibetan Government Education Department," the young woman suggested, her tone implying not so much the promise of a job as a desire to be rid of us. We were not the first wishful travellers to plague them and we wouldn't be the last.

We found the Education Department with difficulty. It was a row of concrete rooms with only a sign in Tibetan and Chinese suggesting that it was any different from the row of houses on the other side of the muddy yard.

Inside, four officials were huddled around a bucket of hot coals, their chairs pulled up as close to the warmth as the smoke would allow. They looked surprised at our entrance and not a little perturbed.

We launched into a speech about our desire to help with the development of Tibet; the importance of English for tourism; our work in Wuhan and our lack of concern for creature comforts, to forestall any excuses of this sort. Talking fast to give an air of fluency to our Chinese and taking turns to speak, we kept going for about fifteen minutes.

We seemed to be impressing them. They asked us about Wuhan, how we got there, what we thought of it, how we adapted to the climate and then about England: Mrs "Satcher", the fog, Dickens. The interview was drifting away from the point. It would be another hour before we realised why.

"Miss Catriona, Miss Rosemary, please come back tomorrow, our leader is not here today," one of them said eventually. We had simply been helping four bored clerks to wile away their morning.

The following day the clerks were again eager for conversation. Again, their *lingdao* would be there tomorrow. It was not until two days later that we succeeded in presenting him with our proposition. Politely interested, he gave us a jam jar of green-leaf tea, but such decisions were not his responsibility.

"Try the Lhasa City Government," he said, writing us a letter of introduction.

Armed with this new credential we set off, cursing the distances of the sprawling town and fearing that their help would consist of either telling us to come back tomorrow or sending us on somewhere else.

It did both. Our introduction was not sufficiently impressive to prevent the "I'm sorry our leader isn't here, please come tomorrow" from a clerk. And when we arrived next day, the leader sent us back to the Education Department:

"Mr Morse has just come to teach at Tibet University," he smiled. We knew.

"There is the Agricultural University, but that is not my responsibility," he said, focusing his gaze on the cigarette he was squashing into the ground with his foot.

"Whose responsibility is it?"

He yawned and leaned back in his chair. "The Education Department. I can write you a letter of introduction if you like."

"We have been to the Education Department," Rosemary said. It was obvious that he had nothing more to suggest so we left with the formulaic farewell.

"Why didn't they tell us about the Agricultural University?"

"I should think it means that we are not allowed to go there."

We made our way slowly back towards the Education Department. Still scrupulously polite, the *lingdao* offered us tea and sunflower seeds, and told us that we could certainly go down to the Agricultural University. "Yes, Yes. Maybe they will want teachers."

It was in Ba Yi, an isolated Chinese-built town, two days truck-ride from Lhasa. They would write us a letter of introduction, if we wanted to go there. We were beginning to wonder what these letters of introduction contained. If the Agricultural University was under Education Department control, permission to employ two English teachers must surely come from here. The sudden enthusiasm of these leaders seemed to have little to do with our chances of success.

We were not getting anywhere. Nor were we seeing anything of Tibet. So, abandoning for the second time our plans of working in Lhasa, we went to Ganden Monastery with Jigme, a Tibetan whom we had met in a restaurant the day before.

Seven a.m. The darkness shuffles with frozen shadows. Dogs which during the day have no other thought than to stretch themselves out in the sunniest spot prowl in warring packs. As they speed invisibly into attack, the night echoes with their cries, fuelling my imagination. Among travellers stories of attacks by dogs abound. To the Tibetans, Lhasa's hundreds of strays are part of the community, and at the slightest rumour of a purge by the authorities they drive them to the monasteries for protection.

Jigme was waiting for us at the pilgrim truck on the Jokhang square, his unusual height distinguishing him from the other passengers even in the gloom. He helped us clamber up the wheels into the back, and insisted on paying. It cost double: we were foreigners. But he didn't argue; not wanting to embarrass him, we, too, kept quiet. Jigme explained his height by the fact that he was born in Kham. "Yesterday my hair was unusually curly too," he grimaced, feeling his scalp with his fingers. Today it was bristling in tufts.

"The leader of my work-unit told me to get it cut. He said that I looked like a hooligan."

I asked him where he worked, but he was reticent: his job was boring.

At both ends of the Lhasa bridge, People's Liberation Army soldiers were dozing against their bayonets. Their heads, raised momentarily as we approached, drooped as we passed. We headed out along a dust road: the only road east to Central China which for a thousand miles clung to a spectacularly perilous landscape hardly more than a truck's width.

Judging by their coats – thick yak skin *chubas* – the other passengers were nomads from Kham. Beside me a family was breakfasting off bowls of buttery tea and *tsampa*, which the father kneaded to pellets of dough in a leather sack. A baby, tucked naked into the pouch of his mother's *chuba*, stared up at her as she ate. Now and then she put her lips to his, and fed him with food from her own mouth. They were smiling at each other.

For a long time I watched, strangely moved. I must have drifted into reverie for the next moment a bowl was being thrust into my hand.

"*Söcha chö.*" The husband was smiling at me: have some tea. It slopped over the edge of the bowl as I drank and froze on the floor of the truck. Quickly, I swallowed the rest. Now that the vapours of altitude sickness were beginning to clear, butter tea no longer floundered miserably in our stomachs. Today in the biting frost of early morning, it tasted thick and warm.

People disapproved of us eating butter on bread: butter should only be drunk in tea. Nevertheless, under Lhamo's tutelage we were becoming connoisseurs. The secret lay in the sampling which was something of a daily ritual. Aristocratic Lhasa ladies would bustle up and down the alley where nomads stood behind blocks of butter. Only the freshest, the most expensive, would do for them – and they had to taste it all. Stripping the blocks of their yak-gut skins, the nomads offered slivers of butter to everyone on the end of long ornamented knives. Lhamo kept trying to tell us only poor people bought the butter that we liked. To no avail. Mottled with veins, it reminded us of Stilton.

This tea was Stiltonesque too. The man offered another bowl to Rosemary who decided that it was less cloying than Lhasa tea. "A good warming broth." The wind whipped ice into our nostrils, and froze her words almost before they were out. For a while we were numbed into silence.

Ahead of us the Lhasa valley stretched out flat and frozen. Sand glittered with frost. The river twisted like tinsel through its braided bed. I caught my breath. It was not just the cold. Elation: I had felt elated so often that I was beginning to wonder whether the scenery could be inspiring me, unaided. Might the altitude also have a physiological effect on one's brain? Perhaps we were high on oxygen deprivation? I turned to ask Jigme, but he and Rosemary were talking with the nomad.

Rosemary had asked the man about a badge with a picture of the Potala which was pinned to his belt. Almost all the passengers were wearing them.

"Propaganda." Jigme sneered. "It's for the twentieth anniversary of the Tibetan Autonomous Region." When the T.A.R. was created in 1965, Jigme's family home in Kham was cut out of Tibet and absorbed into the neighbouring Chinese province. Like many Tibetans in Kham and Amdo, most of which was also split off at this time, Jigme was bitter. "These people think the badges must have some religious meaning because of the picture of the Potala. The leaders were handing them out at the celebrations last month." He frowned, and then added, "Panchen Rinpoche came from Beijing."

"We saw him in Shigatse on our way from the border," I said.

Rosemary said, "I don't think you can say we saw him. But he seems to inspire enormous devotion."

Jigme was contemptuous. "Not in me. People say he eats meat early in the morning and often gets angry. Anyway he's married to a Chinese woman so he's not even a real monk any more. Shigatse people don't believe it, of course. They think it's Chinese propaganda."

I wondered how much of Jigme's ire was inspired by the traditional rivalry between Lhasa and Shigatse, and how much was due to his belief that the Panchen Lama was *go niba*.

After the Dalai Lama fled in 1959, the leaders in Peking used the Panchen Lama to communicate with Tibetans. They knew that his status as a religious leader would always draw crowds. He openly criticised the Government on occasions, but he was their only spokesman.

On the day that he died in January 1989, I was having lunch with a Tibetan friend in London. The Chinese Government had just announced that they were intending to search for the Panchen Lama's new incarnation in the traditional manner. They would consult oracles and look for religious signs. After that, a search would be mounted for a child who had been born around the time of the Lama's death.

"They're really making fools of themselves now," my friend scoffed. His manner was very similar to Jigme's. "This is the Communist government which, for forty years, has condemned our religion as idle superstition. Now they're appointing a leader to their Communist parliament by Buddhist *hokey-pokey*. When this child, this incarnation of the Buddha Opagme, grows up, he will be a vice-chairman of the National People's Congress Standing Committee."

The sun rose. It fought the wind, and eventually won. Our faces began to thaw. After four hours, from a mountain ridge a thousand feet above the valley, two threads of smoke curled into the blue.

"Ganden," Jigme shouted through the wind. Scrambling to our feet with the other passengers we hung over the side of the truck; children were lifted up to catch a first glimpse of this sacred place. But all we could see were the two threads of smoke.

Jigme beamed, his anger now dissolved. "It's behind the mountain. We'll be there soon."

Turning off the road into a side valley, we followed the narrow track to a village where the driver stopped to talk with a friend. The houses were built in walled courtyards with entrances barred by wooden doors. They had a strangely fort-like appearance. Made from the surrounding earth, they seemed as though they were about to melt back into it; they probably had for centuries. The suns and moons and swastikas, painted on the doors at New Year to bring good fortune, were pale. Prayer-flags were fluttering in the colours of the landscape, their dye long since dissolved by the sun and wind. The scene was monochrome. Yet the sun scattered light into innumerable shades of brown, even the darkest of which were vibrant.

The monastery was still hidden as we began to zig-zag up the side of the mountain. Another three-quarters of an hour had passed since Jigme had said we were nearly there. The bends in the road were only a few feet above each other. But eventually the road straightened out and crossed to the facing slope. I looked back.

There was nothing left. An expanse of ruins jutted from the ridge like an outcrop of rocks; the sky above it was cut by jagged lines. Around us, some people prostrated themselves on the floor of the truck. Most, like me, just stared.

Time had softened nothing. The mania, the terror, the despair that had destroyed the whole of this monastic town over twenty years before, still made themselves felt. I looked down the mountain. I found myself imagining the Red Guards shouting revolutionary slogans as they climbed towards the monastery, and the suspense of the monks waiting.

But Ganden's death was slow. It was first bombarded after the Dalai Lama's flight in 1959. Later the gold roofs were melted down, and the most valuable artefacts were sent out to Hong Kong to be sold on the international market. The final blow only came with the Cultural Revolution when local villagers, caught up with the terror of the times, took pickaxes and sledge hammers to the gutted ruins.

"The monks suffered more than anyone at that time," Jigme said, as we warmed ourselves in the monastery kitchen. "Many of them were sent off to labour camps or were executed. They bore the brunt of the attack against our religion, continually being forced into committing acts of sacrilege. They were made to destroy their own temples, fish the holy lakes in Tibet to feed the Chinese army. It is against our religion to kill anything, but catching fish is particularly bad because people often bury their dead in rivers." He broke off. His eyes expressed pain yet he talked quietly, without emotion. "Everybody suffered then, my family did too. My brother stood up in school and said that Tibet was an independent country. They said he was a counter-revolutionary and executed him. He was only sixteen. My mother had to watch him being shot. And then she had to pay before she could take his body away. They didn't waste bullets on counter-revolutionaries." I looked at Rosemary.

"They were bad times," Jigme continued. "But things are better now. Three years ago I couldn't have talked to you like this; I wouldn't have dared go to a monastery." He looked at us, his voice lingering over the words as he spoke them. "Compared with before, life is paradise now."

Life is paradise compared with before. Far longer than his voice had lingered, his words would linger with me – far longer than our acquaintance with Jigme even, for he was sent off to Peking shortly after this.

In the months after I left Tibet, every time another report filtered out, describing pro-independence demonstrators being imprisoned, tortured, or summarily executed as counter-revolutionaries, his words would cut deeper into my memory. Opening a document by a human rights organisation one morning, following the suppression of demonstrations in Lhasa in March 1988, I read that Tibetans were being forced to pay 600 yuan – £100, a year's salary for some people – to claim the bodies of their dead.

I recalled Jigme's face, the timbre of his voice. The whole scene came vividly into my mind. The monastery kitchen, the copper cauldrons of tea, boiling on the fire. The two novices, watching us from stools by the door, vying with each other to keep our glasses filled. They had come to Ganden three years previously to help with the furtive restoration of the monastery. But at this time they were optimistic. Reconstruction was being carried out openly with funds from the Religious Affairs Office, the state department which controls religion in Tibet. The Religious Affairs Office was also turning a blind eye to the fact that they were under eighteen and didn't have permission to be monks.

The whole day was optimistic. As we wandered through the crumpled ruins of the monastery later in the afternoon, we came across temples which were being rebuilt. Monks and volunteers were painstakingly working to recreate the past. Murals had been re-painted, a few statues had been saved from the rubble, new statues were being made, and new brocade decorations hung up. The colours were garish, the gold and jewels of the statues fake. But their purpose was not artistic.

In this land where everything served religion, reverence for an-tiquity, or art for its own sake, had never been valued. In the past, an artist's work would often have been destroyed on his death. Often, temples would be renovated as an act of devotion, with no attempt to preserve the existing art.

To Jigme it had seemed miraculous that these images were here at all. As we walked around, I watched pilgrims filing through the newly painted rooms. I thought of the Danish tourist's scorn about religious belief inside Tibet. There seemed to me little doubt that these gods, however gaudy, inspired as much devotion as they had before.

We ambled to the top of the ridge. Way below, mountains and rivers spread in far-swinging lines to the horizon. The landscape was empty of human life, empty too were the open skies.

In the vast exalting solitudes of the place, I found myself imagining how Ganden had been the Joyful Paradise that its name had once implied.

Chapter 3

CHINA'S SIBERIA

On our return to Lhasa, we found a note under our door. "Came to see you four times, Li."

I assumed that Li must be someone from the Education Bureau wanting to offer us a job, for in a country where no one leaves messages, nothing else could be urgent enough to warrant one. Rosemary looked at the note. "Mr Li? He's not from the Education Bureau. He's the man whom we met last week with the delegation from Canton." My heart sank. I had thought for a moment that someone had changed their mind, but I remembered Mr Li now, at least I remembered the grating giggle. He had come up to us when we were negotiating the price of some Tibetan cloth with a trader. Peasant cloth! Having tried in vain to stop us from buying it, he laughed at us all the way to the Friendship Store where he demanded to see some *good quality Chinese nylon* to prove how deluded we'd been.

"At last! You are returned home!" Mr Li burst in. "We have been waiting for two hours. My friends have spent all day preparing a banquet and you don't come back."

"But Mr Li, you didn't invite us," I protested. He took no notice.

"My friends have cooked a lot of expensive food – beef, preserved eggs, balls of the pork."

"Balls of the pork. Mmmm, sounds delicious." Rosemary's voice was shaking with laughter. "But why didn't you warn us?" I recalled an evening in Wuhan when the University leaders had telephoned during dinner with friends. A banquet. There had been no question but that we would cycle the hour's journey home to eat a second meal. It was useless to argue.

Mr Li kept up a constant banter as we set off on bikes. He had managed to borrow one for us but with the tradition of taking the whole family on the back now illegal, Rosemary had to jump off every time we saw a policeman. Eventually Mr Li stuttered into silence and rode ahead, leaving us to the mood of the streets.

An occasional street-light cast a darkness more impervious around it. Trucks trundled sightless down the middle of the road; glowing cigarettes marked its edge. With the tarmac invisible beneath the bike, I trusted to Mr Li's pedalling outline to guide me through the rocks and dogs and open-manholes. Trees threw stark shadows against the high white walls of the work-units: male figures entwined with branches, women at a decorous distance.

An hour passed before we reached Mr Li's unit. In a bluster of reprimands and apologies we entered his dormitory. Forgiven, seated on the bed, plied with sunflower seeds and boiled sweets, the questions began. Wuhan, famous place: one of China's four *hotpots*. Do we know the other *hotpots*? Chongqing, Nanjing – no we couldn't get the fourth. Rosemary turned to the man next to her, a small thin-faced man.

"Mr Jin," he said, smiling warmly.

"Were you sent to Lhasa by your unit?" Rosemary asked.

"No, we volunteered to come." Mr Jin was thirty and had been in Lhasa since he was twenty-three. But Mr Zhou who was next to him sneered.

"Yes, I volunteered too, but if I hadn't volunteered to come here for eight years I would have had to go to Sichuan province for life." Mr Zhou was older than the others and had left a wife and child in Canton.

Most of the group were teachers on two-year postings. They had been sent to Tibet on a programme which the Government described as the developed provinces helping economically and culturally backward provinces. And there was no question in their minds that Tibet was culturally backward. They all hated the climate and the scenery, and for them the only buildings of any interest here were the newly built Lhasa Theatre and the Tibet Gymnasium, a Stalinesque monolith with concrete statues striding towards a radiant future.

It was true that life here had little to offer them. Photographs of their families fought for prominence on shared desks. The walls flaked copies of *The People's Daily*. There was no water and the single light bulb, even at moments when the electricity was not cut off, left us peering at each other through the gloom. They went to the cinema as often as their unit issued them with free tickets. Most of their time and money, however, they spent preparing elaborate meals for themselves.

"Life is difficult here. But we will soon be leaving for good." Mr Zhou pointed to a calendar scored with crosses, hanging above his pillow. The party, it transpired, was a celebration of their seventy-second week in Tibet. They celebrated every week, Mr Wang, a

round-faced man with tendrils of moustache trailing from his upper
lip, told me. His *hukou*, the permit that restricts your residence to a
particular place, would be transferred to Beijing as a reward for his
two years here. Mr Zhou had been promised that his sister would be
able to return from the countryside where she was sent during the
Cultural Revolution.

They showed us what they had bought to take back with them –
blankets, tape-recorders, musk. The availability of consumer goods
such as these, and salaries that were often four times higher than in
central China, compensated for their being sent to Tibet. For Mr Li at
least, only his growing collection had made the eight years in Lhasa
worth while.

"This period has been a complete waste of my life," he said, "but if
I'd stayed in Canton I would never have been a rich man." Mr Li made
no idealistic claims to be helping Tibet. Like many people and
ironically even some of the Government work-units in Lhasa, he was
following the reformist slogan "Fa Cai, Zhi Fu", Make Fortune, Get
Rich. He had taken a year's unpaid leave and a loan from his unit to set
up in private business. "My unit is happy," he grinned. "They take a
third of my profit."

Mr Wang and Mr Li began frying the feast of twenty dishes which
covered the floor. As each was cooked, it was arranged on the table of
joined desks. For a few minutes steam would rise from the dish, and
then slowly it would begin to congeal. We were getting hungry,
conversation began to pall. Mr Li suggested borrowing a stove from
the dormitory next door.

By the time the first dishes were reheated, another hour had strewn
the floor with sunflower husks. With the two beds drawn up as seats,
we sat down to our banquet. A banquet indeed it was, both in quantity
and delicacy: chicken, beef, eel, turtle, fungus, seaweed, eggs preserved in lime, not a thousand years old, only a few months but
already a translucent blue, and slimy. Mr Li's "balls of the pork" were
meat balls. We contained our laughter, but then, spearing his chopsticks into another bowl and grinning pitilessly, he offered us the balls
of the cow.

Everyone made speeches and toasted *China and England, The Four
Modernisations, Sacher and Deng Xiao Ping*. "*Gan bei*," we shouted, or
"Bottoms off" as Mr Li translated, and downed our glasses Russian-
style, in one. Mr Wang and Mr Jin were collecting up the chopsticks,
sweeping the bones and gristle from the floor. Rosemary began telling
Mr Li about our unsuccessful attempts to get jobs.

"Yes, it's impossible. Foreigners are not allowed to live in Tibet."
Why on earth did we want to stay here anyway?

"We like the mountains," Rosemary suggested.

The mountains! Hadn't we been to the famous mountains in China:
Emei Shan, Wudang Shan, Jiuhua Shan. I caught Rosemary's fleeting
grimace and remembered the five-hour queue toiling up the stairway
of Wudang Shan; the souvenir stalls with their cork pictures and
plastic longevity Buddhas; the shrine at the peak where we picnicked
with our students among the eggshells and pop bottles of other
people's picnics.

"Yes, but we like Tibetan mountains too," Rosemary said with
characteristic diplomacy.

Everyone began suggesting alternatives to Tibet which, they
assured us, would be far more comfortable and more rewarding.

"You'd never be able to teach English to Tibetans anyway," Mr
Wang said. "It's hard enough for us, and we're Chinese." They all
laughed.

Perhaps it is *because* you're Chinese, I wanted to say, suddenly
angry.

"Why couldn't we teach Tibetans?" Rosemary asked, her bantering
tone turned cold.

"Their minds work too slowly."

"They are very dirty, you know," Mr Li added.

Although since the Fifties the Government had railed against what it
called Han chauvinism, we would meet few Chinese in Lhasa who did
not agree with Mr Wang and Mr Li.

"But we don't want only to teach Tibetans," Rosemary said,
attempting to smooth over the momentary discord. "We want to
teach everybody. Maybe we would start night classes where workers
could study English in their free time."

I looked at Mr Li. With a suddenness that bordered on caricature he
seemed to have grown interested. "Yes, yes. I know someone who
works in the Government; he will help us. I will go to see him
tomorrow."

They began to discuss amongst themselves where we would live,
whether we could manage to cook for ourselves, how we would
survive on Chinese and Tibetan food, how much we should get paid.
They talked as if everything was settled already, and their excitement
was contagious. For no reason, except perhaps the effect of alcohol at
this altitude, the possibility of living in Lhasa seemed nearer as we
biked back through the empty streets.

"Remember," Mr Li said at the door of our hotel "*Meiyou guanxi, mei banfan!*" No contacts, no hope!

"I'll come and see you tomorrow after we have been to my friend. Oh and by the way, you can keep the bike for the moment. It belongs to friend who has gone to Shanghai. I'll try and find another, you might be needing them now."

Mr Li didn't appear the next day, nor the day after. Not wanting to miss him, we hung round the hotel. Sitting on the roof, lying on our beds, visions of monasteries battled with Shiyan. Lhamo found her relatives and left. We gave up and went out, and returned and went out.

"We'll give up tomorrow," Rosemary said as we watched the sun sink at the end of the valley. But both of us knew that we wouldn't. The last rays struck horizontally through the serrations of a peak, catching the Potala in a blaze of silver, making the mountains glow for a while, then letting them sink back to a rich crinkled brown.

Sounds of Chinese voices came from below. People were climbing the ladder to the roof. Neither of us moved; we had been caught too many times before. Rosemary looked round, studiedly unconcerned.

"Miss Rosemary! Miss Catriona!"

We leapt up.

"They've agreed."

"What?"

"They want you to work in Lhasa."

"What do you mean?"

"Who do?"

Mr Li and his friends grinned at our inarticulateness.

"The Lhasa Government."

"The Leaders."

"The Education Bureau."

"Everyone."

They started talking at once.

"For three days we had a meeting."

"The Leaders agreed just now."

"You worked a long time in China, we said."

"You know many things about our country."

"You are Oxford and Cambridge graduates."

"Oxford and Cambridge best universities."

"The Leaders think we must have Oxford and Cambridge teachers. Very good."

With all the arguments that we had used over the past four weeks, it had never occurred to us that these were the credentials we needed to produce. That, even in Lhasa, we would be caught in Oxbridge snobbery.

Chapter 4

FROM TOURIST TO TEACHER

"Yii . . . errr . . . sannn . . . siii . . . wuuu . . . liuuu . . . qiii . . . baa . . ."

Music, imperious voices shout through my dreams. One . . . two . . . three . . . four . . . five . . . six . . . seven . . . eight. . . . In the confusion of waking, fractured images lurk round my thoughts. The commands insist. Their intrusion is familiar, associations familiarly unpleasant. Wuhan. The Tannoy: directing the university through morning exercise. It must be past six . . .

Panic sharpens my wits. Suddenly I am wide awake. I open my eyes. But not to the greying mosquito net, not to mould on sweating carpets, not to somnambulant students making disjointed movements of military inspiration or wandering rice-bowl and book in hand along sticky paths. I am not in Wuhan. I look round and relax, testing the feel of morning in our Tibetan work-unit. The mound of quilts, halo of frosted breath, prayer-flags fluttering from the house beyond the window – and the Tannoys which still clamour for attention. In Lhasa communal exercise was abandoned long ago, yet the voice, the same voice which harries sleepers even in the remotest corner of the country, barks its clipped commands regardless. I smile to myself as I recognise in them the cause of my panic and the images of Wuhan in those half-waking moments.

There was a time when I found the Tannoys sinister. Terrifying one out of sleep with a clatter of distorted sound; bombarding one all day with exhortations to love the Party, to serve the people, to work hard for the future of Communism. Like most foreigners in China, I saw the Tannoys as the first sign of repression. But soon their sound fades into the background of China's noises. You sleep through even the loudest of them, particularly here where, broadcasting mostly in Chinese, they are incomprehensible to a large proportion of the population. They become silent but for the good tunes and useful information: the time of the unit's film show, the day the coal ration will be issued. Only when they stop are you aware of their noise.

Beyond the next unit where *Jingle Bells* is tripping over its Chinese words, other Tannoys merge into a dim fog of sound. Suddenly from the tree outside my window, a new Tannoy screeches out: *"Lasa Cheng Guan Qu Shi Xun Ban."* Lhasa City Government Teachers Training Department.

Silence.

A burst of childish giggles, its pomposity dissolves.

This is our work-unit. The high wall which surrounds it stares blankly at pilgrims and townspeople plying the path to the river. Emblazoned with red-starred flags it is like every other walled compound in Lhasa. But occasionally the iron doors open to let a jeep or a truck pass, and you glimpse inside.

A garden. A rose blooming in extravagant defiance of the cold, a pump, a tethered sheep. It was once the home of an aristocratic family who fled to India during the uprising of 1959 when the house was destroyed. The buildings are modern yet the eaves are painted with traditional floral designs, and wind ripples the cloth frills above the windows. Children play on the dusty grass; an old man sits with his friends, rolling coils of prayers to fill their prayer-wheels.

Within the ubiquitous crust of Chinese authority, the atmosphere is Tibetan.

So much happened after Mr Li and his friends rushed up to us on the balcony of the Banak Shol. That moment, it transpired, was not the end; just another beginning in another month of disappointments. With a surge of optimism, Rosemary set off via Peking for Hubei Province to collect our possessions, and to tell the truck factory that we wouldn't be renegotiating our contracts. Twice after she left it looked as though we might need to. But we would have no means of communicating in the month that she was away, and by the time she returned at Christmas it would be too late.

More surprising than the lengthy process of negotiation, however, was the fact that the leaders in Lhasa had entertained the idea of taking us on at all. In a country where decisions are shackled to those of superiors in a chain whose end is held tightly by Peking, it was hard to know how high the decision had to go. The meetings, the people, the *guanxi* or contacts: all were hidden from us behind the concrete arches of the Lhasa City Government and the Tibetan Autonomous Region Education Bureau. Knowing nothing, we began creating our own faces, our own leaders, as decisions filtered back in a chain of nebulous *yes's* and *no's*.

One day there was a contract: twelve hours a week each for six months at 350 *yuan*, £60, a month. But with Rosemary's departure came new pronouncements of *impossible* from new disembodied voices of authority. Then quite unexpectedly one day, I was told to pack my bags. I was being moved into a room in the work-unit.

Everything was settled, Mr Li assured me. Everything, that was, except the decision of the Public Security Bureau, the Gong An Ju, the most important, and the most difficult to obtain.

I peer out from the mound of quilts. After six weeks of hotel life, the room has a reassuring permanence about it. The rucksacks are banished beneath the beds. With proprietorial abandon our possessions litter the cupboard, made for us yesterday by the unit's workmen. Near the door shining thermos flasks, buckets with carrying poles, pressure-cooker, candles – necessities of life at 13,000 feet where water can boil without scalding and electricity is a privilege – all shout that we are meant to stay. They speak of the trouble the leaders have taken too. Last week only the mountain-filled windows and the sweep of the Lhasa river suggested that a home might be made of this minute graffiti-scratched shell. The leaders *must* be confident that the Gong An Ju will agree. But the Gong An Ju are answerable and accountable to no one.

A child passes along the balcony, clanking her buckets and slopping water on to the frozen stone. Other sounds follow as people emerge: hissing dung, the hum of prayer, frothing of butter and tea being plunged together in a wooden churn. Next door, a family of four lives in a room as small as ours and, judging by the frequency with which the child is banished to the balcony, life is not always easy. I look round the frosty brightness of our room. How will it feel in six months' time? Will *we* be banishing each other to the balcony? A single room to live, to eat, to sleep; to entertain not only our own friends but each other's too. Are we mad? I could almost touch Rosemary's bed if the numbness of my nose didn't deter me from the experiment. Will we survive this intimacy, this invasion of each other's privacy? Privacy, the word doesn't even exist in Chinese. My thoughts ramble on, deferring the moment when I will have to face the cold; fully dressed but for coat and jeans, I shrink back inside my burrow of quilts. A cup stands on the desk, frozen with last night's tea; damp socks stand stiff inside their shoes.

Outside, my neighbour is brushing his teeth. We greet each other with toothpasty grins and spit down our respective drains. These are holes in the balcony which are there to deposit everything on to the ground beneath. Or so I thought until I emptied my chamber pot, provoking an embarrassed visit from the family below us. Their windows look out on to that patch of ground. Now, with one eye on the gate to make sure that students don't arrive early, I join our neighbours in the morning pot-procession to the latrine.

I continue to brush my teeth after the leader has gone inside. A stain of rose light begins to spread over the peaks. Down the path to the river, a child is driving a flock of goats, imitating their bleat to prevent them from straying. I brush mechanically, thinking of friends in England similarly occupied, but with only the bleary reflection of their faces for view.

"Aja la!" Sister! A voice calls through the quilted door-curtain. It is Lhamo. She walks in and bursts out laughing. Sitting down on a sack she laughs and laughs, loudly, helplessly, until tears make streaks down her cheeks.

Since this morning, I have been battling with the yak dung stove. My face is red from exertion, my clothes are black, the room is filled with acrid smoke – and the dung still hisses sullenly. The stove is a monstrous Heath-Robinson invention made of tin with drawers and grates and a drainpipe chimney which sticks out horizontally through a hole in the door. I can see there is an art to using it.

"You look so funny," Lhamo says, still laughing. "How long have you been trying to light this fire?" She jumps up, retying her plaits briskly across her forehead as if they were shoe-laces and tucking them into each other at the back. "I'll show you." With the deftness of habit she builds a pyramid of paper and twigs in the grid. When I pass her the matches, her face puckers with scorn and she unbuckles a tinder-box attached to her belt. Taking out a few strands of tinder she strikes the flint. It catches immediately. Her eyes glisten; she glances at me, struggling to keep a straight face. Breaking the dung patty into pieces, she arranges it around the flame.

Nothing happens, the dung hisses, the flame droops and goes out. Snatching a piece of dung from the stove, she breaks it again and sniffs. "Where did you get this from?"

"The market."

"Who sold it to you?"

"I don't know. A nomad I suppose."

"It is rubbish . . . didn't you test it?"

"Test it?"

"Yes, it's damp; it hasn't been dried properly. How much did you pay for it?"

"Five *yuan*," I say meekly. It had in fact cost eight.

"Well, you'll have to leave it out in the sun for at least a month."

The Leaders brought 30 jing of flour and rice not long ago, and promised us a ration of coal. They gave us an electric ring too, although as Lhasa suffers from an acute shortage of electricity in winter when the water level falls, it has been of little use.

"Privileges of state workers," muttered a Tibetan woman who was watching through the door while workmen installed the ring. Not belonging to a work-unit she cannot get an electric ring, nor the 30 *jin* of rice that we get. Rations are limited to 20 jing of *tsampa* and flour, for everyone who does not work for the state. They have rice only at New Year.

"Of course they are angry," Lhamo says, and then laughs. "But they are better off than I am. My residence permit is in Kongpo, so I can't get rations at all. My relatives have to support me."

It was not until the beginning of December that our passports were finally returned with a six-month visa from the Gong An Ju. "Everything is settled," Mr Li grinned. I believed him this time. A room across the garden had been filled with desks, and classes had already begun.

Rosemary's class was established at the start. She would be teaching English teachers from Lhasa's secondary schools. They were all Chinese, apart from two. But there was some confusion still about who would attend my classes. Scientists, primary school teachers, Government cadres or officials: everyone had a different suggestion. Every day new students would introduce themselves until the classroom walls refused to make room for any more. It would be an interesting mixture of people, some of them state employees and all, except two, Tibetan. Judging by the snippets of conversations I overheard, a certain amount of bargaining between Tibetan and Chinese leaders determined the ultimate ethnic composition of the classes.

With Rosemary still in Hubei, I was teaching everybody for the moment. The inaugural meeting of her class went off with a volley of speeches, an impressive row of *lingdao*, their velvet chairs borrowed for the occasion from the unit next door.

Having followed the official clichés with my own, I made a suitable pause and then suggested that the class was too big. Fifty students whose knowledge of English ranged from tracts of Shakespeare to a stumbled alphabet might have difficulty learning together. They agreed and divided themselves according to bureaucratic rank. It might have been more useful to divide according to language ability. Impossible. Of course they understood my argument but it was impossible. No one would learn anything, I pleaded. Eventually they agreed, but I lost Rosemary a few leaders who found themselves in the bottom class.

The meeting ended but no one felt inclined to leave.

"I think you should give us a lecture on English intonation," someone said.

I looked at him, hoping he was joking, but his face showed no trace of irony. Intonation? A lecture? I couldn't without preparation. I felt murmurs of consensus around me; rows of comfortable faces waiting to be entertained. For an hour they had been told how lucky they were to have *real* English teachers and now I was going to have to prove it. In my panic the faces seemed to harden. They were testing me, I was convinced. I looked towards the door hoping that some escape might present itself. I looked at the rows of faces. Suddenly, I remembered the text-book. The faces lost their evil intent. "A lecture on intonation would be very interesting, but I think we should decide which books we are going to use." I smiled.

They smiled. "Yes, yes very interesting."

They were happy to talk about anything.

The choice was small. The only book that I had with me discussed the merits of insurance, Mediterranean holidays and fast cars. The alternative was Middle School English with a series of tales about Li Ping. Li Ping on the commune, Li Ping with the Great Helmsman. It was the source of the Chinese English language and the origin of the many colourful expressions that were beginning to blossom even here. "WELCOME YOU TO TIBET," proclaimed a new banner at the main crossroads in Lhasa. At the airport bus station there was a sign by the door which indicated that "THE UNORGANISED TOURIST" should queue at the far counter. It was written for Chinese by Chinese, and it produced a language as rich in sayings as their own. "Please come back tomorrow, I'm as busy as a bee today," was the favourite expression of our leader in Wuhan.

The students knew all six books of Middle School English by heart and the sentiments expressed by Li Ping were no longer fashionable. The glimpse of capitalist decadence which my book gave seemed more alluring.

"Good, that's settled then," the monitor said, turning to me, his eyebrows raised in question.

I looked at him. Was he seeking approval of his English? Or was he about to suggest another lecture?

"Homework," I said quickly and, thinking it would be interesting to find out the attitudes of Chinese teachers in Tibet, asked them to write about their life.

I'd forgotten the classroom was not the place for private confidences; rather, with the threat of informers, a place where most would uphold the accepted public image. Half-expecting Mr Li's virulence, half-hoping for something different, a week later I sat down to mark fifty essays on China's *Sun City*.

"The Tibetan people are brave and hard-working . . ." Five essays opened with the same flourish.

"Tibetans are proud and happy to receive the advanced culture of the Han people. When I meet some of them in the street, they look on me as their very good friend."

Miss Liu was a Party member, still publicly fired with pioneering zeal: "I work hard for building of Lhasa. I must do my work well to make my students men of the Motherland to make our country stronger and stronger."

"There are many ancient buildings in Lhasa. These ancient buildings are all Chinese people's great achievement." Mr Zhou was unusually impressed by Tibetan architecture; credit for it, however, he gave to his own people.

Most of the students missed their families, their homes and the gentle climate of southern China. But the last essay told a different story:

Dear Miss Catriona,

I came to Lhasa since 1983. Then things were difficult for me in my home town. The Leaders criticized my thought. We had the Campaign Against Spiritual Pollution. One night I was dreaming. In my dreaming I think I must go to Tibet, I think life is easier for me there. When I tell my family they all crying. But my leaders think it is very good – I volunteer to go to Tibet is a good thing. They show my picture on T.V. They praise me, say many people should follow my good example. I like Lhasa very much and the Tibetan people are very kind. I try hard to learn Tibetan and to get to know them. But sometimes it is difficult. Many Chinese are not polite so the

Tibetans often don't want to make friends with us. Some Tibetans are angry at us because their monasteries are destroyed. It is not my fault, I think their monasteries are beautiful. Sometimes I am very sad.

> Your honest student Sui.

The irritation that had been rising in me as I marked the essays evaporated. It wouldn't be long before I met other people in Sui's position, some of them were intellectuals who had come to Tibet because, for Chinese, Tibet was freer than Central China. They were sensitive people, wanting to understand the Tibetans and their culture, wanting to be accepted by them but facing, instead, continuing suspicion and rejection.

Chapter 5

ECHOES OF THE RAJ

"Hello! I say!"

I was biking to the post office one afternoon in early December when a voice called after me.

"You must be Catriona la," the voice continued, adding the honorific particle to my name with a polished drawl redolent of the Raj. I nodded, more in question than answer at this anachronistic apparition, and turned round to see an elderly Tibetan pedalling alongside.

"Basang Dorje," he said doffing a battered Homburg. "I was told you'd come to live in Lhasa. Aren't there two English ladies?"

Yes. Rosemary would be back from Hubei at the end of December; I was surprised he didn't know. To me Lhasa had the feel of a sprawling village, I was getting used to everyone knowing who we were. We'd often meet people in the town: some would become friends, others were simply curious, like Basang Dorje, and we wouldn't see them again.

As we biked together through the dusty glare of streets I became mesmerised by his voice, by the mellisonant tones of an era now relegated to the realm of novel. It was as though, through years of silence, the essence of the Forties had been preserved in him like a chrysalis. "Can't remember a word of English now," he said as we reached the post office. He had been educated in India like many of the nobility. But over the previous twenty years he had had to force himself to forget, for anyone who had connections with India was *an imperialist spy*.

He said he'd wait as I fought my way past the troughs of glue, past the outstretched fists with notes for the limited stock of panda stamps, past a man who hadn't heard a single word of what his wife had said from Peking and was refusing to pay for the call, past a nomad bewildered by all the signs in Chinese, to the counter.

The counter was wide and tall, and in the maddening peace that reigned on the other side, clerks read comics and finished their conversations.

Poste restante? Nothing. Could I have the poste restante book please? Nothing. The book, it's just there. I raised myself on my elbows and leaned over the edge. A pair of eyes looked up, momentarily. "*Bu zai.*" I don't need the clerk, just pass me the book. The eyes had gone. Please. "*Ta xiuxi.*" But the book's by your elbow.

There was no response. The same thing had happened yesterday – today I was certain I'd avoided the poste restante clerk's *xiuxi*, her nap. Why had I come?

I vowed I would go to the post office only once a week, and went every day. It took fifteen minutes to bike, thirty-five walking along the river which I preferred; then there was always a battle and maybe a letter at the end of it. Maybe not.

A letter, a letter which I would guzzle like chocolate, not reading properly, and then reread and reread trying to recapture its first thrill. Sometimes a whole afternoon would be wasted, just for a letter. Why were they so important? Our Chinese friends were shocked when we shook our heads at "*Xiang jia ma?*" Do you miss home? There was no question of our wanting to exchange our life here for the life of the letters. I thought about it as I made my way outside to Basang Dorje. Was it the distillation of distance and absence, perhaps, that gave them their addictive appeal?

"No luck?" Basang Dorje called from the market which spread beneath the walls of the Potala. He was heaping apples into a string bag.

"No."

We paid the cycle attendant outside the post office one *mao* for looking after our bikes, and set off towards my room; Basang Dorje had wanted to see it. There was a kind of easy assurance about him, an arrogance almost, which reminded me of the English aristocracy. He dropped the name Hugh Richardson – British representative in Tibet before 1949 – with the familiarity that assumed I must be part of the coterie. "Damn fine parties he gave," he said, chuckling to himself. "He'd invite us down to the British Mission at Dekyi Lingka for tennis and bridge." Later, he pounced on a pot of Nivea that was lying on my desk.

"Antiques!" He laughed. "We could buy this in Lhasa, once. Our ladies wore it, and Elizabeth Arden."

In Basang Dorje I sensed a nostalgic warmth towards Britain which I had met in several other older people. Although there was a cautiousness about him that forbade political discussion, he talked of his school days in India, of the journey home across the Himalaya for the holidays.

"Did you know your neighbour's father went to school in England," he said.

I looked at him in surprise. "Which neighbour?"

"Over the wall." He pointed through the window to the house below.

"Was he one of the four?" I had been reading in Sir Charles Bell's *Portrait of the Thirteenth Dalai Lama* how four Tibetan noblemen were sent to be educated at Rugby in 1912.

"Yes. Ringang was the best of lot," he smiled. "He was trained as an engineer and later installed electric lighting in the Potala."

Many months later, after my return to England, I was curious to know how these boys had survived in an English public school, and rang the archivist at Rugby. The project wasn't a great success from the British point of view, for its aim to increase British influence in Tibet was thwarted by the fact that all four were given lowly positions on their return. The archivist didn't seem to know much, but she said that a lump of gold lay in the school safe, still wrapped in a *katag*, the ceremonial silk scarf. It was payment of school fees from the Thirteenth Dalai Lama.

Basang Dorje went on to talk about western influence in the dress and pastimes of the aristocracy, and the suspicion with which this was viewed by the ruling monks. He was not uncritical of the past, however. He described the power struggles in the Tibetan oligarchy: intrigues between the monasteries and noble families who formed the government. In 1947, Tibet was nearly plunged into civil war when Reting Rinpoche, the ex-regent and abbot of a monastery to the east of Lhasa, attempted a coup d'état with monks from Sera.

There was much more I wanted to talk about, but our conversation was cut short by the start of afternoon classes. Reluctantly I told Basang Dorje I'd have to go, and asked if we could continue later.

"Of course. I am sorry." He picked up his hat and leant over to shake my hand in the western way. "Now I have made you miss your luncheon."

During the class, I kept recalling his expressions and smiling to myself. But I wondered about the attitude to Britain of Tibetans like him.

The British first set foot in Tibet in 1904 when a military expedition led by Colonel Younghusband was sent up to Lhasa. A treaty was to be agreed with – in the event, forced on – the Tibetan government.

This prevented other foreign powers from political intervention in Tibet, and gave Britain exclusive rights over trade. Not long before I met Basang Dorje, I had been reading Hugh Richardson's *Short History of Tibet*, and had found the text of the treaty in the back. There were no British casualties. But the Tibetans were armed only with primitive weapons – catapults and stones probably – and 780 of them died. The last clause of the treaty concerned an indemnity of £187,300 which the Tibetan Government was to pay "for expense incurred in the despatch of armed troops to Lhasa and for insults offered to and attacks upon the British Commissioner and his following."

For several days after reading Richardson's history, I found myself pointing out to everyone the pompous barbarity of the Younghusband Expedition. In fact, I must have apologised so much for being British that someone eventually said to me, "Don't you like your country?" British accounts justify the operation by the belief that Russia had designs on the country. It was rumoured that a Russian monk in Lhasa, known to be a confidant of the Dalai Lama, was a Tsarist spy. And anyway, we are told, the British soldiers' behaviour was exemplary. They didn't shoot until forced to defend themselves.

To the Chinese government, on the other hand, the Younghusband Expedition is a brilliant example of imperialist aggression. And Lhasa people are still reminded of it. Standing with Mr Li in front of a lurid painting in the Lhasa museum one afternoon, I imagined the hostile glares of the other museum-goers as he explained loudly that its life-size figures depicted Tibetan heroes bravely enduring British imperialist atrocities. It did nothing to restore my confidence.

The hostility, however, was largely my imagination. People seemed to overlook this period. In fact they overlooked Britain's fickleness in its forty-five year friendship with Tibet altogether, or perhaps didn't know about it. At one moment Britain would be acknowledging the Tibetan Government's claim to *de facto* independence and supporting it against the Chinese. A few years later it would be describing Tibet as a state under Chinese suzerainty and urging reconciliation with Peking. The mood was determined always by the current tenor of Britain's relationship with China.

But Tibetans seemed to have forgotten the machinations of British politicians, remembering only the warmth of the handful of officials who had lived in Lhasa – and a jumble of English words. One day I was miming an explanation of the word *army* to my class. I wasn't having much success; they didn't seem to understand. Then suddenly, one of the students stood up, grinning.

"Quiiickmuchlefrilefrilefrilefbowwwwwtun," he barked, striding towards me through the desks. The whole class burst out laughing; it was my turn to look bemused.

"Army?" I asked.

"Yes."

In 1914 the British had established a garrison in Gyantse to train Tibetan soldiers. The training was in English and these drill commands, along with parade tunes like *Auld Lang Syne* and *God Save The King*, were used by the Tibetan army right up until 1959. But somehow, even after the army was broken up by the Chinese, the expressions stuck. It wouldn't be the last time that I was a target for this volley of incoherent parade ground abuse. Even people who were too young to have known the army, knew its language. Beyond entertaining us, I never discovered why.

The representatives whom the British Government had periodically sent up to Lhasa developed a great respect for Tibetan culture; some made deep relationships with Tibetans. Sir Charles Bell, British political officer for Tibet from 1908 to 1921, was a close friend of the Thirteenth Dalai Lama and became an eminent Tibetan scholar, as did Hugh Richardson who headed the mission which was established in Lhasa in 1937. I imagined that we owed our warm reception from older people partly to these men. Perhaps we owed it simply to the fact that Britain was linked with the nostalgia for the past.

"Of course people are nostalgic," Basang Dorje said later. "It is the same everywhere. How do you say it? The good old days, isn't it?" But, like Jigme, he said that his life was better than it had been ten years ago. "Many of us feel lucky to be here."

That the aristocracy survived in Tibet, that its members retained their identity whilst working within the Communist system was, for me, one of the greatest ironies of the situation. The snobs were still there; now they hobnobbed with Government leaders. And, for a few, even the old hierarchy was important. "He's only a small noble," an aristocratic friend said scornfully once when I was telling her about someone I'd just met. In the Sixties and Seventies they all suffered persecution, many were executed or died in prison. But although some had still not been rehabilitated, most of the old noble families that we came across had a considerably higher standard of living than ordinary Tibetans. Their children attended the classes of Chinese children which gave them a greater chance of being sent to university in Central China, and most went on to work in the Chinese administration.

From the start, the Communist government had wooed the ruling élite. "The Seventeen Point Agreement for the Peaceful Liberation of Tibet", which was signed in 1951, stated that neither the political system, nor the status of officials would be altered. Although this fragile alliance between the Chinese and the Tibetan Government collapsed with the Dalai Lama's flight in 1959, "patriotic nobles", those who were considered not to have taken part in the uprising, retained their privileges until the Cultural Revolution.

However ironic, I suppose it was not surprising that over the sixteen months that I was in Tibet, the people who expressed to me the most vehemently anti-Chinese sentiments were not aristocrats like Basang Dorje but ordinary Tibetans. For them, Communism had simply grafted its own hierarchy on to the existing one, and privilege was still beyond their reach.

Among the aristocracy there were those who were considered collaborators, who continued to exploit the system for their personal gain. But I got the impression that, far from wallowing in nostalgic inertia, most of the aristocrats in influential positions were working to win concessions for Tibetans, while trying to avoid getting themselves accused of "local nationality chauvinism". Basang Dorje talked of "building bridges", of working quietly to encourage reform. He was cautiously optimistic.

Chapter 6

ADAPTING TO LHASA AND WINTER

The weather has turned icy. For the first time, the sky is hung with swathes of cloud, like temple banners. Wind rasps, crazing the earth with a fine, steely snow, crusting sheltered corners. After weeks of living under the glare of infinity, the sky has enfolded us. The mountains, no longer dwarfed by its height, loom huge and sullen, their disembodied peaks almost closing over us. And Lhasa, once the crown of twelve thousand feet of world beneath, disowns it now, floating weightlessly on a chiaroscuro of curving mists.

Chinese and Lhasa people pass voiceless behind ubiquitous surgical masks as if the cold had visited a plague upon the town. Khampa traders beam under fox furs, tied in a knot behind their heads – nose through the tail, paws dangling rakishly round their ears. Kongpo people, from warmer climes, pull down the brocade of their small felt hats and add a layer of padding at their waists. Only the nomads make no concession – they sit and sleep outside as they do in summer, one brazen shoulder bared to the elements.

I found myself envying the nomads, their weather-beaten beauty, their hardiness, their dirt even. Chinese and Lhasa people scorned them for it, others pitied them. "Poor, sad things they are so filthy," an English tourist said to me one day. Sad? Cleanliness could hardly be a virtue on the bleak plateau of the north. It might be healthy, but not in this climate. To bare your body to sub-zero temperatures, to torture it with icy water, to spend hours scrubbing clothes which froze in the wind and were dirty again in hours: this was beginning to seem a dangerous madness. I tried to conform to the higher standards of Lhasa people, but found myself being drawn towards the nomad's nonchalant acceptance of dirt. For them, washing in the river acquired the importance of a ceremony – *chang*, tea, picnics, stories – a whole day would be devoted to this rare event. But grudgingly I washed like Lhasa people from a bowl in the uncertain seclusion of our room. Passers-by would peer through the ill-fitting curtains, students walked in unannounced, for only in the afternoon was it warm enough to undress.

Rosemary returned, and our fears that we might invade each other's privacy were quickly dispelled – there wasn't the time. We taught alternate sessions during the day. And when a Tibetan asked us to help with a night class he'd set up at the Banak Shol we began teaching on alternate nights as well. We ate lunch together, that was all.

By lunch-time the sun would be strong, for even in the depths of winter overcast days were rare. Bowl in hand like everyone else, we sat in the wind-blown remains of the garden reheating after the classroom's concrete cold. In the market there was little fresh produce left. Most traders displayed only small heaps of potatoes or radishes in drums of brine. Occasionally a Xinjiang trader would turn up with apricots; the walnut woman still stuffed our pockets with walnuts. And, to the consternation of our neighbours who warned that yoghurt ruined the digestion in winter, we still found yoghurt to buy. We ate meat rarely. Not because it wasn't good – it was delicious. But we had used up our ration of coal, and cooking with yak dung was an art which we still had to acquire. Around this time, however, the unit made an acquisition which transformed our meals.

"*Genla dé pe da!*" Come and have a look! The child from next door called up. It's magic. There was a large silver disk in the garden, circled by three old men in *chubas*, plaits hanging loose down their backs. The wrinkled arms which reached towards the centre, recoiled as hands were burnt in the concentration of rays. A solar cooker, our *lingdao* beamed. We too, burned our hands and marvelled at the kettle puffing rings of steam into the air.

"*Chu khol ba! Kama sum du!*" The water's boiled! Three minutes! In a confusion of ancient rite and brave new world river-bound nomads surrounded the silver disk, admiring the sun's power.

I kept expecting to wake up and find that our life had become routine. In a way it had. We rose with the Tannoy, coaxed water groaning from a frozen pump into metal buckets, lit the stove – there was electricity if we were lucky. We'd cross the garden to the classroom, return for lunch, wander along the river, go round the market, see friends. Novelties became chores which took longer than in England yet, surprisingly, they were no more irksome. Washing up at the pump became as unmomentous as putting plates in a dishwasher. The pile of dirty clothes rose with no more menace than if it had been destined for the launderette. Even the most tedious tasks were alleviated by the company of friends. I had expected that as novelty wore off, a humdrum existence would be exposed. But it was hard to imagine the humdrum when eagles circled the mountain peaks above your washing, or the first sun caught the gold of the Jokhang as you carried rubbish out to the latrine. Or when the latrine itself had a view over the roofs of Lhasa and in the late afternoon an unusual slant of light would turn the Potala silver.

The latrine, an unpartitioned eight-holer, was used by the whole neighbourhood. As communal latrines went, however, it was one of the most salubrious. The earth floor was swept daily, everyone's rubbish stemmed the sickening tide of slurry, and the cold provided a disinfectant. It was nothing like Wuhan where a fetid aura surrounded the latrines in summer. But there, we had never had to squat with students.

For the first few weeks in Lhasa, the younger girls would crouch a decorous number of holes away looking embarrassed – and particularly when we could hear the men on the other side: *toe, foot, leg* – the lesson was being repeated through the cracks in the mud wall one morning. *Knee, thigh* . . . Silence. Guffaws of ribald laughter.

The girls' talk of warm clothes shrivelled around us. I sensed Rosemary's mirth, I studied the view.

For a while I had noticed that people were bemused when we greeted them. They looked blank or giggled, stumbling over their reply as if it was an apology. Thinking that they were shy I smiled reassuringly and continued to address them as we'd been taught by a Tibetan in Nepal. But eventually, Lhamo came up with the reason for their embarrassment.

She burst into the room one day and collapsed on the bed.

"The gateman has just told me . . ." She stopped, unable to get the words through her giggles. "He told me that, every morning you . . ." She broke off again.

"What social blunder have we committed now?" Catching her laughter, Rosemary turned to me. The previous week, a particularly devout student had been with us when, in a moment of absentmindedness, I swatted an insect that was crawling across the table. Too late I had remembered, as he was carrying it outside, that Buddhism proscribed the taking of life. "What have we done, Lhamo?"

"Tashi delek."

"What?"

"Everyone says that you say *Tashi delek* whenever you see them."

"So? It means hello, doesn't it? That's what Tibetans told us in Nepal."

"It means good luck," she said stifling her giggles. "And in Lhasa we only use it at New Year."

"What! You mean we have been wishing everyone a Happy New Year for the last two months and no one has even told us?"

"Not only that," Rosemary said, looking at me. "They have always wished us a Happy New Year in return."

Sometimes it felt as though we were children in an adult world, and we didn't know how to behave. Even the most insignificant act seemed to be complicated by religion and ritual. To the novice, each moment was fraught with social danger.

We were learning slowly, but I suspected that being accepted would require more than learning Tibetan manners. As foreigners in Wuhan, we were rarely treated as equals, we were not in the same scale of things as the Chinese. The decades of isolation and the legacy of xenophobia which the foreign concessions left behind them, had reduced foreigners to the embodiment of Maoist slogans. To many of the Chinese we knew, foreigners were, without exception, capitalist, decadent and immoral.

In Lhasa there was an old man who wandered into the unit from time to time who, knowing that we were foreign, communicated with us as if we were deaf. One day he rushed up to our room and started blowing into the air. I didn't understand. He made vomiting gestures with his hands: it was obviously urgent. Was someone ill, I wondered. No. Someone was talking. Did he want to talk to me? Getting desperate he caught hold of my arm and dragged me down the steps. The telephone was ringing.

Later it became a game between us. He had heard us speaking Tibetan but remained convinced that the only way to communicate was in sign language. Two circles made with his fingers and held in front of his eyes was not, I discovered on another occasion, *"Do you wear glasses?"*, or *"I've got glasses"*, but *"Have you developed the photos that you made of me?"* And by taking so long to decipher his signs, we proved his point about our strangeness.

I was resigned to the fact that for most people we would always be foreign, and yet the desire to be accepted was strong. Sometimes I felt as though I was becoming someone else, someone who was not me at all: meek, giggly, nervous of alcohol and unable to do anything alone. And sometimes, as we were drinking beer, with our backs to the window so that the neighbours wouldn't see as we slipped off, feeling

ridiculously guilty, to that exclusively male domain, the teashop, I
wondered why I was doing it. In summer it would be worse –
perspiring politely inside a winter jacket while the men sat around in
their T-shirts; watching them swim in the waters of the Tsangpo,
sitting coyly on the bank with the girls. And yet for all that, when
people told us that we were "not like foreigners", I felt absurdly
pleased.

But Lhasa hadn't always been like this. There was a time when
Tibetan women were more liberated than women in the West, when
they ate, talked and got drunk with their men. Among early western
travellers they were legendary not only for their openness, but for the
high position they held in society. It seemed to me that while older
women and country girls like Lhamo had retained this easy assurance,
the new generation of educated Lhasa girls were growing up inhibited.
It seemed that they had caught an urbane coyness from their Chinese
colleagues. In class they giggled when we addressed them and hid their
heads in their hands. As break began they flitted into a huddle away
from the men. Even at social gatherings they had to be cajoled into
talking. It was as though a cloud of Communist puritanism had
enveloped the town and smothered their traditional sparkle.

Chapter 7

A MODEL RED GUARD

"Ah ha! you are here at last. I have brought you raw duck's organs –
expensive delicacy." Mr Li pokes his head through the window bars
and drops a bundle on to my bed.

It is half past one, *xiuxi* or rest time. Rosemary is out and I don't feel
inclined to get up. With now daily visitations from Mr Li, we have
discovered the drawback of our vista of mountains: every passer-by
has a vista of us, and there is no escape. The room locks with a padlock
on the outside, so we can't pretend to be out even when the curtains are
drawn. Yesterday Mr Li brought me a sheaf of newspaper articles
reflecting the official view of the old society – proof, he said, of its
barbarism. The articles were filled with grisly descriptions of alleged
tortures: "hamstrings used to rip out hearts, and knives to split noses";
"serf-owners throwing their serfs into pits of scorpions", "gouging
their eyes out simply because they happened to see their masters
raping their daughters."

The logic of the articles eluded me at first. Few of the Tibetans, I
knew, wanted a return to the old Tibet. While Shangri la was, as far as
I could see, a western creation, Tibetans also dismissed the ghoulish
image which the Chinese created. But whatever the old society may
have been, its fabric had been destroyed more than a generation ago.
And with the example of a modern Tibetan society just over the
border in India, this Hell image, which the Chinese government used
as a deterrent or as a means of legitimising its presence in Tibet,
seemed an anachronistic absurdity.

"Hey, Miss Catriona! Miss Catriona!" Mr Li is banging on the
door. "Hey Mimi wake up!" he goes off into peals of laughter at the
thought of my Chinese name – I was christened by a student in a
frivolous moment, with the word used to summon cats.

"Mimi, Mimi – I am here!"

If it weren't for a conversation that we had yesterday, which made
clear his intentions, I would feel guilty: "I must see you often," he said
to me, clasping my hand in a prolonged handshake; I was beginning to
feel quite tender towards him.

"I need to practise my English every day."

No, I am not going to get up.

"Miss Catriona wake up."

I should get up, I know. In China people call at any time and can expect to be welcomed. I know I am being rude, but the sacredness of privacy is deeply ingrained: I resent his intrusion.

"You've woken." Laughing at the ungraciousness with which I open the door, Mr Li saunters into the room.

"Ah, I see you're reading," he says picking up a book from my bed. "Tibetan history, why this?"

"I am interested."

"Huh, it's a waste of time."

I say nothing.

"You should read English books, I have read so many English books . . . Dickens, Jack London, Galsworthy . . . do you know these great persons?"

"Yes."

"Ah, yes, yes. I must come many times to practise my English with you – we are both in tractors."

"In tractors?" I look at him blankly.

"Yes, we are in tractors," he repeats with conviction. "In Lhasa it is terrible for us, Tibetans are not in tractors."

"I am sorry I don't understand."

"In tractors, you know – Marx, Lao Tzu, Shakespeare, Dickens. . . ."

"How are they connected with tractors?" I ask, wondering whether I'd understand if I were feeling less grumpy.

"No, not tractors," he says laughing at me. "In tractors – you know – clever, intelligent."

Suddenly it dawns on me and I can't help laughing too: we are intellectuals. The word in Chinese embraces anyone who is not a manual labourer – except, of course, Tibetans.

It is pointless to argue. Mr Li just thinks I am ridiculous; Tibet is officially described as *culturally backward*, so I suppose I should not be surprised at his attitude. Anyway, today I am determined not to argue and not having anything else to offer him, I suggest a glass of *chang*. This provokes another outburst of derision.

"*Chang!* Oh no, no. I never drink *chang*."

"Have you tried it before?"

"No, certainly not. You mustn't drink it, it is bad for your stomach."

Opposite: Ganden Monastery

When I tell him that I like it, his scorn is turned on me. Its milky colour and grainy texture remind me of lemon barley, although, like almost everything at this altitude, it is deceptively powerful.

"Tibetans have bad stomach-ache all the time, you know." A look of smug superiority settles over him as he sits fingering his leather jacket, a symbol of the status that his term in Lhasa has bought him. I stare gloomily, making no effort to talk. . . . But it is not always like this; usually we get on, in a bantering sort of way . . . and he did wake me up . . . and I have had a stream of students all morning.

"I want to show you some pictures of my family," Mr Li says, undaunted by my silence. He takes a handkerchief-wrapped bundle from his string bag and pulls his chair closer, making its metal legs rasp across the concrete. "This is at the Western hills in Kunming . . . my unit . . . this one is in Beijing . . . the Temple of Heaven . . . Tiananmen Square. . . ." As he shows me each picture he points not to the scenes, but to himself draping the foreground with a stiffly theatrical pose.

"Where's your family?" I ask.

"In a minute," he says lingering over the picture of himself in Beijing. He points to a studio portrait of a family group with scenic backdrop, rosy cheeks and lipstick added by the photographer. "My wife and daughter. And me."

The others aren't important – he flips through them quickly: faded photographs of his parents who died a long time ago, classmates, young pioneer friends and finally a ragged miniature, which he tucks behind the rest before I can see it.

"What's that?"

He looks coy and fumbles, trying not to find it again.

"That one. Who is she?"

The photo, faded almost beyond recognition, is stuck with glue across the back. He holds it away from me so that I discern only the branching pigtails and mouth, disfigured now by the tear.

She was his girlfriend once, long ago. She loved him, but she was a bad girl and he left her. Mr Li looks at me, waiting for me to ask more, enjoying, it seems, his own evasiveness. "I think you are very interested to know about my past," he says incongruously and without giving me time to answer, launches into his story. It occurs to me that he might have planned the whole conversation before he came. Yet why should he? His English is almost fluent and his few mistakes so funny that I sometimes wonder if they are deliberate.

Opposite: Monks at Ganden

"I lost my youth in the so-called Great Cultural Revolution," he says, his expression growing tragic. "I was a Red Guard, you know. A very good Red Guard. I was there in Tiananmen Square when Chairman Mao started the so-called Great Cultural Revolution.

"It was August 1966. It all seemed so exciting then – there were thousands and thousands of people, all gathered in the square, all shouting: 'Long live Chairman Mao.' I think most of us didn't understand what was happening. Perhaps nobody understood, but we felt important. Suddenly we had power like grown-ups. Suddenly we didn't have to go to school, we travelled all over China, exchanging revolutionary experiences with other Red Guards." Mr Li closes his eyes as if savouring the memory, and a note of old excitement counterpoints the disillusion in his voice.

"For the first time in my life I went on a train; I saw places I never dreamed of seeing and I never paid a thing – not for tickets, not for food, not for sleeping, nothing – we were in the great struggle for the future of Communism." As he talks, the old clichés tumble out, shining with retrospective bravura.

For him, as for millions of others, the Cultural Revolution began as a big adventure. Since early times China's young people had been bound by the Confucian concept of filial piety, and now, in his bid to regain nationwide power, Mao was allowing them to rebel. He urged them to struggle against the Four Olds – old culture, old ideology, old customs and old habits. He encouraged them to criticise their elders, to use violence to defend the revolutionary line.

"Later we had to stop travelling," Mr Li continues. "We went back to school, but we didn't have any classes, we just had political meetings.

"Some of the teachers weren't popular with the students, some who had been strict with us before. Now we got our revenge – we said that they were counter-revolutionaries. We drew big-character posters with lists of their crimes, and sometimes, when we couldn't think of any, we just made them up. We made them kneel before us in *Pi dou hui*, struggle sessions, and forced them to make self-criticisms, while all the students attacked and humiliated them."

As he talks, I try to imagine him in the situation. So often, I find myself looking at people in the streets, looking at the streets themselves and wondering what it was like then. What happened here? What did this person do? But, like a calm sea which lulls with its reflection of normality, the surface has closed over the violence of those years.

"The Headmaster had much worse punishment," he continues. "He was beaten every day and forced to clean the latrines; we hung a car radiator around his neck and made him wear a cast-iron hat with 'revisionist' written in big characters. It was so heavy that he could hardly stand up, you know – he often used to faint and then we would throw water over him to make him wake up."

"What about your girlfriend?" I ask remembering that he was going to tell me about her. He laughs.

"She was the headmaster's daughter! So, you see I couldn't love her any more. I couldn't be in love with the daughter of a reactionary. I ignored her. For a long time she tried to see me but every time I walked away. Then the Red Guards broke into their home and destroyed everything. They beat her mother and made my girlfriend eat er . . . night-soil. After that she ignored me too."

Mr Li picks up his mug, sipping his tea through the floating leaves. I watch, trying to discern the feelings behind his words; behind the barrier of his laughter. It is almost as if he is telling me anecdotes from someone else's past. Most people blame the "difficult times" and "The Gang of Four" – Mao's wife and her henchmen – for the excesses of the Cultural Revolution, but Mr Li says he doesn't feel remorse.

Later, however, when he talks about his own misfortunes, his attitude changes.

"The so-called Great Cultural Revolution destroyed my youth," he announces. "Ten lost years they call it now, and so it was. It was a bad time, a very bad time, but for me it was awful."

"For you? I thought you were a model Red Guard."

"I was, I was a very good Red Guard," he says, rancour flooding back into his voice with this aggrieved refrain. "Perhaps I was too good. Anyway, things suddenly changed. They sent me to the countryside, to a terrible mountainous area: Re-education, they said I needed re-education. Terrible, terrible."

"Why? Did you start taking the capitalist road?" I ask, unable to resist the taunt.

"Oh no, no, no," Mr Li titters. "We were in Beijing and my Red Guard unit, The Fighters-Till-Death-For-Mao-Zedong-Thought Revolutionary Regiment, were helping to smash up buildings and temples: smash up the past. Bombard the old and build the new – that is what everyone was saying. It was then that the British Legation got burnt."

"Burnt?" I look at Mr Li in surprise.

"It wasn't me," he says defensively, an old fear jumping in the muscle below his eye. He looks, suddenly, as if he wished he hadn't spoken.

He didn't burn it down, he protests. He got lost on the way to the foreign quarter. He missed the glory of the moment, the praise for this great revolutionary act. But later, when these acts were reinterpreted as excesses, his friends denounced him and he became the scapegoat for his Red Guard unit. He was sent off to the wilds of Manchuria to atone for their counter-revolutionary crime, their crime against Mao and Communism.

"Oh, it was terrible. I had to live with the peasants," he says, spitting the words as if even their sound were distasteful to him. "They are so dirty, their food is poor and they made me work so hard: I am not a peasant, I was not used to physical work . . . cleaning pig's houses, digging, planting. . . . Ugh, I can't think of it."

Mr Li's contempt is virulent, dismissive, but it is not unfamiliar. As his indictment of rural life continues, my thoughts turn to similar experiences last year. I recall the disbelief of my students when they learned that I, their teacher, came from the *countryside* in England. Then the broad face of Xiao Ye comes into my mind. She was our star pupil, her English was nearly fluent. We gave her the top mark in her finals, which meant that she would stay on to teach at the university. But she was a peasant. The leaders told us that her accent in English was strange and surreptitiously deducted several marks from her papers to ensure that a "town student" stayed instead. Since 1949, the Government has worked to eradicate this élitism. In the Seventies the *xia fang* campaign which sent town youths to live with the peasants was partly aimed at this. But listening to Mr Li's vehemence, I realise the enormity of the task the Government still faces in narrowing a divide which has stretched between town and country for thousands of years.

Mr Li is still talking, still talking of his ignominious life in the countryside; of the terrible peasant family whom he had to suffer. How did they suffer him, I wonder – this arrogantly sophisticated youth who hated everything about them and their way of life; who, by his own accounts, was wilfully inept and simply another mouth to feed?

Mr Li is getting up to go – a very important meeting. He is sorry to leave me, but in the future we will often have fun together. He grins: a new idea comes to him.

"I kindly invite you to spend New Year with me," he announces pulling his white mask across his nose. Throughout our conversation, it has been dangling from one ear, flapping across his face each time he moves his head.

"I am sure you have never met such a kind person as me," he whines, his face close to mine.

"No, Mr Li."

"Good."

"But I can't come, I have promised to go out with some students," I tell him.

"What?"

"I can't come."

He looks crestfallen, making me feel guilty again. But he persists. "Spring Festival then."

"Yes, all right."

As I watch him prepare to face the cold – leather jacket, gloves, "good quality" watch – I can't help wondering how his peasant family has fared in comparison.

"Ten lost years," he sighs again as he goes out of the door. "Ah, how I suffered. Every day, you know, every day I nearly strung myself up and committed suitcase."

Chapter 8

A TIBETAN CHRISTMAS

We had planned to forget Christmas. The year before I had spent it vicariously, travelling across southern China on the top bunk of a hard-class carriage. Fighting the train's public address system, I directed my thoughts towards home, imagining mince pies, mulled wine, midnight mass, and everyone emerging from the rubble of wrapping paper in the dusk of Christmas afternoon. But our students were convinced that we would feel homesick. For several weeks they had been accosting western tourists to find out how to celebrate. A party was planned, and a driver on his way from Kongpo with his unit's apple rations delivered a fir tree.

On the morning of Christmas Eve, however, an anxious delegation appeared at our room. "We didn't realise that Christmas was tomorrow," a voice blurted through the door-curtain, before I had even opened the door. It was one of the younger students, the one who had had the idea for a party. He had once seen Christmas in a film.

The party had been planned for the afternoon, but Christmas, it transpired, coincided with Political Study. Work could be shirked, classes skipped, but no one in Lhasa missed Thursday afternoon's political meeting or Saturday's communal labour. State employees were summoned by the Party secretary of their work-unit, ordinary citizens by the leaders of their Neighbourhood Committee.

They were tired of politics, the students often said, echoing the cynicism of our students in Wuhan. And that of the local Party secretaries, it seemed. Every Thursday new directives were intoned to an audience engrossed in its novels, its knitting or the latest gossip. If you didn't attend you had to stand up and make a self-criticism. Provided the Party secretary could tick your name off his list, you could do what you liked.

The student was worried. He wouldn't believe that we didn't mind celebrating Christmas on Christmas Eve. But our persuasion over five cups of tea was so effective that, suddenly, he thought he'd been mistaken. Perhaps Christmas wasn't important after all.

"No, it is just that we don't want you to miss Political Study," Rosemary consoled him. "We can celebrate on our own tomorrow."

I suggested flippantly that we could start the party in the meeting, and he left laughing.

But even in the more relaxed atmosphere of that period, we would never have been allowed to attend Political Study. We asked at liberal moments in Wuhan, and were told with a firmness that forbade protest that it would not be interesting for us. Too often the directives concerned foreigners or the perniciousness of West-inspired bourgeois liberalism: and they changed with unnerving rapidity.

In Wuhan we only had experience of life in the state work-unit. In Lhasa, where most of the Tibetan population did not belong to a work-unit, the Neighbourhood Committee was the main organ of political control. But at that time, like Political Study, these too were more relaxed. Meetings were held in the courtyards of homes. The leaders were concerned less with ideology than with matters of local importance. People were being urged to keep the streets clean, to lock their houses, to take precautions to avoid starting fires. Meetings had become a routine chore, a far cry from the Sixties and Seventies when surveillance was a significantly more important part of the Neighbourhood Committee's role. At that time the meetings were a forum for *pi dou hui*, or *thamzing* in Tibetan, the "struggle sessions" like Mr Li's headmaster had had to undergo.

No one wanted to think about those days. "The horrors of the Cultural Revolution have gone, never to return" was a favourite slogan of the time. But already by the summer, there were signs that the apparatus of political control hadn't been dismantled at all. Political Study became serious again. People were told that they should "unify their thinking", that ideological education should be improved. It was to be a foretaste of things to come. By the end of 1987 Political Study had fallen back into the Cultural Revolution mould; citizens were again being arrested in meetings for refusing to toe the Party line.

A friend of Lhamo's knew a Muslim who would sell us some mutton for the party. Yak was not special enough and poultry, as Mr Li said, was expensive and nearly impossible to find in Lhasa. Tibetans rarely ate birds because, compared with yak, where the sacrifice of one life would sustain a whole family for weeks, poultry was religiously uneconomical. Tibet's harsh climate prevented them from adhering to the Buddhist law of not eating meat. But they left most of the butchering to Muslims.

On the morning of Christmas Eve, Lhamo and I went off to the market before sunrise. The air, purged of market smells by the cold, was entwined with warm threads of incense. Among the carcasses of meat, the blocks of butter in their yak-gut skins, people were performing their devotions before business began.

We found Lhamo's friend on the Barkhor, doing a *korwa*, a circumambulation of the Jokhang. For five hours he had been stretching himself out on the frozen ground, advancing, not by lengths of his body but by widths, to acquire extra merit. As he neared his beginning, his prostrations were growing heavy with exhaustion. His bare torso was smeared with grime; a religious badge, pinned through the skin of his shoulder, told of unusual dedication.

Lhamo went up to him.

"Shouldn't we wait?" I said, not wanting to interrupt.

"Wait!" She laughed. "Why?"

Why? I didn't know. The man didn't give the impression that we had interrupted him.

"The sheep?" He smiled and took us to the end of the meat alley where two Muslim women were leaning on their elbows, flapping languidly at imaginary flies with their yak tail whisks.

"They want some sheep," Lhamo's friend addressed one of them.

"We only need a piece." Lhamo turned the carcass over to find the best meat. To me, it looked no different from the other heaps of meat around us, but the Muslims had built up their reputation as butchers in Lhasa since the seventeenth century.

Wabarling, the Muslim quarter, was given to them by the Fifth Dalai Lama. According to tradition he fired an arrow from the roof of the Potala. At the place where it pierced the ground, he allowed them to build a temple and worship in their own way. Today the Muslim community has been swollen by immigrants from the Chinese provinces of Qinghai and Gansu who have come to seek their fortunes.

The Tibetans never interfered with the Muslims' religion and there had been few converts to either side.

"Life has been difficult for them," Lhamo's friend said as we returned to his prayer-beads which he had left on the Barkhor to mark the place where he left off his prostrations. "In the beginning of the Sixties, their situation was almost worse than ours."

"Worse than ours?" Lhamo looked at him.

"Well, bad anyway," he said, turning his attention to his prayers again. Now it was my turn to waylay him. I had had a conversation with some Muslim girls, not long before, about the Arabic which since liberalisation they had been taught at primary school. Now I seized the opportunity of talking to Lhamo's friend. I plunged in rather unsubtly:

"Did they have a worse time than other people in the Cultural Revolution?"

"No, it was before that," he said, wrapping his prayer-beads around his wrist. "In 1962 the Muslims said that they wanted to go back to Kashmir. The whole community demonstrated in front of the Government offices. They said they weren't Chinese and refused to have anything to do with them. Their children left school, state workers stayed at home. Even the Muslims who had been sent to universities in China came back. For several years they refused Chinese *hukou* and ration books. They just did manual labour and helped each other by scavenging what food they could."

"Did they remain apart during the Cultural Revolution too?"

"No. Then, they were the same as all of us. They too had struggle sessions and street committee meetings like everyone else."

We stood watching him for a while as he returned to his prostrations. Each time he raised his hands above his head his prayer was repeated, sinking chromatically as he fell, melting away into silence as he threw himself on the ground. I listened. For a long time afterwards its sound would return to stir this moment in my mind, recreating the whole scene in his single falling note.

The excellence of the meat was not apparent to me, covered as it was with the dust of travel. Nor was it to Rosemary who met us at the gate. But Lhamo knew and we took her word for it. As we arrived home, the neighbours came out to inspect our purchase, bringing their meat cleavers to help us.

"What are you going to do with it?" Lhamo asked, as we finished cutting through the bones.

"Boil it, I suppose."

The neighbours were scornful of our cuisine, of our domestic capabilities altogether, in fact. Our pots were deprived of the hours of sand-scouring that their pots received. The concrete floor, instead of shining like polished wood as most people's did, was traced with the mud of students' boots. Books and papers littered the beds. We would notice pitying glances, but everyone made excuses for us and told each other that we were worked too hard.

"You shouldn't cook the meat," Lhamo said. "It's fresh." She took a piece from the pile and put it in her mouth.

★

After Lhamo leaves Rosemary and I join a group of people at the pump. We don't know them but, conscious of their scrutiny, and enjoying the gossipy camaraderie, we wash the meat more thoroughly than we might have done.

"Midon's husband has written again from Beijing. He wants more money – his student allowance isn't enough, he says. Of course, you never know: fond of dancing, he is. He won't come back, some people think. Lhasa is too backward for him now. He's becoming like a Chinese."

In the stone trough by the pump, a child is trampling a carpet. Above the socks, her legs are mauve and mottled from the cold water. "She really shouldn't be made to work so hard. They treat her like a slave, that family."

"Yes, and you'd think Yudon was religious, the way she's always telling everyone how she took her in!"

"So she's a servant too," Rosemary says to me, as the child continues to tread, indifferent to the remarks around her. Several of the Tibetan aristocratic families and cadre families we have met kept servants. They were girls from rural villages, sent to Lhasa by their parents in the hopes of a better life. Not all were treated like this child, however. One family we had met recently was using their *guanxi* – contacts – to get their nanny a job as a secretary in order to transfer her *hukou* – resident's permit – to Lhasa. But their attempts had failed, as the girl didn't speak Chinese.

The conversation turns to a tall Amdowan just out of earshot who is washing her hair in a bowl of cold water, her breasts bared with the insouciance of a country girl.

"Now, there's one who has made a good marriage. The family had connections in Lhasa – arranged it through a cousin."

"They certainly did well."

"Yes, and now they have sent the sister to live with her so that she can go to school."

I watch the husband helping her untwine her hair from ornaments of coral and turquoise, from silver medallions that run down her parting. She is stunningly beautiful; he is old and his face is set in a permanent scowl, but he has a Lhasa *hukou*. With extreme poverty in the rural areas, the appeal of Lhasa's facilities is great, although it is rare for someone to have this good fortune. But he has done well too. According to Lhamo, country girls make better wives than Lhasa women: they expect less and work harder.

After a while the voices peter out and sounds of work take over:

clothes frothed and frotted and slapped against the rocks; the rattle of rice rinsed in enamel bowls; the creak of the pump-handle. As the sun comes over the wall, everyone stops to rest in its first warmth. Silence is broken only by the clicking of ice which cracks around us on the thawing ground.

At three o'clock on Christmas eve, our Tannoy joined the mêlée of other Tannoys with Wham's Greatest Hits. A student had bought it in Shanghai. It made a change from our own voices which the Tannoy had been broadcasting recently for the benefit of the students: "No. . . .se, Mou. .th, Foooooot, To. . . .e": they would echo round the garden, taunting us like some preying madness.

By six o'clock, with the beds pushed back and the Christmas tree relegated to a corner, our square of floor was filled with shyly contorting male bodies, proving their trendiness with disco dancing. The girls clasped each other in a stylish Chinese foxtrot. A few of the braver ones were dragged, protesting on to the floor by the men, where they danced with eyes averted, backs stiffly arched.

"Teachers, you should show us disco, you should teach us how to dance."

Suddenly the floor cleared. Everyone was looking at us expectantly.

"The music is too slow," Rosemary said hopefully.

"Miss Rosemary, Miss Catriona, you dance, we think you must be good dancers."

"You can't teach disco," I protested. "You just do what you feel like."

But there was no escape. We found ourselves jiggling self-consciously on an ocean of empty floor as the faces, pressed back against the wall, analysed our fumbling movements.

"You see, there is nothing to learn."

"Teachers continue, very interesting."

"Maybe for them," Rosemary grimaced.

Eventually our embarrassment was brought to an end, but on a note of discord. Although most of the guests were Tibetan – the party was their idea – we had also invited some Chinese friends. Among them was Sui, the student whose essay I found so moving. We had been promising to introduce him to the Tibetans we knew. Suddenly, as we were dancing, I noticed him standing with a group of other Chinese outside the door. They were too shy to come in. The Tibetans offered them tea and beer, but their politeness was strained.

"Come and dance," Rosemary said, hoping to dispel the tension.

Crushed together the two nationalities danced apart, the Chinese facing Rosemary's bed and the Tibetans mine. I introduced Sui to Lhamo, thinking that she, if anyone, would put him at ease. But she mumbled a few words and turned away. Even their shared distaste of English food provided no warmth. After an hour, all but Sui had slipped away.

Shortly afterwards, he came up to me. He, too, had to go. My protests faltered under his hurt expression, there seemed little point in persisting. I accompanied him to the gate.

"Do you know these stars?" I gestured half-heartedly at the encrusted night.

"Some of them."

He looked at me. I felt I had let him down. I wanted to hug him, wanted to show him I understood, but he pushed off on his bike, swinging his leg over the saddle with balletic grace, disappearing down the lane.

Afterwards, we tried to persuade ourselves that it was because they didn't know each other. But we both realised, and it would be proved again until we gave up inviting Tibetans and Chinese together, that there was more to it than that. In class and at work Tibetans and Chinese got on because they had to. But with so much suspicion on both sides, any social contact became a duty.

We were no longer in the mood to celebrate. The students were ready to go on into the night, however. Sonam, a friend of Lhamo's, had plaited his hair with a red silk tassel for his role as Father Christmas. He had been our supporter throughout the evening, helping himself to the mutton stew, to Christmas cake, and yak butter fudge when everyone else refused. We found ourselves struggling again between the etiquette of two cultures. We should press the food on them, force them to eat. This was only Tibetan politeness, but our Englishness argued that they might not like the food. Now it was lying cold and congealed on tables around the room.

I went next door to stoke the stove and found Sonam glowing with *chang*. *"Maya khoroshaya uchitelnitsa."* My good teacher, he said, complimenting me with the Russian he substituted for English.

"But I'm not your teacher."

He was undaunted and he turned to the old man next to him: *"Ona maya khoroshaya uchitelnitsa."* She is my good teacher.

The old man looked at me apologetically. "He's drunk."

"You don't understand what I am saying. But she does." Sonam grinned at me. We communicated in a mixture of the Russian he learnt after Stalin's rapprochement with China, my meagre Tibetan, and one word of English:

"Classmate." He pointed to the old man, holding up his little finger in the Chinese gesture of disapproval.

"You are supposed to be giving out the presents," the old man growled. "And now you are so drunk that you can't even get up."

"*Maya* . . ." Sonam's head lolled forward, exposing the dirt-filled wrinkles of his neck.

"Gone." The old man took the container of *chang* and shambled off to join the end of the party in the other room.

Chapter 9

PROBLEMS OF EDUCATION

There were times when we found teaching very demanding physi-
cally. A declamatory style at twelve thousand feet was guaranteed to
have you gasping after a few sentences. Leaping round the blackboard
miming a word instead of translating, because it was better for the
students, would leave us purple in the face, and them in fits of
laughter.

The night classes were particularly strenuous. In the first lesson I
taught A, B, C, D, E and F to a class of seventy. Shaking hands
vigorously, repeating endlessly "Hello I'm . . .", the class extended
three people deep beyond the windows. Six nights a week, by
gas-lamp and candle when electricity failed, these private classes were
offered to the whole of Lhasa. The price was high but so were the
incentives: a better job perhaps, an alternative to the *chang* shop and
cinema. It was only later that we discovered what, for some of our
students, was the most important incentive.

The Government acknowledged that there were serious problems
with the education system in Tibet. The 1982 census which Mr Li was
fond of quoting showed a national illiteracy figure of 23 per cent. In
Tibet, 78 per cent of the population could neither read nor write. By
1985 the figure had fallen to 51 per cent, Mr Li said, and praised
himself and the rest of his Canton delegation. They were "giving
intellectual support to Tibet", it was one of the current slogans.

Everyone agreed that education was in a bad way, and everyone
pointed their finger in a different direction. One thing was indisput-
able. Tibet's rugged size and scattered population would be a nightmare for any government. "There were two people per square
kilometre in Tibet – on every square kilometre in Central China, there
were a hundred and five Chinese" (Mr Li).

Mr Li was a fount of statistics, most people were. Statistics gushed
forth from Political Study meetings, carrying the authorities on a tide
of official benevolence and promises.

Since the arrival of the Chinese, Tibet had acquired three institutes of higher learning, fourteen special secondary schools, sixty-four ordinary secondary schools, and 2,380 elementary schools. Altogether, 147,910 students – Tibetan and Chinese – were in full-time education.

With our own experience limited to Lhasa, it was difficult to find firm ground in this wash of statistics, particularly as most of the Chinese we knew let themselves be carried unquestioningly by the flow, while many of the Tibetans refused to believe any figures.

At the level of higher education there was certainly a significant amount of serious research in the field of Tibetan studies, even though it might sometimes be hampered by the need to adhere to the official line. The Academy of Social Sciences concentrated entirely on Tibetan history, and language. And at Tibet University there were large departments devoted to the study of Tibetan art, Tibetan medicine, and Tibetan history. Here, education seemed dynamic, there was great drive among scholars to preserve Tibet's cultural heritage.

However when we began talking about the teaching of science and technology, rhetoric and reality parted company. Officials told us that Tibetans were sent off to train in Central China. Some were, it was true. But if we pressed them on why the science and maths students at Tibet University were almost all Chinese, we would provoke our bête noire: Tibetans were stupid.

Despite talk of reform, everyone agreed that the situation was bad. But just how bad, was hard for us to know. And who, or what, was most to blame? The Central Government? Han chauvinism among local officials? Bureaucratic inefficiency? The Tibetans? The reforms themselves?

Tibetans don't want to study, Chinese would tell us. This may have been true of rural areas, where in many families the need for the children's labour had to come before education. The opposite was true as far as our students were concerned.

As the months passed we were met with such a barrage of statistics that the obsession became contagious. We were told that 65 per cent of the children at Tibet's middle schools were Tibetan. If this statistic was right, I began to argue, it meant that Chinese children who, according to the 1982 consensus were 3.8 per cent of the child population, occupied 35 per cent of the places in Middle Schools. Mr Li laughed on these occasions; education wasn't anything to do with him. But I would insist. I knew that in the best schools in Lhasa far more than 35 per cent of the pupils were Chinese. Yi Zhong, where I would teach summer classes, had twenty-seven forms. Only twelve of them were for Tibetans. We talked to the Chinese teachers who said it was unfortunate, but there were not enough classrooms to have more Tibetans.

Despite official rhetoric, most of the Chinese we met expressed similar views. It was natural that their children should take priority. They were already suffering hardship by being in Tibet, and they saw no reason why they should be further deprived.

Problems for Tibetan children began early, before they even started school. If they got into primary school life would run smoothly until they were twelve. Most of the primary schools in Lhasa were divided according to nationality. Tibetans would be taught in Tibetan, with three hours of Chinese tuition a week from the age of nine. Chinese children would be taught in Chinese, they would also study Tibetan. But then the entrance exam for middle school would loom, and parents would be running round the best schools with favours for their *guanxi* – those all-important contacts. The problem for Tibetans was that, as most of the leaders were Chinese, their parents were less likely to have good *guanxi*. *Guanxi* was important, but so was the exam itself. The pupils would have to take papers in all their subjects, as well as in Tibetan and Chinese. But while the Tibetan paper was not important – Chinese children would drop it at middle school – the Chinese paper was crucial for everyone. All secondary education in Tibet is taught in Chinese.

So, this was why teachers thought Tibetans were stupid. After learning Chinese for only three years, they had to compete against children who were using their native tongue.

It was only the beginning. Once they had made it to Middle School, those that did, Tibetan children would find that, in effect, what they had learned at Primary School was useless because they could not express it in the language their teachers understood. From then on lessons would continually be held up while the teacher taught the necessary words of his language before he could communicate the lesson.

Chinese and Tibetans were segregated because of this, and, in-evitably, with as much as half a lesson devoted to learning Chinese instead of, for example, history, the Tibetan classes would fall behind.

All over China students use the same text-books, and the final exam which determines whether you can sit for university entrance or not depends on completing all the books in every subject. Children in the Tibetan classes could never hope to finish the number of books each year. So, in the final exam, which is a national exam, they would encounter even more problems than on graduating from Primary School. Now, not only would their Chinese classmates be using their mother-tongue, they would also be answering questions on topics which the Tibetans had never studied.

It was incredible to us that the Chinese teachers ignored this handicap. But what was worse, the authorities only acknowledged it indirectly. An allowance was given to Tibetan children in exams: to enable them to get on in life, we were told. We were not told that it was to compensate for the topics in the exam which they had not covered. The allowance – which was irrelevant to the majority of Tibetans who never reached the final exam anyway – was presented as a magnanimous gesture on the part of the Government. It existed to help Tibetan children because they were less intelligent.

Already we could see how this structural imbalance in the education system had reached into Lhasa society. With poorer results than their Chinese classmates, Tibetans had greater difficulty in getting into state work-units where, despite official rhetoric, Chinese was still the working language. Even if they managed to find work, once on the fringe of state society, they would be deprived of its privileges: bonuses, holidays, maximum rations. Many westerners believed that the Chinese, on arriving in Lhasa, were automatically given better accommodation and higher salaries than their Tibetan counterparts. But salaries in Tibet were higher than Central China, for all state workers. Tibetans generally did not get paid less for doing the same job, nor did they get allocated poorer accommodation than Chinese of a similar standing. The problem, beyond nepotism, was that few Tibetans received enough education to be able to compete with the Chinese.

It wasn't that the Government was unaware of the problem. More funds were apparently being spent on education in Tibet than in any other minority region. There were a lot of plans, it seemed to us. But, at best, little co-ordination. Tibetan medium primary schools were part of the new reform programme, as was the stipulation that Tibetan children at Middle School should study six hours of Tibetan a week. In principle both were important developments. But Chinese pupils studied English when Tibetans were having to study Tibetan. So both reforms, instead of helping them, simply created extra hurdles for Tibetans in a race which was already unfair.

We had imagined that our night-class was largely entertainment. For some of the students it was, but others were deadly serious. They

wanted to go to university. And for most university courses in China –
for science it was essential – you had to know English.

The reforms included a quota of places being reserved at universities
in China for students from Tibet. But it was not an ethnic quota, it just
referred to residents of the Tibetan Autonomous Region. And most of
the places were taken by the children of resident Chinese.

Given the obstacles in the school career of most Tibetans – not
studying in their mother-tongue, not being able to complete the
syllabus, and finally not being able to take an English paper – it seemed
remarkable to us that any got to university at all. They had to be
extraordinarily intelligent, which some of them were. Or have *guanxi*.

Some Tibetans did have *guanxi*. Tibetans who worked in the
Chinese administration often managed to get their children streamed
with the Chinese. It was advantageous in many ways. Not only would
they be able to learn English, they would also – and no secret was made
of this – get better teachers and better facilities. But these people had to
confront a different problem.

"They become like Chinese," a Tibetan cadre said to me once. He
wanted his children to be able to compete for jobs and acquire a similar
standard of living as the Chinese. But they were growing up unable to
read and write their own language. "Just by being in classes with
Chinese children, they learn Chinese habits," he said. He thought his
children had lost traditional Tibetan modesty and filial respect.

But his loss was nothing compared with that felt by some parents of
the children who were being educated in Central China. Part of
China's education policy for Tibet included bringing up Tibetans in
schools in inland provinces. They would be sent at the age of twelve,
and although they would have Tibetan lessons every week, they
would spend their formative years speaking Chinese, in a Chinese
environment. For some families the advantages outweighed the dis-
advantages and they willingly let their children go; others refused, and
suffered the consequences, both in terms of reprimand from the
authorities and often the resentment of their own children.

Four thousand Tibetan children were studying in China at this time.
Undoubtedly these children benefited academically. Given the still
very basic resources in Tibet, it might be an effective way of educating
Tibetans, in the short term. But this policy dates from the 1950s.
Now, instead of reducing the number of children sent to China, and
investing more in improving facilities in Tibet, the Government has
announced plans to send as many as ten thousand children by 1993.

For many Tibetans we met, the policy posed the most serious threat to Tibetan cultural identity. With more and more young adults returning to Tibet, ignorant or scornful of Tibetan traditions, some people saw the policy as a conspiracy on the part of the Government to erode Tibetan cultural values from within.

The authorities dismissed these accusations. And you couldn't deny that they were now trying to preserve the Tibetan culture. But for all the research into Tibet's history, its religion and traditions, there was a danger of it being preserved as museum-piece folk culture, while being destroyed as a way of life.

Chapter 10

SLEET CHILDREN

For hours, the darkness had been exploding with sadistic glee as the spirits of the old year did battle with the new. It was 31st December. Even the moments of respite jittered with anticipation of their next assault. "Don't close your mouth or your ears will hurt," Lhamo had warned half-playfully as she left our room through a minefield of fire-crackers. I lay awake with thoughts of past, less frivolous fighting, while beyond the window the Potala flared through the smoke, green and yellow and red.

"It's not *our* New Year." Lhamo was adamant next morning as Rosemary left to celebrate with some Chinese students. Lhamo and I were setting off to spend the day with her friends who were having a party anyway.

Through the back streets of the old town burnt-out crackers covered the mud in a petalled mildew. Children scoured the ground for unexploded prizes from the night before, greeting each with a shout of glee, and protracted squabbling over who should light it.

A ring-leader emerged, a tall boy of six or seven, filled already with the pomp of officialdom. "A cadre's son," Lhamo said as we watched the other children defer to his authority.

He surveyed his henchmen with a conciliatory smile, wondering on whom to bestow this next favour. The boy next to him? As his glance fell on a small girl at the edge of the group, something, malevolence perhaps, stirred the placid smugness of his face. He gave her the fragment of cracker.

"Throw it into the air before it explodes," he warned, striking a match. The little girl blinked and almost drew back, but a sneer lurked round his face. Hers twitched faintly as she watched him, hovering between fear and shame. She looked round and, sensing the testing glares of other faces, thrust the cracker towards the flame.

"Kupa!" Idiot!

The laughter was shrill, but Lhamo laughed too and there was no malice in her. I looked at the cracker lying unexploded on the ground; at the girl rubbing the nape of her neck like a cat in the peculiarly Tibetan gesture of embarrassment.

"I knew you wouldn't dare hold on to it." The boy sniggered, hurling the exploding cracker into the air.

The web of alleys that radiate from the Jokhang Temple drew me particularly that morning. Narrow and muddy, with doorways sunk deep beneath the debris of decades, they became the embodiment of many long-imagined scenes. Medieval London, or Gogol's Russia even with its puddles and pigs and barefoot children.

We crept along the slithering edges where the ice and mud was half-congealed. Lhasa ladies in high-heeled shoes clutched at the walls and each other to avoid the sewage that ran down the middle. Nomad children squatted in the path with their mothers, decorously hidden beneath long-skirted *chubas*. Men relieved themselves into stone troughs in the walls, chatting and eyeing the passers-by. The new public conveniences were spurned by these country people. From habit I suppose, or was it? The barricades of excrement which piled up around the doors effectively protested against the sacrilege that had built latrines on the ruins of their temples.

"Yangzom's father is Chinese," Lhamo said as we neared their house. I knew Yangzom and her brother quite well by this time. I had met them with Lhamo while Rosemary was away. Several times since then they had been to our room. I had assumed that they were Tibetan.

"Their mother is Tibetan but their father was a P.L.A. soldier," Lhamo explained.

"No, not one of those marriages," she added quickly, following the direction of my thoughts. She had just been telling me how, in the Fifties, Tibetan women were given as brides to Chinese army personnel.

"Yangzom's parents loved each other. Of course, it is difficult for their children. My friends feel completely Tibetan and technically they are because their mother is Tibetan, but people still think of them as half-Chinese. The leaders call it Friendship Nationality, but we have another word in Tibetan. I don't think you'll understand."

"What?"

"*Khang ma char*. It means they are not pure snow, but not rain either."

Diluted Tibetans. I laughed, the analogy seemed apt.

"Sleet, we say in English."

"Sleet . . . sleet," she giggled, rolling the word around her tongue as if testing its unintelligible sounds for expression.

"Yar pé." Come in, a voice calls down from a balcony as we push open the heavy door from the street and cross the courtyard through sacks of *tsampa*, large earthen jars of brewing *chang*, bicycles gleaming with ritual care. A cow belches as we pass, looking up from a meal of fermenting barley.

"Yar pé."

We exchange greetings bowing with hands together. Yangzom, dressed in a long Tibetan *chuba* for their party, ushers us up the ladder to their door. At other doors, dimpled faces appear: children of the eight families who live in this house where one aristocratic family lived before. Inside Yangzom's family's room, the ceremony follows its prescribed pattern:

"Söcha chö." Tea?

"Mei." No thank you.

"Chö, chö." Oh, please do.

"Mei, mei." No, I won't, thank you.

"Dikts chö." Just a little.

"Mei, oné mei." No, honestly.

"Chö." Do have some.

"Mei." No.

"Chö, chö." Have some.

"Mei." No.

Yangzom stands in front of us bowing slightly, proffering with both hands a bowl of frothing butter tea. With protestations failing under her insistence, I take the bowl with one hand, the fingers of the other resting lightly on its edge as custom demands. I am full, I have had five bowls of tea this morning and don't want any more. Resistance, however, is only a formality, genuine refusal is an insult. Enemies refuse a bowl of tea, and only enemies, I remember with a sinking heart, refuse a second.

"Mmmm . . ." It is good.

Yangzom hovers over me, waiting to refill the bowl as it leaves my lips. "Mmmmmmmmmm" she mimics, uncomprehending.

"Shimbu shirra du." It's delicious, I say, enjoying the onomatopoeic tones of the word.

"What's delicious?"

"The tea."

She looks bemused.

Lhamo laughs. "Foreigners always make that noise, they say everything is delicious. It's their custom. Thank you." Lhamo is convulsed with fresh giggles. She is mimicking my pronunciation: *tooocheeechay*. "Thank you is a full-stop for foreigners, they add it to every sentence."

If I had sometimes felt inhibited by Tibetan politeness, Lhamo was quick to show up the absurdity of mine. But as far as "thank you" and "delicious" were concerned, I suspect that I used them so often because I liked the words. Tibetan was still more music than meaning to me. Although we had been having lessons and were making progress, the language was not yet so familiar that its words had become silent, their sound had not yet been lost behind their significance. Although Tibetan is tonal, the tones are so slight, they create a language which is unusually mellifluous. I could still listen for hours to the music of people's conversations without taking in a word.

Yangzom disappeared into the kitchen leaving Lhamo in charge of refilling my cup.

"Don't give me any more," I pleaded. "I've had enough."

She filled it to the brim. "You'll never be a real Tibetan. Yangzom's mother makes the best tea in Lhasa."

"Are her parents here?" I was curious to meet this couple whose "Friendship marriage" was genuine, who married for love at a time when many Tibetan women were married against their will.

They were lucky, Lhamo said. She was thinking of Yangzom's mother, but her father was lucky too. In the Fifties, thousands of Chinese troops were sent up to Tibet many of whom had not returned home, but not all were given wives, or found one as he had.

Was the situation better now? I thought of Sui. He had told me that people were beginning to think there was something wrong with him because he wasn't married: at thirty he was nearly an old man. But there weren't enough women in Lhasa, he complained, at least, not enough Chinese women. His unit had arranged meetings with Tibetan girls but none of them were interested.

Certainly for Tibetan woman the situation had improved since the Fifties, although even then not all the women who married Chinese soldiers were married against their will. Girls from families who had been branded as reactionaries thought that a link with the army would help their situation. And many were simply attracted by the prestige that was given to the Friendship marriages.

"The soldiers were polite then," Lhamo said. "We still say, you know, that Chinese make better husbands than Tibetans." She was giggling.

"Do they?"

"No, not that." She blushed. "They are better at helping with the housework."

I looked round the room; there was little evidence of Chinese influence here. The carpeted couches cradling a low central table, ornate dressers around the walls, wooden pillars painted with flowers of religious inspiration, the frills of coloured silk floating between them: all these were Tibetan. Yangzom's father was beginning to intrigue me. Who was this man who had spent his life in Tibet, yet had made no mark on his own home?

His picture stood on the dresser, a studio portrait with khaki cap, red star, fixed expression. It revealed nothing, nothing more than I knew already. Above him, Dolma, the goddess of wisdom, gazed omniscient from a newly carved altar, but his stare remained impassive. Did he condone this religious belief? Did he share it, perhaps? I looked at his red-starred cap, surrounded by offerings: the heap of *tsampa*, water brimming in silver bowls, the two thin spires of incense which were rising from a latticed holder on the floor, and had, for so long, that the furniture breathed its fragrance. I searched the sepia face for signs of expression, but the camera had created a mask. A P.L.A. soldier like all P.L.A. soldiers returned my stare.

On the balcony outside I found a child setting out the family flower garden. With her face fixed in an expression of responsible gravity, she was arranging her twisted pots and broken fruit jars along the wall. A moment later as the sun came over the roof, they caught its first rays in a cloud of coloured blooms. I wanted to ask whose child she was but she was busy, her expression told me, and she couldn't be disturbed.

Lying back against a heap of cushions, a small boy was following her movements with a look of dreamy idleness. His homework lay half-finished at his side, the haphazardly drawn letters of the Tibetan alphabet smudged across his writing slate. As I joined him, his gaze drifted over me and then was re-absorbed in himself, in his fingers tracing the filigreed shade of apricot branches on the floor. Like him I lay back, letting my mind drift with the senses, following a sound for a while, a smell, a sight. Gradually, in the sun's warmth, my mind slid into thoughtlessness.

Yangzom's parents were back, Lhamo called out some time later. I watched as they crossed the yard, her mother walking ahead, taller than her husband, her plaits dangling grey and wiry down her back. Suddenly, Yangzom's father noticed me and skipped up the ladder.

"Welcome you to my house," he said in English, shaking my hand. He looked older than his photo, his face, no longer pulled smooth to a mask of authority, was lined with crinkled laughter.

"Do you speak Chinese?"

"Yes, but not well."

"Good. I speak only broken English, you see."

His voice was lush with the coastal tones of Fujian province, although he hadn't been there for forty years.

"Don't you miss your home town?" I asked, knowing how important roots were in China, how people usually talked with nostalgia of their ancestral town, even when they had never lived there.

"Why should I? I have everything here."

I was expecting my conventional question to receive its conventional answer, to be told how wretched Tibet was. I looked at him in surprise. "Wouldn't you go back even for a holiday?"

"I have thought about it. I could go every two years now, the unit would pay my fare; but I am an old man, you know, and the journey is too tiring."

He took a cigarette from a packet squashed in his top pocket and offered it to me.

"I don't smoke," I said noticing, or perhaps only imagining, his look of approval: in China only *bad* women smoke.

"Of course, there is a road out of Tibet now," he continued. "And a plane to Chengdu, but when I first came up there was nothing. Nothing but mountains, cold, sickness, hunger, and endless marching."

He looked at me, beyond me, perhaps, to his year-long march into Lhasa with the People's Liberation Army.

On New Year's Day in 1950, Peking announced plans to liberate Tibet from the feuding landlords and foreign imperialist influence, he explained. Not long afterwards, thousands of troops were despatched to its eastern borders which had long been in the hands of the Nationalists. The P.L.A. was still in its infancy, its troops ill-equipped to face the rugged conditions of Tibet. Winter, debilitating altitudes and the effects of snow-blindness soon took their toll. But worst of all was the shortage of food. The men had been instructed not to take anything from the locals; they could carry little themselves and the food packages, dropped in by plane, often fell into ravines or disintegrated as they hit the ground. For months rations were reduced to

six-and-a-half ounces a day; but the forced marches continued
through increasingly barren country. As the bands of Khampa guerrillas became better armed, as morale amongst the troops fell, attacks
became more frequent: the number of casualties was enormous. Only
through discipline and the sheer force of numbers did the first
battalions of the P.L.A. reach Lhasa by the end of 1950.

Yangzom's father fell silent. I wanted to ask him about his arrival in
Lhasa when, as someone had told me, the road was lined with
Tibetans clapping, not in welcome as the Chinese assumed, but in an
age-old ritual to drive away evil spirits? What was he thinking as he sat
there, his face growing gradually to the mask of his photo.

"How did you . . . ?" I began tentatively, torn between curiosity
and the feeling that I was rummaging around in someone else's past.

"Oh, it's all long ago now," he waved his hand dismissively. The
subject was closed.

Yangzom's brother came in. He had just returned from the market.
As he crossed the room, I looked closely for the Chinese features I had
missed before. He was tall like his mother, with her prominent
cheekbones, only a lingering softness reflected his father.

"Her heart is no good," he observed, sharing a wistful smile with
his father as he sat down.

"Whose?"

"Xiao Li's. There is nothing, we are finished."

I was confused. Tsewang – he used his Tibetan name – was in love:
his girl was kind, beautiful and good at housework. He wanted to
marry her but his father refused to allow him. She was Chinese.

I had understood when he told me before, but, then, I didn't know
that Tsewang's father was Chinese too.

"She was a bad girl," he addressed his son in Tibetan. "No morals."

"Yes, my father is right. At the time I . . ."

But his father didn't allow him to finish. "Young people now are no
good. They are only interested in money; girls don't want love, they
want to improve their social position."

Tsewang tried again; but his father, seemingly oblivious, talked on.

"Tsewang is too kind-hearted. Many things he doesn't understand."

"My girlfriend has met a cadre's son," Tsewang explained quietly.
"He is going to university in China. I am only a worker, you see."

"Is that why your father wouldn't let you marry her?"

"Oh no, that's not the reason, I only found out recently. No, he
didn't want me to marry her because she is Chinese."

"But . . ."

"Well, not exactly because she is Chinese,' but because . . ."

"My son is much better than a cadre's son." The old man's face leaned towards me, his face working with anger.

Tsewang blushed. "No, it's because she wanted to go back to China, and my father couldn't bear me to leave home."

"Could you have lived in China?" I asked, noticing his pointed, high-heeled shoes and flared Shanghai trousers.

"I don't know really. It would have been difficult to get transferred to a unit there. Anyway, my friends who have been to China said that every day they missed Tibet. But Tibet is very backward. There are no opportunities for young people here."

"No, I won't allow him to marry her." The old man glared at me as if I were doubting the justice of his decision. "Not just because she is going back to China."

"Xiao Li didn't get on with my mother," Tsewang explained. "She didn't like Tibet, and she always complained about everything. But I loved her then, you see."

"There are many people like Xiao Li who are not respectful to Tibetans," the old man said to me, his eyes flashing with the indignation of the pioneer, who had lived too long and had seen his ideals trampled by the next generation. "They don't listen to the Party. We are here to help Tibet, but they just criticise, complain and do nothing. When I came to Tibet I learnt Tibetan, but many Han people refuse, some have lived here for years without being able to speak a word. The Party says Han cadres must learn Tibetan. The radio broadcasts Tibetan classes every day. And who do you think uses them? Tibetans trying to learn Chinese."

I was sure he was right. I thought of the handful of words Sui boasted. He was the only Chinese person we had met who spoke Tibetan. But could you expect ordinary Chinese to learn the language, I wondered. Most of them didn't like Tibet, Tibetan or Tibetans. They hadn't come here out of choice. I began to think of Wales, of India, Africa: where had colonials ever learned the language of their colonies?

Tsewang's father broke into my thoughts. "But there are many bad Tibetans too, you know. Reactionaries who do not help Tibet, who do not like Han People."

Leaning towards me, he lowered his voice. "Do you know . . . ?" He hesitated, wondering perhaps whether he was talking too freely in front of a foreigner. "Do you know that, until recently, many Chinese people never went out alone, they were too frightened . . . But now it is different," he said quickly. "The situation is good now, people are happy. You have seen for yourself – Tibetans can go to the monasteries and make their offerings, they say their prayers . . . just look at this room." He stretched his hand towards the altar, palm held upwards in the Tibetan gesture of respect. I imagined a note of reverence in his voice as he pointed out the goddess, the different offerings, the incense. I looked back at the photo lying amongst them – its young mask of atheism – I looked at the old man. Dare I ask?

Tsewang went out. We sat silent for a while. He smoked another cigarette and I found myself staring at him. I suppose my thoughts must have expressed themselves in my face, for suddenly he smiled, his cheeks crumpling into lines of amused recognition.

"I don't believe in Buddhism, if that's what you think." He laughed, not shocked, but pleased, I think, that I had mistaken his respect for reverence. "Tibetans are free to believe in Buddhism now, we Han people must not despise them for it. Respect is very important. I believe it is only through mutual respect that the problems in Tibet can be solved and a higher stage of Communism achieved. We must serve the people, love the Party and work hard for the Motherland." He ended with a familiar flourish. Yet these slogans which dribbled vapid from other people's lips, glowed with his sincerity.

For the rest of the day I found myself carried by his idealism. Guests arrived, some of them I knew. They were friends of Lhamo; friends from Kongpo mostly, on pilgrimage in Lhasa. We sat, talked, drank tea and later, much later, we ate.

The table is heaped with *momos*, the yak-filled dumplings, dishes of vegetables, stew bubbling in a copper charcoal burner of Mongolian origin. Everyone helps themselves – and everyone helps me. Chopsticks appear on all sides clasping morsels from dishes beyond my reach: curried potato, pickled radish, a piece of fungi, dried yak, some peppers with beef. "Help yourself," "Help yourself," the cries persist as my bowl rises higher. "No, no you have that piece . . . no, really . . . yes, I *am* helping myself."

They are restrained and pick politely at the dishes. Conversation is dwindling, chopsticks slowing down – one or two desultory mouthfuls of rice and the dishes are removed, still laden.

The afternoon dissolves; moments melt into each other. Like in some Chekhovian tableau, time is cast adrift. Guests play mahjong, doze in corners, talk or do nothing. It is evening, perhaps. Another meal appears: the same meal, the same toasts and, gently, drunkenness seeps in. From guest to guest a loving cup of *chang* is filled and passed and filled again. Drinking with courtly ritual, each man is serenaded by the women, each woman by a group of men. They gather round me now: bold, alluring through mists of alcohol, drifting in the romance of another age. But the mood changes. The songs breathe memories of old Tibet and night sinks slowly into *chang*-charged melancholy filled with ghosts of half-forgotten dreams.

Chapter 11

DEMONS OF THE OLD YEAR

Losar, Tibetan New Year, was nearly upon us by the time anyone knew when it would be. This week, next week, around the beginning of February: everyone told us something different. The confusion arose because although Lhasa now ran on the western system, the festivals were still calculated according to the Tibetan calendar. Matters were further complicated by the fact that the Tibetan calendar itself is not fixed. Based on a lunar calendar, it inserts an intercalary month roughly every thousand days to keep it in line with the seasons. Each year the astrologers calculate the dates that will be auspicious, and these may happen twice. Any particularly inauspicious dates are deleted. There were going to be two Julys this summer, and August, or the eighth month, had been left out.

Lhasa is being scrubbed for the New Year. The icy edges of the river are churned by stockinged feet as people tread their carpets in the water, wash themselves and all their clothing. The threadbare frills of cloth that have fluttered in the streets from window-tops since this time last year are torn down and replaced with iridescent new ones. Shops teem with people buying material to make clothes and quilt covers. Everything must be bright and clean and new to greet Losar. From the dark and jumble of tailor's shops comes a whirr of sewing machines as *chubas*, blouses, hats are hurriedly run up. In every kitchen *khabtse*, the Losar pastries, are made by their thousands: a heap for the New Year altar, some to give beggars and the rest for guests in the week of festivities to come.

One day at the beginning of February we walk into an empty classroom: we are on holiday. Everyone is preparing for Losar and will not be back until the end of the prayer-festival in two weeks' time. Rosemary has a friend arriving on the second day of Losar, and since the the *lingdao* are reluctant to allow other foreigners to stay in our unit, she will be spending most of the holiday at the Banak Shol.

On the day before Losar Eve I am invited to the home of a Tibetan woman whom I met with Lhamo not long ago.

Deyang is a classical Lhasa beauty: tall, with high cheekbones and hair which reaches almost to her knees. She was married six years ago, but her husband has been sent to work in Dram, four days away on the Nepalese border. Deyang prides herself on her *khabtse*-making skill, the intricacy of her designs is legendary amongst her friends. We spend the day in her dark, smoky kitchen, piping the thin paste into boiling butter, spinning it into delicate lotus flowers, boat-like ears of Buddha and a tracery of complex patterns. Her brother works round us, decorating the sooted walls with flour drawings of the Eight Auspicious Signs: conch shells announcing Buddha's enlightenment, wheels of Dharma, eternal knots of love and harmony. The front door is chalked with a swastika, the symbol of luck and eternity; the roof-beams are covered in white dots for longevity and good harvests.

On the day before Losar Eve the evil spirits of the old year are driven out. Deyang's mother sweeps the house with a vengeance, summoning demons from their lurking world of dusty corners. On top of the dust, swept into a piece of broken crockery, she places effigies of the demons made from dough.

Deyang's mother is in her sixties, old by Tibetan standards but still beautiful. Today her hair is braided with new tassels, and the recent gaps in her teeth lend a roguish charm to her already expressive smile. With the final preparations being made for the New Year, everyone – son, daughter, nephews, nieces – scurries around under her instructions. No one is allowed to rest until the evening when we all sit down to *guthuk* – the 29th day soup.

"Look, she's got a black heart," Deyang's son shouts, stretching out across the table and diving a grimy finger into my soup.

"Catriona la is bad isn't she?"

I am unprepared for this game and watch bemused as he fishes a lump of coal wrapped in dough from my bowl. Deyang laughs and explains a tradition similar to that of putting charms in a Christmas pudding; everyone has something hidden in their soup.

"You can't escape, your true character will be revealed," she taunts.

"Pu! Behave!" Deyang's mother scolds her grandson, striking her finger across her cheek: you should be ashamed, the gesture means but in a gentle way. Pu – boy, as everyone calls him – looks defiant and continues round the table peering into bowls, plunging his fingers in, as he spots a new charm.

Uncle's bowl. Nothing. "Uncle! Stir your stew." Deyang's brother

Dawa dutifully complies. "There's a chilli," the boy squeals. "Ama la, what does a piece of chilli mean?"

Everyone laughs. "Chilli means that Uncle is talkative and likes to argue."

"Is that right?" I ask Pu, watching Dawa smiling from a contemplative distance.

"Er . . ." he looks at his uncle and then back to his mother and me. His face gathers into a frown. "Is it right Ama la?" He asks not knowing which holds more truth, the 29th day soup or the face of his uncle.

I find the piece of wool as I am struggling through the obligatory ninth bowl of *guthuk*. I am kind and soft like wool. And black-hearted too?

Pu begins to get upset by these contradictions. When his own bowl produces a lump of salt he lets out a howl of rage. Salt means you are lazy, his mother explains. Lazy people's bottoms are heavy like salt, so they sit all day and do nothing.

Pu screams, pushing his bowl off the table, squelching the offending *guthuk* into the ruts of the mud floor. I try to humour him. I stroke his head, shaved as many children's are to ensure that the hair grows thick in adult life. But this irritates him more and he pulls away. Dawa drinks his ninth bowl in silence, the rest of us laugh, but grandmother looks stern.

"Pu, you must pick up all your *guthuk*," she warns, placing the piece of crockery with the dirt and *tsampa* demons in the middle of the table. "If you don't offer the last of your *guthuk* to the demons they will be hungry and angry and won't go back to hell."

Pu stares at her for a moment, his long dark eyes growing round with fear, then without a word he begins scrabbling around on the floor. In a moment of playful solemnity the rest of us empty our bowls over the demons.

Deyang's mother sits back on the carpeted couch and, tucking her legs under her, summons us in turn. With an expression of matriarchal pride she rubs a ball of *tsampa* dough over our bodies, drawing out headaches, back pains, ulcers and any spiritual ailment that might have afflicted us over the past year, all the time murmuring prayers for good health during the coming one.

"*Tonsha ma! Tonsha ma! Tonsha ma!*" Out! out! Get out! Suddenly she leaps off the couch, picks up the devils in their piece of crockery, and disappears through the padded door curtain into the moonless night.

Above left: Pilgrims encircling Lhasa in a series of prostrations
Above right: Pilgrims from Amdo before the Jokhang
Below: Amdo women shopping in Lhasa

"Where are we going?" I ask as we all stream after her through the courtyard and out into the lane.

"To send the devils back to hell. Here, take this." Deyang passes me a lighted torch of straw and runs ahead to catch up with her mother.

"Out! out! out!" we shout, drawing after us the spirits and demons and all the evil they have brought to the house over the year.

"Don't look back," Deyang calls, "or they will return to haunt next year."

"*Tonsha maaaa* . . ." We run yelling through the darkness to the end of the lane, to an auspicious place where three roads meet.

Other families emerge with their devils and firebrands. I recognise students but there is no time to greet them. At the crossroads the dirt is sprinkled in a swastika to bring good fortune, and the demons are thrown to the flames of a communal fire. Everyone shouts, howling at the shrivelling dough, letting off fireworks, goading dogs into barking: creating enough noise to drive the devils away from the world.

A group of students have just arrived, and fire a volley of rockets at us. We hide behind the wall of the old bank. Pu comes up to me, clutching with both hands a "flowering rainbow." "Here Catriona la, throw this at them." It fires before I can let go and sprays my hand with sparks. From the other side of the road the salvo of rockets intensifies and I shrink behind the wall. My heart is pounding I realise with surprise and not a little shame as I watch adults and children tossing lighted roman candles, catherine wheels, crackers, at each other like toys.

With the fog of firework smoke, the darkness becomes opaque. The devils have vanished in the ashes of the fire. Groups of people bent and plotting, gleam momentarily as they light their next missile and then dissolve again into the night. A rocket whistles past my ear and hits the wall; crackers split around me like breaking stars. Suddenly I notice that my pocket is hot. Too late. It explodes. A cracker jumps out through the side of my coat.

"Pu!" I turn round to him accusingly, but he has gone. He is running home with the rest of the family to prevent the devils from returning in our absence.

Opposite: Making an offertory fire at Sera Monastery

Chapter 12

LOSAR FESTIVITIES

Losar, once the most important festival in the Tibetan calendar, resonated with echoes of the past. In the Potala pilgrims pointed out the balcony, far above the main courtyard, from where the Dalai Lama would have watched the ritual dances of Losar Eve. Old people talked of horse races, archery competitions, the review of the army, its soldiers dressed for the day in the ceremonial armour of ancient times. There was no longer any of this medieval pageantry. Only recently had Tibetans been allowed to revive their traditional New Year at all. Yet for all the talk of the past, it was hard to imagine how the spirit of excitement could have been greater. I wondered if there was an edge to it now. In some people I sensed a certain defiance – a determination to uphold traditions which had been banned for ten years, traditions which were seen by many Chinese as proof of a backward society.

"You must get up early to greet the New Year," Deyang's family had told us. And to ensure that we did, they arrived on the first morning, bearing *goldan*, the alcoholic New Year porridge made from wheat and *chang*.

"*Tashi delek! Tashi delek!*" Voices called through the door curtain.

"*Tashi delek*," we mumbled, wary of the word now. Although, since Lhamo had told us to stop using it, I had discovered that it wasn't really a mistake. One day, at supper with a friend whose cousin was visiting from India, we realised that we were not the only ones to get confused. There were moments of misunderstanding between them too. The reason, the cousin explained, was that Tibetan spoken by Tibetans in exile was beginning to drift away from the language spoken in Lhasa. Words of Hindi and English were stealing into the exiles' vocabulary, words of Chinese into that of Tibetans here.

"Don't worry, you can say *Tashi delek* today." Deyang laughed at our nervousness as she placed a *katag* around our necks. Rosemary remarked on the fineness of the silk.

"You are our guests, we should respect you," Deyang said, explaining how a different grade of scarf was offered according to the status of the person being greeted. The finest ones were given only to high lamas or draped over religious images in a gesture of greeting to the god.

"It is difficult to get good quality *katags* now," she added. "You have seen the ones they sell in the Barkhor – only those gauze things or very poor silk."

Deyang's family was followed by Lhamo, Yangzom, and Tsewang. All arriving with kettles of especially potent New Year *chang*, they vied with one another in making us drink the most of their brew. Dawa held out a glass.

"*Chö chö.*" Drink.

I dipped the tip of my third finger three times into the *chang*, tossing the droplets into the air in offering to the gods. He sang as I drank, a song in praise of dark-eyed women, and smiled darkly with his own eyes. I was caught off guard. Today he was in Tibetan dress to honour the New Year: full-skirted *chuba* drawn in round the thighs with a red silk sash, tall boots, silk hat with fur peak and ear-muffs, slipping forwards on his newly washed hair. I watched him, too long, the song had finished and he looked embarrassed:

"*Gen la, chang chö da.*" Teacher, drink the *chang*, he said turning away, absorbed suddenly in straightening the pleats of his nephew's *chuba*.

Deyang offered me the *chima* – the wooden offering box filled with wheat and *tsampa*. It was piled up like a mountain, and decorated with small banners of silver paper and coloured butter. I took a pinch of the wheat and *tsampa* and threw it into the air. I was wrong. Rosemary took a pinch of each, and ate it. We were both wrong. But everyone was too polite to tell us. Only after the ritual had been repeated at every house in the neighbourhood did we learn that you take a pinch of each, throw them three times into the air in offering to the gods, and then eat the remainder.

Deyang's family were on their way to the Potala and suggested that we went with them. In the past, the Jokhang was the focal point of the first morning of Losar, but now many people visited the Potala as well to pay homage to its exiled incumbent.

Dawa offered to take me on the back of his bike as the one Mr Li lent me had a puncture. "*Terge!*" Let's go, he shouted, pushing off and motioning me to jump on the back. As we careered over the ruts, he turned round to talk, making wide arcs into the middle of the road, grazing the riders in the languid stream of bicycles around us. I clung to his waist and watched Tibetan and Chinese girls behind their men, riding side-saddle with enviably demure composure.

The town was filled with bands of revellers: youths whose self-conscious swagger suggested that, like Dawa, they too were wearing Tibetan dress for the first time. There were girls with pinched waists, whose hands hidden in silk sleeves floating beyond the ends of their fingers would once have distinguished them as ladies of leisure. Even Lhasa dress could be seen amongst the sheepskins of Kham and Amdo as Lhasans discarded Chinese clothes in honour of the New Year.

"Everyone says that Wu Jinghua is wearing Tibetan dress today," Dawa remarked as we followed the high wall which hid the apartment of Tibet's top leader. Wu Jinghua, a Yi from Southern China, was considered to be sympathetic by Tibetans. By the Party he was eventually considered to be too sympathetic. Nicknamed the Lama Secretary, two years after my return to England he was removed from office for failing to quell Tibetan unrest.

"Why is he wearing Tibetan dress?" I asked.

"People think that he wants to show his support for Tibetan traditions. It is because of him that so many Lhasa people have worn Tibetan clothes today."

Not all of them had, however. Just before the Potala we met one of my students who instead of being wrapped in the thick wool of a Tibetan coat was shivering beneath the flimsy cotton of his Chinese jacket. When I asked him why he wasn't in a *chuba*, he muttered something about it being too cold. He was a Party member and apparently stood aloof from such displays of nationalism. Perhaps, like many people, he was afraid that this liberal period would pass and such a gesture would count against him. Perhaps he was cynical about the Government's encouragement of Tibetan dress.

"They think that by getting everyone to look like Tibetans, they can prove that freedom has returned to Tibet," someone had said to me the previous week, after our class had been interrupted for the second time by a Chinese reporter, who having arrived unannounced, sent the students home to get their *chubas*: he was going to take photos for the newspaper. There were mumblings of dissent as the classroom emptied: it was a waste of time, and the reporter was unpleasant. But a few of the students expressed deeper anger. They were proud of their national dress, they said, but it was humiliating to be made to wear it when for years they had been told that it was a sign of backwardness and when many Chinese still saw it as that. A few days later when most of the students were poring over the *China Daily* to see whose faces were on the front page, these few sat outside, smoking with studied indifference. Dawa listened as I recounted the incident but he wouldn't be drawn into discussion. Today he was proud of his *chuba*.

From where we left the bike in Shol, the Potala towered above us. It was like a huge white bird, nestling in its solitary hill, reaching upwards to the heavens. Dawa turned to me and smiled.

"When the great flood comes that will end the world, the Potala will rise up on its wings above the waters and float away."

We stood for a while, watching the dark tracery of pilgrims climbing above us against the whiteness of its stone. Then, half way up, we rested again and looked below. The valley spread out in a dazzle of tin roofs, and mountains cut sharply from the sky.

"The flood could drown all that," Dawa muttered in a moment of spleen. "But still, it is better than Ngari, I suppose." He frowned.

Most Tibetans talked to us of Ngari in tones of reverence; within the province of Ngari lay the centre of the Buddhist world, the place to which every religious person dreamed of making a pilgrimage. Mount Kailash, Khang Rinpoche in Tibetan, stands in the province of Ngari. But for Dawa its name held no mystique. He had been assigned to work there for the rest of his life. At this time, while taking his biennial three months' leave, he was trying to get transferred to a work-unit in Lhasa. Without success.

"Shall we go on?" He shrugged and turned the conversation back to the Potala. He pointed to the Red Palace rising up out of the White Palace. Its cranberry bricks and yak-hair curtain, cascading down seven floors, showed its particular sanctity. It was here that the Dalai Lamas lived, here, too, that most of the shrines and chapels were to be found.

"In that part," he pointed vaguely to the west, "the Dalai Lama's own monastic community used to have their quarters. But the monks are only caretakers now," he added dismissively. "The Potala no longer functions as a monastery at all."

We rested again in the fragile shadow of a tree growing from a crack in the wall. The steps were tall as if they were meant not for mortals but for the gods that inhabited this Paradise of Buddhas, as the Potala was known. We are nearly there, I told myself, keeping my eyes on a huge portico at the top of the flight. But as we got closer I noticed grass and weeds growing up around the door. Steps, untended, were crumbling into each other: the stairway turned and swept up another flight.

Blaming the *chang* for my breathlessness, I joined the others at the top, leaving Dawa to turn the great prayer-wheel alone. As it rumbled round on its axis, oiled with butter and clogged with offerings of barley grains, I asked him what prayers were written inside the wheel; each rotation would send these prayers to the heavens. But he didn't hear, he was concentrating on turning it in order to concentrate his mind on his own prayer.

"Teachers, hello!" Sonam and Kelsang, two of our monk-students, emerged from a doorway as we entered the inner courtyard. I hardly recognised them in their monastic regalia: new maroon robes, yellow coxcomb hats tossed nonchalantly over their shoulders, heads freshly shaved.

"You look fantastic." Rosemary walked round them, admiringly. Sonam's grin rippled to his temples. I thought of the grimy, yellow, knitted hat that he usually wore as a substitute, pulled over a stubbly growth of hair; and the brown nylon trousers, stiff with the grease of old butter.

"Today no work," Sonam said in English. "Today monk."

"Guide." Kelsang joined in. "We show teachers Potala."

"Come."

They led the way across the sun-bleached courtyard and up the left side of the three flights of steps leading into the Palace itself. A group of cadres from the Kunming Education Bureau – so the red badges on their breast pockets announced – were sauntering down against the stream on the far side, simultaneously reaching for their dark glasses as they hit the glare of the courtyard. The middle flight of stairs was cordonned off, polished and shiny.

"Waiting for the Dalai Lama," Kelsang said as we entered the hallway at the top.

Sonam came up behind me and pointed to the muralled walls. "Here you can see how they built the Potala."

From the time before the Dalai Lamas, when the world was a great ocean and the first king of Tibet came down on a cord from the sky, to the enthronement of the fourteenth Dalai Lama in 1939 where, amongst the crowds, the British representative is depicted in minute detail with his wrist-watch and a diminutive Union Jack, Tibet plays out its religious history on the walls of its monasteries.

"This is King Songtsen Gambo," Dawa pointed with palm up-turned to a turbanned figure. "He built a fortress on the Potala hill one thousand, three hundred years ago."

But it was the fifth Dalai Lama, or the Great Fifth as he is known, who was responsible for the Potala's present magnificence. Thirteen storeys high and nine hundred feet long. It was started in 1645 and took forty years to build. The Dalai Lama died before it was completed, but for twelve years his Regent, knowing that the workers would never endure the hardships involved in its construction for anyone but the Dalai Lama, kept his death a secret.

Deyang's mother was impatient to reach the shrines and had already taken a butter lamp and a handful of coins from her *ambac*, the pouch of her *chuba*. We worked our way back into the queue coiling upwards, ladder by ladder, to top the Potala. Eventually, from the gloom and the warm crush of sheepskins, we emerged among the pagoda roofs and the sky. I caught my breath. Suddenly the confusion of colours, images, smells were resolved in a blast of gold and cobalt blue. Rosemary seemed to be as affected by its simplicity as me. We stood at the edge of the roof, looking out at the frozen peaks beyond Sera.

But Kelsang came over, concerned that we would miss the Fourteenth Dalai Lama's apartments which he had coaxed an old monk into opening for us.

"This way please, teachers," he grinned and then waved us on with an exaggeratedly western flourish. I looked at Rosemary:

"Yesterday's lesson?"

She laughed.

We found the others prostrating themselves on the polished wooden floor of the Dalai Lama's audience chamber. There was no altar here before which to bow, only the tall silk-covered throne from which the Dalai Lama would once have given audiences. On the seat a saffron robe stood in a cone as if its owner, deep in meditation, had momentarily spirited himself away.

Deyang's mother had finished her prostrations and was looking at us. I turned to Rosemary, wondering whether we should prostrate ourselves. People often asked us if we believed in a religion: although not theirs, that would have been strange. A western monk appeared in my night-class once. The students had stared at his robes and pale scalp. "What is his religion?" They asked me afterwards. He couldn't be Buddhist, he wasn't Tibetan.

The idea of proselytisation is foreign to Tibetan Buddhists. So foreign, in fact, that when a group of Capuchin missionaries arrived in Lhasa in the eighteenth century to convert the Tibetans to Christianity, they were allowed to celebrate mass in the monasteries. In thirty years they converted twenty-six people: their servants. To be Tibetan was to be Buddhist, or Bonpo, and that was the end of it.

But prostrating was a sign of respect, and with everyone prostrating round us, it seemed an affront not to prostrate ourselves too. Deyang's mother clearly expected it of us, I realised as I stretched myself somewhat clumsily on the ground. Today it was particularly appropriate to show respect for this man whom only Deyang's mother had seen, but whose absence filled the place in our imagination. Dawa pointed out the silk-covered window from which the Dalai Lama once watched the New Year dances in the courtyard below. Deyang imagined the pilgrims who, on this day, would have filed awestruck past the throne to be blessed according to their status, either with a tasselled stick or with the young Dalai Lama's own hands. Into my mind came a scene from the Dalai Lama's memoirs: a small boy lost in the vastness of his throne, grown tired of reading, and following instead the events of one of his previous lives which animated the walls around us.

We passed through his private rooms to the roof again. Once more muffled by the thick *chubas* of the shuffling queue, we descended through chapels and apartments of other Dalai Lamas. There was too much to absorb. On every stretch of wall, frescoed deities fixed me with their painted stares. Sitting on lotus thrones, the symbol of purity, they gazed with gentle compassion. Others, garlanded in freshly severed human heads and cloaked in human skin, were dancing on living bodies to crush the human ego. Yet the murals were only the backdrop to the gilded images of gods and kings and Dalai Lamas which thronged the narrow chapels. Festooned with *katags*, offering of boiled sweets, plastic bangles, grains of barley crammed into the folds of their robes, blackened with the grease of fervent foreheads, they each commanded attention.

In one chapel the darkness withheld everything except the face of the caretaker monk, which glowed in the myriad flames of a vat of butter. Bent over it, adjusting the wicks with silver tongs, he stood up as we passed, to pour saffron water into our cupped hands. We took a sip and sprinkled the rest over our heads. It would purify the body and the mind, Deyang explained. In another chapel the monk, skating round the floor on woollen polishing cloths, told us of a fire which had broken out the previous year, destroying many of the religious paintings, the *thangkas*.

"We managed to save the books," he said with obvious pride as he slid off to the far end, leaving shiny tracks behind him in the patina of butter and grime. "These are the collected works of the Fifth Dalai Lama." He took a long, narrow volume from the stack of pigeonholes which lined the wall and unfolded its cloth wrapper. Like all Tibetan books, the fibrous pages inside were loose between two intricately carved wooden covers. Deyang's mother placed her forehead against it and encouraged us to do the same. Like the needles which she had been sticking into the robes of the statues, this would sharpen our intelligence. As we wandered on, crawling under book shelves, being tapped on the head with sacred relics, I began to feel that I was participating in some kind of religious obstacle course. But it occurred to me that in all religions there were people whose faith was centred on acts such as these, and others who performed them as a way of focusing the mind, but whose understanding went beyond.

Kelsang disappeared. Sonam led us on, introducing us to the monks in charge of each chapel, sharing a private joke with them and then taking us to the next. He seemed to be a favourite amongst the older monks and had no qualms about wresting them from their meditation to explain the significance of each image. The Buddhas, too, were treated with the same jovial familiarity.

"This is Tsongkhapa, founder of the Gelukpa sect," he said, patting the statue on the knee as he took us through the gaunt pillars of a deserted ceremonial hall.

At the end of a gallery Kelsang reappeared. "Please come this way, teachers!" he called, leading us from the queue which was already disgorging its pilgrims into the white glare of the exit. Back down a dark passage. My mind, a blur of the morning's impressions, registered that this was just a fraction of the Potala's riches. Somewhere off these corridors must lie the hundreds of store rooms which once were filled with priceless scrolls and ancient armour; the libraries of illuminated manuscripts written in inks of precious metals; the cellars which housed the government stocks of butter, *tsampa*, tea and cloth.

How much was left? It was impossible to know. Zhou En Lai sent the army in to protect the Potala, during the Cultural Revolution, but I remembered someone telling me that, like the Jokhang, it had been the backdrop for battles between Lhasa's two main Red Guard factions. On one occasion, the celebration of a victory in China's border conflict with the Soviet Union had ended in riot when the Lian He Pai, the United Wing, began raining rocks on to the Zhao Fan Pai, the Revolt Wing, a mountain slope below them. The person who told me had been on his way to the hospital and had sat for hours not daring to pass, in the trench that had been dug down the middle of Beijing road. The Lian He Pai, everyone believed, had the support of the army which secretly supplied them with arms. Using the cinema as a rendezvous, soldiers would leave after the film, "forgetting" their guns, and members of the Lian He Pai would be waiting to steal them.

I had been out of the conversation for a while, drifting on my own thoughts, and hadn't grasped where we were being taken. We reached the end of a long passage. Ahead of us a massive red door with antique padlock and snow lion knocker seemed to defy entrance.

"It's the Thirteenth Dalai Lama's tomb," Rosemary said as we waited in the light of Deyang's mother's butter lamp. "None of them has seen it before."

All around, to the edges of the flame, gold gleamed darkly. Still gleaming, and strewn with turquoise and rubies, it stretched upwards for fourteen metres until, in the gloom above us, it burst out of the Potala in a cluster of pagoda roofs.

"The tomb of the Thirteenth Dalai Lama," Sonam intoned, with pride.

"Over a ton of gold was used to make it," Kelsang chimed in, not to be outshone. "And all of it came from presents given to the Dalai Lama during his lifetime."

"These were presents too." Sonam pointed to the porcelain and cloisonné jars, the silver chalices which surrounded the base of the tomb. "The Thirteenth Dalai Lama had a very long life, and he received many presents so his tomb is very beautiful."

But the charred wicks had drowned in their vats of butter; ice had sunk deep in the silver offering bowls. Even the familiar smells of incense and butter vapour had gone, long ago, for they had left no lingering fragrance in the walls or hangings. Deyang's mother looked round for a place to leave offerings, but there was nowhere. There were no lamps to feed with butter, no heap of *tsampa* to add to, no vigilant monk. It had become a place for tourists, a museum, a mausoleum.

The week that followed was filled with festivities. Students, friends, acquaintances – everyone invited us to celebrate at their homes. Not knowing, we accepted all their invitations, only to find that everyone expected us to spend a whole day with them. Confusion, embarrassment and interminable leave-takings. From one four-hour banquet we were forced, bloated and soporific, to launch ourselves into the next.

At the house of a Lhasa noble family, roast chicken and roast potatoes were served in our honour from a silver dish, hall-marked in London at the beginning of the century. Another aristocratic family invited us to a traditional Tibetan banquet, inspired, as the formal cuisine of the upper classes always had been, by Chinese cuisine.

It was with Jampa, a Party member, that we ate a real, almost provocatively Tibetan feast. The Chinese couple who were invited with us picked scornfully at the large hunks of dried meat, the *tsampa* cake with cheese and sugar, and warned us not to drink the *chang*.

Jampa lived in a modern flat in his work-unit. But, despite the privilege of running water and electric cooking facilities, he would have preferred to live in a Tibetan house in the Tibetan part of town. The rooms were too narrow for Tibetan furniture and in summer you couldn't hear yourself speak for the noise of rain on the tin roof. Chinese-style buildings were unsuited to the climate, he told us emphatically. Unlike Tibetan houses which, with their large windows and thick mud walls, absorbed the warmth of the day, these rooms were permanently freezing. But part of the problem, Jampa conceded, was that although the state had built a few Tibetan houses around the Jokhang, they were more expensive to build than the Chinese blocks.

No one called Jampa *go niba* – a collaborator. The first time I met him he made his position clear. Slightly inebriated, he told me in defiant gestures the difference between Tibetans and Chinese. He struck his hand out in a straight line from his nose. That was the Tibetan way of doing things. Then again from his nose, he moved his hand forward in a series of snaking bends: that was the Chinese way. He was fiercely Tibetan and, like many others, he said, he became a Party member because he believed that it was only by working with the Chinese that life could be improved for Tibetans.

But it was at an official Losar reception that the pervasiveness of Tibetan discontent was brought home to me. I was introduced to two Tibetan Party members and spent most of the afternoon with them. Having been to university in China, they now worked in the Administration. I don't know what sparked it off: it may have been the singer who began singing, under his breath, the nostalgic songs of the Tibetan exiles. But both men were suddenly pouring out their bitterness, the resentment they felt towards the Chinese, the difficulty of their own position. One of them eventually broke down and, although we were sitting in a corner, his sobs threatened to attract the attention of two army officers sitting near us. We left through a side-entrance.

On the third day of the Losar, not the third of February, nor the third day of the week as I had understood, I visited Tsultrim and Ngodrup:

theirs was not the only invitation to get lost in the confusion of the two calendars.

Tsultrim and Ngodrup were students who had recently come to Lhasa from eastern Tibet. To all appearances they confirmed the fears of older Tibetans, that the younger generation was becoming sinicized. In class they conversed in Chinese; everyone teased them when they tried to speak Tibetan. "Four and a half words Chinese, half a word Tibetan," the other students joked with me, although their Tibetan was liberally sprinkled with Chinese words too.

Having no family in Lhasa, they lived in their work-unit, in one room at the end of a concrete row. On the narrow metal beds their quilts were folded Chinese-style: turned at an angle across the corner, the pillow and head-towel arranged neatly on top. The walls were decorated with calendars of Chinese pin-ups, open at July and August: the months with the prettiest models. Between them a picture of Tsongkhapa hung as a token gesture to Losar. Arranged beneath him, however, were offerings not of *tsampa* and *khabtse* but the silver trophies that Tsultrim had won in sporting competitions.

We talked in Chinese about disco music and drank bottles of Qingdao beer, yet their feelings towards China were complex. Both had spent three years in Peking where they said they were constantly made to feel inferior. Ngodrup told me how he had gone into a shop once, near Tiananmen Square, and two Chinese women, noticing him enter, had left their purchases on the counter and walked out. "I heard them telling each other to get away quick," he said. "They thought I might be dangerous." But Ngodrup and Tsultrim were ambitious and they knew they would go back.

I returned from their unit through the Tibetan part of town where celebrations had moved to the roof-tops. A forest of new prayer-flags had sprung up over the silvery ghosts of last year's. Streaming from branches at the corners of each house, sharp-edged and freshly blocked with prayers, they challenged the boldness of the sky. Red and green and blue and white and yellow: the colours accorded with the element of the years in which the family was born.★ But they were not "flags" in Tibetan. They were wind horses who carried their printed prayers on the wind to the heavens on behalf of all sentient beings.

★ 1986 was year 2113 according to the Tibetan calendar, or the Fire male tiger year. Tibetans start counting from the birth of Buddha, basing their calendar on a sixty-year cycle. Each cycle is named after one of the five elements – wood, fire, earth, iron and water – combined with two successive animals, the first female and the second male.

As I walked home through the Barkhor, whole families, joined like chains of paper dolls against the sun, walked in procession round the roofs of their homes. At rhythmic intervals, a silhouetted arm rose from the groups of figures, and for a moment the sun would be pitted with grains of *tsampa* and libationary droplets of *chang*.

"*Lla ge lo.*"

"*Lla ge lo.*"

"*. . . ge lo.*"

"*. . . lo.*"

Vaporised by the wind, their cries drifted down towards me, dying before they reached the ground. *Victory to the gods*, their words proclaimed with the prayers on the flags. But there were other flags coiling in the background, redder and larger with the stars of the P.R.C.

Chapter 13

THE GREAT PRAYER

Dawn. The Jokhang Temple. Beneath me, on the frozen flagstones of the inner courtyard a thousand monks huddle turtle-like inside their garnet robes. Softly ageing faces muse a contemplative distance. Among them, the prickling crowns and finely arched napes of younger monks suggest sleep.

The Jokhang opens to the sky in petals of balconies and golden roofs which catch the first sun in a sudden moment of glory. It is an auspicious time of day, says an old woman next to me: the sun is rising straight upwards and the mind is still unclouded. She doesn't understand the prayers but she is not concerned; she will acquire merit just by attending this Great Prayer, the Monlam Chenmo.

Monlam Chenmo began in the fifteenth century as a yearly rededication of Tibet to the Buddhist faith. Traditionally, the Jokhang would be filled with twenty thousand monks from Lhasa's monasteries who gathered for three weeks to pray for the world, that it may have prosperity and abundant harvests. Like most of the festivals, Monlam had been grafted on to the indigenous New Year celebrations, giving them an additional esoteric significance.

The world is now considered to be in a period of decline in which, with growing evil, Buddha's doctrine is becoming obscured. The Prayer Festival was intended to lessen the evils of plagues, war and famine, in preparation for the new age when Jampa, the Future Buddha, would descend into the world. During Monlam the Tibetan government traditionally distributed, among the monks, alms of symbolic significance: medicinal plants as an antidote to disease, pieces of silk against the danger of weapons, and meat, soup and money against the threat of famine. On the last morning a statue of Jampa would emerge from the Jokhang and be taken on a ritual circumambulation of the temple to symbolise the epiphany of this Buddha at the conclusion of the present cosmic period of decline.

★

Monlam had been reinstated this year for the first time since 1959. But its reappearance would be brief. Two years later after Jampa had returned to his shrine and I to England, the police would enter the Jokhang, ending the prayers with bloodshed such as the temple had not seen since the Cultural Revolution.

When we were there, the excitement of Monlam's revival momentarily masked discontent. China's Central Television showed pictures of government officials distributing alms to the thousand monks taking part, and told the nation that Lhasa had been swelled by a hundred thousand gaily dressed Tibetan pilgrims enjoying their quaint culture and religion. "What an inspiring atmosphere of harmony!" exclaimed the glossy brochure produced for visiting Tibetan exiles. But, in their delight at the revival of Monlam, few people cared that the authorities were making political capital. Whatever the motives behind its reappearance, the individual acts of devotion were powerful. Lhasa *was* bursting with pilgrims, many of whom had travelled for weeks over frozen passes to reach what was still the Holy City.

The storerooms of the Jokhang bulged with their donations: whole yaks, prized sheep from the northern plateau, blocks of butter, sacks of *tsampa*, and money. I went with Yangzom to offer a donation from her mother. The man in front of us, as we queued between towering walls of animal carcasses, was donating the equivalent of four years' salary. Few people seemed to have been deterred by the cadre from the Religious Affairs Office – the State Bureau which controls the monasteries – who took the donors' names and issued them with a certificate, allowing entry to the Monlam to those whose donations were large enough.

At night the concrete pavements were filled with pilgrims, clustered tentless under the icy stars. Their children slept naked in the *ambac* of their sheepskin *chubas*, while they drank and sang and prayed round anaemic fires. They lent gaiety to the desolate similitude of Lhasa's streets and the token Monlam, as some people saw it, seemed to have been made real by the strength of their devotion.

At first I want to understand the ceremonies, I want to know what was going on, I keep expecting something to happen. But little *happens*.

From before dawn until far into the night, the courtyard of the Jokhang is filled with a perpetuum of chanted prayer. "Dry Ceremonies" flow into "Wet Ceremonies" with offerings of tea and soup; "Wet Ceremonies" flow into "Dry Ceremonies". Processions of

donors swathed in silk *katags* and incense pass through with petitions
for prayers. The scene changes briefly; the prayer continues. The rows
reform, fanning round parasols of yellow silk while the ceremonies
turn into doctrinal debates. Questioned by the elders, aspiring *geshe*★
drive their arguments home with theatrical strides and stylised clapping. The scene changes again; the prayer continues. By the third day I
no longer need to understand. I open my mind to the smells and sights
and sounds around me, and the ceremonies have no length. Their own
rhythm imposes itself on me now: the rhythm of the music.

The chants begin on a long dark note from the precentor, so deep
that before you become conscious of it as sound, you sense the
movement of air. I search my mind for comparisons but none come,
save those of the elements. A distant wind, an echo of thunder. Over
this note, the other voices rise slowly, tapering to the trebles of the
child-monks. The chants swell, growing from the precentor's voice
louder and faster, reaching their climax, and then sinking back again to
the soundless depths of his single note. There is no harmony, most of
the music hovers around three notes, but the hypnotic rhythm gives it
an emotional power which stirs the soul.

The carpets on the roof beside me begin to fill with the families of
donors. Beneath us the sun spills on to the courtyard, raising somnolent heads. The wind stirs notes of the prayers and strands of incense.
Ruffling the bells along the pavilioned roofs above us, it mingles their
sound with stray voices from the market and the ritual music of the
monks.

Later among the gold pinnacles, the sun silhouettes two figures in
embroidered robes and hooked hats like crested birds. Their conch-
shell horns throw an eerie call to the skies, symbolically announcing
Buddha's enlightenment and the "Wet Ceremony": breakfast. Monk
children tear down the lines of sedately sitting elders, robes flying,
yellow coxcomb hats askew. In the rush to reach the kitchens first, one
trips on a mischievously extended foot and falls headlong into the laps
of those still praying. Laughter ripples down the rows until it dies
under the tread of the proctor monk who stalks the aisles like a huge
eagle, his hooked hat pulled forward, his shoulders padded with thick
brocade.

The monks return in procession, bearing copper vessels of tea.
From the depths of his robes each monk takes a wooden bowl and a

★ The Geshe degree is like a Doctorate of Divinity. Traditionally it was awarded after
monks had followed the full course of philosophical training which would take from
fifteen to twenty years.

Opposite: Towards the Changthang Plateau

Above: Monlam Chenmo, The Great Prayer Festival

Below: Monlam. Young monks at dawn in the outer courtyard of the Jokhang

small sack of *tsampa*. The spirals of incense, now wreathed in butter vapour, lose their sharpness in the sun's heat. The lightness, the stillness and the early morning dies with this pungent aroma.

There is a refreshing geniality about the way the ceremonies are performed, enhancing the impression of religion as a way of life. Dogs wander in and slump down amidst the monks, children lean precariously over the edge of the roofs to get a better view, men and women pray and drink tea and talk and pray. There is no incongruity in this, and all are acknowledged with easy-going cheerfulness as if they are a part of the ceremony. And, in fact, they are. Although the laity do not participate in the rituals themselves, their individual prayers and acts of homage acquire merit for the whole community, whose future welfare the ritual ensures.

How different is the atmosphere from church services at home. Empty cathedrals pass through my thoughts. Clergy gliding through congregations, distant with sanctimonious solemnity. Choristers, stern and disdainful as if childhood were beneath them, as if playfulness were somehow a profanity. How remote it all seems here, where brief moments of fun are not denied, nor do they detract from the seriousness of the ceremony. I watch a silk *katag* float down from the balcony on to a monk who is deep in prayer. Everyone smiles. Others are drifting down now, containing petitions and gifts of money. Thrown by the young monks to the feet of the head lama, they float over heads like paper planes.

Opposite: Monlam. Monks announcing the start of a ceremony with the echoing call of the conch

Chapter 14

THE PANCHEN LAMA

On the second day of Monlam I found myself in a crowd on the Jokhang Square. It was waiting for something; or just waiting, perhaps. The people around me spoke a strange dialect. When I asked them why they were there, I didn't understand their reply, but their words communicated excitement. I waited in an atmosphere of expectancy which, in the Tibetan way, was refreshingly free of urgency and frustration. Something might happen.

I sat. We all sat: we were surrounded by platoons of police. They were brandishing electric batons, shouting through megaphones. "*Tongzhimen zuoxia! Zuoxia, zuoxia!*" Comrades sit down! Sit down, sit down. Only policemen used "comrade" now. Around me children were playing a game with pebbles, juggling them on the backs of their hands; most of the adults were turning their beads and prayer-wheels, watching the roof of the Jokhang. Panchen Rinpoche might come out, I heard someone say. From time to time throughout the day the crowd surged to its feet. Immediately, a kind of frenzy would run through the police, making their loud-hailers crackle with staccato shouts, their electric batons flash across the sun. And then from these pockets of agitation, ripples of panic would spread out through the crowd.

The security operation for the Monlam had been formidable. The army, the *Wujing* – the People's Armed Police, who would be responsible for crushing the demonstrations after 1987 – the plain-clothes men and the network of informers, already made up a large proportion of Lhasa's population. But before the start of Monlam plane-loads of reinforcements had been sent in from Chengdu. Riding along the Linkhor, the previous day, I had found people queuing in single file to receive the blessing of the Panchen Lama. They were guarded on the other side of the road by a line of almost as many policemen.

I stopped to watch and fell into conversation with a P.L.A. man. He was bored. He had been there all day and was ready to be distracted.

He was from Chongqing and had been sent to Lhasa sixteen years ago. He had no idea when he would be allowed home.

I expressed a casual interest in the electric baton which hung from his belt.

"It looks just like a stick, doesn't it?" he said, holding it out to me. It was made of rubber, tipped with metal, and was about the size of a large torch. "But it's very effective." He smiled. "You see these two nodes here." He pointed to the metalled end. "These send out the electric current."

I remember Mr Li telling me once that, although it was supposed to be only temporarily disabling, the *dian ban* could cause brain damage, and I asked the policeman if this was true. Realising, perhaps, that he was getting on to dangerous ground, he ostentatiously lit a cigarette and turned away.

What was becoming clear as Monlam continued was the inappropriateness of the techniques of crowd control. Whenever I had been in a crowd, the antagonistic attitude of both the Tibetan and Chinese policemen contrasted starkly with the crowd's docility. One day I was near the front and more than once I was thrown back against the people behind me. Using their batons, the police hit out indiscriminately. As people struggled to avoid their blows, pushing others down behind them, a mood of panic set in. It was obvious that the police lacked training in crowd psychology. But it occurred to me one day as I watched an old woman being tackled that their aggression and fear still lay in the belief that Tibetans were barbarians. Today, with thousands of people packed into the square, the police were more nervous than ever.

"Where are you from?" A voice in English was interrupting my thoughts. He was from Lhasa, the voice told me. I turned to see a tall Tibetan whose dark skin and unruly hair made him look more like a nomad. I was enjoying being alone and responded reluctantly at first.

But then the conversation moved on to the Panchen Lama and became more interesting. I wondered why so many Lhasa people had come to hear him. Although he had broken his monastic vows by marrying, the man explained, he was still the incarnation of Opagme – the Buddha of Infinite Light.

"And anyway," he said, lowering his voice slightly, "many people think that the Chinese forced him to get married."

We had become the diversion of the moment, people turned towards us, enclosing us in an attentive circle, rapt by a conversation that they didn't understand.

"What do you think of him?" I asked.

"I don't know really. People in Lhasa spend many hours arguing about the Panchen Rinpoche. We feel angry when he criticises the Dalai Lama, and sometimes it seems that he just says what the Chinese want him to say. But I think that he is in a difficult position. If he is too outspoken, then the Chinese won't trust him, and he can't help Tibet at all. He has had a very hard life," he said. "He has to live in Beijing and can seldom come to Tibet. Last year when he came for the twentieth anniversary of the T.A.R. it was the only the second time he'd been since before the Cultural Revolution. Everyone was excited then. Many people waited in a queue for a whole day to see him. But some people complained that he only blessed them with one hand, other people said that his Tibetan is not good – people always gossip like this. I think when he came that time, he helped Tibet a lot. The Leaders wanted to make a good impression on him, and for weeks workers had been preparing the sports stadium for the opening ceremony. Then three days before he arrived, they decided that the ceremony should look Tibetan and everything had to be moved to the People's Palace."

"That's a Chinese building too, isn't it?"

"Yes, but it is under the Potala. A team of workers were up for the next three nights building a Tibetan monastery, complete with gold roofs, to hide it. There were many, many beggars at that time, I remember. They used to camp round the Barkhor. Then suddenly, the day before the Panchen Rinpoche arrived, they all disappeared."

"Disappeared?"

"Yes, there wasn't a single beggar left in Lhasa," the man said.

"What happened to them?"

"I don't know, people said that they were sent out in trucks to the countryside."

I looked at the faces around me. This time the beggars certainly hadn't disappeared. Scores of children with twisted locks and scabbed with dirt were weaving through the crowd; "*Kuchi, kuchi, kuchi,*" they begged with thumbs thrust upwards, intoning their pleas like the prayers of their benefactors.

"*Kuchi, kuchi, kuchi.*"

"Yes, the Leaders tried to make things look better for Panchen Rinpoche," the man continued. "He was taken to a village where everyone had been dressed in new clothes; new thermos flasks and radios were put in their houses. But they couldn't trick Panchen Rinpoche. He knew it wasn't real. He was very outspoken; in a big meeting, he told everyone that there were many things wrong in Tibet, that Tibetans were suffering. Then I realised that Panchen Rinpoche does not forget about us. Do you know what Panchen did?" Laughing suddenly, the man held his thumbs together like the children begging. "He went like this, '*Kuchi, kuchi*' he said, and begged us to work hard to prove to the Chinese that we aren't a backward nation."

Around us people burst out laughing at the man's gesture, thinking that he was trying to beg money from me. But he was absorbed in his own thoughts and didn't notice. Two young Amdowans grinned, edging closer in anticipation of further entertainment.

"He does care about us, you see," he said; the Amdowans followed our movements, wondering why I was so stubborn, why I didn't offer him money. "I think Panchen Rinpoche has had a hard life. I think he is very brave. Even before the Cultural Revolution he spoke out about Leftist attitudes in Tibet. He wrote a report to the Central Government pointing out the mistakes that were being made. For this he was publicly denounced and later he was accused of trying to start a rebellion against the Motherland. That was 1964. I can still remember it very clearly. I was in the first class at school then."

"What happened?"

"I don't know what happened at the time, but after he was denounced they set up an exhibition at Tibet University. They showed lots of photographs of so-called counter-revolutionaries. The guns that they were supposed to have been going to use were laid out on tables, with the coded messages and pictures of foreign spies who, they said, were helping him. We all had to go to the exhibition, the whole of Lhasa, unit by unit. We were told to learn from his mistakes. He was openly criticised and labelled anti-people and anti-socialist. Later during the Cultural Revolution he was imprisoned for nine years."

As he went on talking, I grew afraid that someone might be listening to us. But suddenly we had been forgotten by our neighbours. Everyone scrambled to their feet again. This time the petulant loudhailers shouted in vain. The crowd, buffeted by its noose of policemen, refused to obey.

"Tongzhimen zuoxia! Zuoxia! Zuoxia!" Comrades sit down! Sit down! Sit down! Commands whine boorishly through the silence. I feel a surge of anger, but no one else seems to notice. No one seems to notice anything; the people around me are transfixed by a silhouetted group

of monks and officials that has appeared on the roof of the Jokhang.
For ten minutes no one moves, the hats and regional head-dresses
which a moment ago made the pageant of the square, turn into
a monolith of black heads, of faces tipped above clasped hands. The
group on the roof stands close together, staring down at us. I wonder
which of them is the Panchen Lama; but then their ranks open and
a figure dressed in yellow silk moves to the parapet.

There is no room to prostrate. Men, like sleep-walkers, unwind
their plaits in greater reverence. Beside me a man clasps his prayer-
wheel so tightly that the sinews stand out on the back of his hands. The
Panchen Lama begins to speak; he tells the crowd that he misses Tibet,
that he misses the Tibetans and suddenly I notice that people are
crying. I look at the tilted faces of the young Khampas near me, the
tough, rugged faces so feared by Lhasa people and see tears running off
their cheeks. An old woman is sobbing quietly. What thoughts has the
Panchen Lama stirred up, I wonder. What suffering is mingled with
their religious devotion?

"He looks like a Buddha," the man whispers, his eyes still fixed on
the portly figure above us. I am too moved by the emotion of the
crowd to reply.

But the Panchen Lama's appearance is brief. Long after his yellow
silk *chuba* has disappeared through the rows of cadre-grey, the eyes
around me cling to the parapet. He might come back, I hear someone
say. But the Tannoys have struck up their peevish chant again.

Slowly the crowd disperses.

One afternoon, after I had spent five days absorbed in the ceremonies
of Monlam, inspired by everyone's excitement, the mood was lost for
me.

As I was leaving for the temple, Xiao Song appeared in my room.
Xiao Song was the monitor of our classes. She had connections with
the Gong An Ju. After the usual exchange of pleasantries, after I had
offered tea and boiled sweets, after she had told me that I must take
a good rest, that I should enjoy the holidays, she went on with the
same sweet smile; "I need a list of all the people you visited during
Losar."

I stared at her, too appalled for a moment to say anything.

"I need a list of all the people you visited during Losar," she
repeated.

I continued to stare, and then drawing on all my reserves of
sweetness, I asked her why.

"Why?" She thought for a moment, still smiling. "The Leaders want to thank the people who welcomed you to their homes – they should do that."

"Don't worry," I said brightly. "We thanked them ourselves." Gloom crept over me as I thought of the implications of the order. How were we going to avoid getting our hosts into trouble? Perhaps we should never have gone. But we had been visiting people since we arrived in Tibet; most of them, Tibetans and Chinese, insisted that it was not dangerous. Tibet was open now, they told us. Were they just being polite? Among some officials, particularly in the Public Security Bureau, suspicion of foreigners was still deeply ingrained. I remembered Sui telling me, not long before, that he had been seen outside the bank, helping an American tourist with his suitcase. He had been summoned by his unit leaders. What was he doing with a foreigner? Where did he meet him? How long had he known him? What had he said to him? An hour later he had been dismissed with the warning that next time he would have to write a self-criticism.

Xiao Song, ignoring my excuses, asked me to have the list ready by tomorrow. Not knowing what to say, I said nothing. I kept my naïve smile; that was important I thought.

"I want to go now," Xiao Song said. "Welcome you any time to my house." She placed her arm around my shoulder. "You don't eat well, I will cook you some very good food."

Later, on the roof of the temple, my mind was in turmoil. I couldn't see a way of avoiding writing a list of our hosts without arousing suspicion. What would the police do with the list? Would our hosts be criticised? Or was it that they wanted to know who our friends were, so that they could keep track of us? I thought back over the previous week, of all the people we had met at different houses. Tibetans, Chinese, high-ranking officials, and ordinary workers. Everyone was relaxed, and it had seemed quite natural that we should be there. But it had been the same in Wuhan. For weeks we would visit friends, they would visit us and we would be lulled into thinking that things were getting freer. Then the policy would change and we would be reminded that we were always a potential danger for the people around us.

I tried in vain to immerse myself in the religious ceremonies. Today I found my attention drawn to the Dalai Lama's apartments on the opposite balcony with their glowing ornamentation and pinnacled roofs. They were being used by Party leaders and the officials from the Religious Affairs Office. Now and again as someone passed across the sun, the tableau of monks and silken canopies, which had been reflected in their windows, would dissolve. The scene opened briefly to the rooms behind: green uniforms of security personnel, officials in cadre-grey Mao-suits, desks, spittoons, smoking ashtrays.

It was from here that the Monlam was being organised. The Religious Affairs Office had staged its revival. But it was the Religious Affairs Office, I reflected gloomily, which limited entry of monks into the monasteries and which, above all, restricted the teaching of religion. I forced myself to concentrate on the prayers in the courtyard below. But the pattern of heads, the grizzled crowns interspersed with adolescent ones, only reminded me of the generation that had been lost in twenty years of repression. Already religious wisdom was having to leap a generation. People told us that there were ceremonies which only the old monks could remember now. Today it brought home to me the fact that, if the restriction on teaching continued, there would be little hope of Tibet's monastic tradition surviving much beyond the death of these old men. It was true that the authorities were encouraging popular devotional practices of Tibetan Buddhism. But they were starving it of the deeper wisdom which sustained these practices. I thought of Mr Li pronouncing the official view of religion as a superstition which would die when Tibetans were less backward. Suddenly his words had an ominous truth. For without the learning of the monasteries, it could not be long before religion in Tibet fitted the Chinese Government's description of it. A blind faith.

I stared at the mosaic of heads in the courtyard beneath me. Time seemed to be running out.

Chapter 15

THE BUTTER FESTIVAL

I went to the Banak Shol, where Rosemary was still staying with her friend, to tell her about my visit from Xiao Song. She was concerned. For a week I stayed away from our room during the day, hoping that Xiao Song might forget. Once she caught Rosemary in the street; Rosemary told her that she had forgotten whom we had seen. Xiao Song must have known that Rosemary was lying; her ritual smile prevented her from exposing the lie. We decided that if we reached a point where it became too obvious, we would give them the names of Party members, since they would probably have already informed the Public Security themselves.

But we heard no more about it. And we just had to hope our hosts hadn't either. If they had, we would never know, for they would be too polite to tell us.

Full moon brought Monlam to a close with the Butter Festival – "The Offerings of the Fifteenth Day". The making of sculptured butter offerings originally comes from Bon, Tibet's pre-Buddhist animist religion, but the festival probably dates from the time of the Great Fifth Dalai Lama. According to Deyang's mother the Dalai Lama dreamed of paradise and, in order to show his subjects, realised his dream in butter. From that time until the early 1960s, when religious offerings of any kind were banned as an extravagant indulgence, every monastery and every noble family had to create a sculpture for the Festival of Butter.

Speculation had been running high for days. Would the Butter Festival be allowed? Who would make the sculptures? Were there any monks left who remembered the art? Stories of past festivals were being told like legends. There used to be over eighty sculptures rising high above the Jokhang; some of them even moved like puppets.

As I was leaving the temple one day I noticed a door, which had always been bolted before, standing open. It was cold inside, and the sunlight which seeped through the silk blinds at the far end created an atmosphere that was strangely unreal. On the floor among mounds of butter, the rounded backs of monks expressed silent concentration. Sitting surrounded by bowls of water, they held wooden palettes covered with knobs of coloured butter and were deftly adding the finishing touches to their works of art. One was embroidering the edge of a robe, another was making a filigreed ear-ring. Even when sculpting the most intricate shapes, fingers were their only tools. As I stood there unnoticed, sounds from outside came muffled. Only the gurgling of tea broke the silence as a novice refilled their bowls. I felt as if I had stolen in on a secret. It was hard to believe, as I watched them work, that the twenty-year break had diminished the skill and ingenuity of their art.

Behind the blockade of buses that seals off the Jokhang, excitement is mounting. Not knowing that the exits are blocked, pilgrims continue to force their way into the alleys which lead to the Barkhor, crushing the rest of us against the barricades. I can't fall, nor can I stand straight. I have lost sight of Lhamo. Behind me a woman is praying aloud, spinning her prayer-wheel. With each revolution the prayers inside the wheel are repeated – and the pendulum swipes the back of my head. Panic hovers round the edge of my thoughts. But they are suffused with a shared exhilaration as our breath hangs above us in the frozen air.

By the time the buses are moved it is dark. The alley disgorges us on to the Barkhor in a seething mass of bodies. I catch sight of Rosemary with her students, but there is no chance of joining her. "Keep running or you'll fall," I hear Lhamo shout behind me. Other alleys eject their crowds. The momentum is broken: we are on the Jokhang square.

Dragons, their giant scales moulded in a kaleidoscope of colours, glower down at us from wooden scaffolds. Flowers bloom in sculpted shades of red and pink. Religious and mythological figures dance on altars beneath. And among them all sit Buddhas in every manifestation from the benignly fat to wrathful demons with reddened eyes and terrifying scowls.

"They can't be made of butter!" People around us are saying. Lhamo gazes up at the sculptures incredulously. From the small pieces that I saw the monks working on yesterday I could never have imagined a spectacle of this size and grandeur.

"They are so realistic," Lhamo wants to touch one to make sure.

At altars in front of the sculptures, thousands of flames are dodging the wind which threatens to extinguish them. Rows of monks are keeping a night vigil, their crested figures silhouetted against the full moon. As we skirt round them, I reach out to touch a statue of Jampa. Immediately I am accosted by a monk guard and given an unholy shove backwards into the crowd. I trip and fall, taking a Tibetan girl with me to the ground.

Behind us pilgrims laugh, several younger monks snigger through their prayers; the guard continues to berate me. Returning her tea and bundle of dried meat to her *ambac*, the girl moves on rather crossly.

"I thought non-violence was important to Buddhists," I say, unable to resist the taunt. The monk scowls, giving me a look of almost theatrical ferocity. But it is his job. In the past the *dop-dop*, the monk police, used to take over the maintenance of law and order from the civil authorities during the Monlam, inspiring terror in the citizens of Lhasa. Although they attended religious ceremonies, these monks were primarily concerned with the running of the monasteries: cooking, cleaning, forming the guard of honour. They had little to do with the scholarly pursuits of the other monks.

"Well, are they all butter?" Lhamo quips blithely. But the monk has already turned his attention to another over-enthusiastic pilgrim, who is being dealt with as roughly as I.

We stay on the Barkhor all night walking round in the crowd. There is an atmosphere of jubilation. The air hums with mantras. Newly rebuilt incense burners send juniper smoke billowing in fragrant clouds about the heads of the monks. Pilgrims turn to shadows in the light of the flames which dance on the walls of the houses.

But dawn comes quickly. The sun rises behind the Jokhang, the gods slide off their pedestals into a muddy heap of melting butter. "What a waste," I remark to Lhamo, as all around us people are scrabbling on the ground for lumps of sanctified butter.

But I have missed the point. These people have been worshipping the gods, not the exquisite craftsmanship of their manifestation in butter. The mounds of smudged colour, inglorious remains of months of work, are a vivid lesson in the ephemeral nature of all things.

On the last day of Monlam, Lhamo and I meet again at sunrise, this time to see the statue of Jampa, the Future Buddha, taken in procession round the Barkhor.

With the first rays of sun on the pinnacles of the Potala, the Buddha image emerges from the Jokhang. It is supported by a body of monks and accompanied by all the instruments of the Tibetan orchestra. We follow behind the procession, squeezing through the alleys filled with music. Slowly I succumb to its power. The air around me is engulfed by it, by the hollow rumble of drums, the drone of the *radung* and, floating above them with the notes of the conch, the piercing wail of oboes. Masters of the art of circular breathing, the monks' notes flow round each other, swelling and ebbing. I don't know whether it is this that gives the music its power, or whether it is vibrations of the drums and *radung*. Whatever it is, like the music of the chants, it floods the soul.

By the time we return to the gates of the Jokhang, the Jampa is already disappearing inside, veiled now in swathes of *katags*. The Lhasa Singing and Dancing Troupe are giving a performance on the square, but the crowd is so dense we cannot see anything. Behind me people are climbing on to each other, on to the concrete flower beds and lamp-posts, to get a better view. One man, a nomad from Amdo, I guess from his clothes, begins to climb a high wooden frame like a scaffolding in the corner of the Barkhor.

I watch him, admiring the agility with which he climbs. Stretching far above his head, he swings himself from rung to rung with sensual effortlessness. Then he sits there, high above us, kicking his legs in front of him, and beaming. In one hand he grips his knife and beckons to his friends with the other. He has got a fantastic view from up there, he can see everything. The costumes are beautiful, beautiful women too, with jewelled head-dresses just like they used to wear. And there's a dancing yak!

"We should try and get nearer the front," Lhamo says. "I want to see." I look at her doubtfully, but begin pushing my way behind her through the crowd.

Suddenly a sharp report cracks the air, sending red flashes across the sky. Around me faces held momentarily in surprise, freeze into expressions of horror. Lhamo turns. "The nomad!" I watch numbed, as far above us the Amdowan is hurled rigid and distorted from the scaffolding. He falls slowly. As I watch, I find myself willing him not to reach the ground, dreading the thud of his body on the concrete.

It is muted when it comes, and so distant that it might be unreal.

"Is he dead?" Lhamo asks.

I don't want to know.

Suddenly everyone is talking, pushing forward to see what has happened. "Did he lose his balance?" "Why wasn't he holding on?" "But what was the flash?" "And the noise?"

"That's the main electricity pylon for the Barkhor," I hear a man behind me say to his friend.

Green uniforms thread their way through the crowd, and some time later a wooden cart is dragged off down one of the side streets. A ring of silence surrounds us. Beyond it people are unaware that anything has happened. They are still jostling to see the beautiful women, their beautiful head-dresses, and the dancing yak.

Chapter 16

SPRING

The arrival of spring was heralded by weeks of dust storms. Every afternoon towards three o'clock the wind rose to demonic heights and a great wall of dust would roll in from the west. Reaching higher than the mountain peaks it consumed everything in its path: the saw-toothed spur at the end of the valley, the sprawling suburbs with their glinting corrugations. As it closed in, the sunlit roofs of the Potala would dim, and be snuffed out completely.

Then it was upon us, dark and chafing. Everyone reached for their masks. Beijing sophisticates pulled printed nylon scarves over their heads and faces, tying them round their necks like cellophane bags. Most people would take shelter indoors until it passed on, leaving nostrils and ears filled with grit.

When the mountains turned green, we were taken by surprise. Since October we had been living in a desert. It was one of the most powerful things about the place. Here was a world stripped to an essential purity where the brute force of nature inspired, exhilarated, killed effortlessly – and yet this world had created a race of rare gentleness and refinement.

That the landscape could support anything was incredible. But that people could survive without possessing its raw ferocity seemed to me miraculous. The earthy and the ethereal, the Ogress and the Monkey, perhaps. Tibetans themselves, found the explanation in their religion: Buddhism had softened them, they believed. Yet when I thought about it, they had developed a form of Buddhism which was less austere than elsewhere. I continued to be taken by surprise.

And now the mountains were proving the landscape did have a benign aspect – at least momentarily. Once in winter, I had provoked an argument among my students by asking whether the mountains ever turned green. At that time their slopes were so powerfully barren, only two students dared suggest that they might. Green was perhaps too strong a word. Now they were like shot silk: they had to be seen in certain lights to catch the hint of green across their rocks.

In Lhasa, trees which I had hardly noticed before sprung buds; snippets of shoots made fields out of the desert. And birds – sparrows and thrushes and hoopoes – appeared as from nowhere. I had seen so few birds since I had arrived that I was beginning to think there was no bird life left at all in Tibet. The Chinese practice of shooting birds, although it was less widespread than it had been in the Sixties and Seventies, was still a cause of resentment among Tibetans.

There was a student in Rosemary's class, a middle school teacher, who was said to have his airgun trained on the tree outside his window. His Tibetan colleagues called him *Chyu Seken* – the man who killed birds – and refused to use his real name. But the practice of shooting birds would have been less of a threat to Tibet's bird life had their numbers not already been drastically reduced by the "Campaign against the Four Pests". This was part of the 1958 Great Leap Forward, Mao's disastrous drive to solve China's economic problems by labour-intensive industrialisation. Every citizen had to exterminate a weekly quota of birds, flies, rats or mosquitoes. Schoolboys were issued with catapults, the girls with fly-swats. Deyang said that she would spend hours at the latrines with her friends, swatting flies to meet the targets set by the leaders. Once a week they would have to queue up with their jars to prove that they had killed their quota. It was a lengthy process. Each pupil was made to tip his dead flies on to the table and count them out one by one before the class leader. Later when the targets were made impossibly high, they started breeding flies themselves. But no one raised birds, that would have been too difficult. Nor were they reprieved in Tibet as they were elsewhere in China where the caterpillar population multiplied in their absence. Now spring reminded people of the fate of Tibet's bird-life. Many species had died out altogether. There were no doves now, no pigeons, and some varieties of duck had not recovered from the attack on their numbers.

Spring, with its hotter days and nights which no longer froze, brought with it new smells. In the lanes around the Barkhor the fragrant clouds of incense and juniper now mingled with murkier odours. Even our meticulously swept latrines were beginning to fester. Maggots in thousands like heaps of white rice clung to every surface. Our rubbish, which had been piling up in the bottom of the pit for months, was beginning to bring the excreta uncomfortably close. Until now I had enjoyed moments passed at the latrine – the views across the rooftops, the changing light on the mountains. And the bizarre snippets of news that might be discussed with our students.

One morning the big story was the robbery which had been announced over the Tannoy – 200,000 *yuan* had been stolen from the Bank of China Lhasa Branch, and from under the noses of the sleeping guards. No one knew any more, and with everyone now less inclined to linger in the latrine, the conversation was curtailed.

After the festivities of the New Year, life returned to normal. Or at least it did until, for the first time in China's history, the clocks were moved on to summer time. There was chaos. The Government work-units changed their clocks immediately; the monasteries refused to change them at all. Everyone else wavered. Half my morning class began arriving at eight o'clock, the other half still turned up at what had become nine.

"Do you mean old time or new time?" "That's old time isn't it?" New time? Old time? Everyone checked now before making any arrangement. But this was nothing compared with the confusion that would occur at the end of the summer when the clocks were turned back again. New time became old time; old time, new time again. Then you had to say whether you meant new old time. Or whether, having made the defiant gesture of non-cooperation, old time was old old time for you.

Rosemary returned from the Banak Shol. We were surprised by the ease with which we adapted to the confines of our room once again. The beds – or couches as they were during the day – became private worlds, and we learned to read, write or prepare lessons, oblivious of the party that might be taking place on the other side of the room. For some reason it seemed that its smallness made life simpler. Perhaps because it imposed a discipline on us. Credit for the harmony which reigned between our two beds, two desks, and the cupboards whose doors had fallen off a week after they were made, had to be given mostly to Rosemary. With her good-natured optimism she was better than I at halting descents into discord. Her remedy was usually a visit with the two-litre can to the old woman near the mosque who brewed *chang*. And a Panda bar of papery chocolate, at such moments it tasted delicious.

Our room never became the hell that I had envisaged on my first morning; it was something we couldn't explain. But in retrospect I wondered whether it was because the room looked, not in on itself, but outwards. Perched on its balcony with windows all round, it became different things at different times. When storms rolled down from the mountains, when clouds swirled around it bringing snow

Above: Awaiting the Panchen Lama's appearance on the roof of the Jokhang

Right: The Panchen Lama appears

and then rain, it had the freedom of a ship. It was disconcertingly like a goldfish bowl, when the neighbours had friends. But with our lives necessarily spent mostly outside, it was, before anything else, a tent. A tent from whose entrance stretched the limitless solitudes of Tibet. And here we could always lose ourselves when confinement threatened.

The classroom took up much of our time too, although memories of classroom life, being the most ordinary, slipped most easily away. I found the mechanics of teaching dull, although the people were always interesting. The classes became entertaining by the Spring. We reached, in the Chinese text-book, exercises for the future: "After a third world war capitalism will be wiped out altogether." And in mine: "Elton Kash has a Cadillac. In it there is a radio, a stereo-cassette, a cocktail cabinet and electric windows. But Elton isn't happy . . . he wants a Rolls Royce."

The Tibetans, I discovered, were extraordinary mimics. Once an English friend appeared in Lhasa. Not having our address, he didn't think he had a chance of finding us. However, a woman came up to him in the street on his second day, wanting to practise her English. "I knew you couldn't be far away," he said to us. "Her voice was unmistakably Bass."

The Tibetan classes continued to grow, but Rosemary's Chinese teachers, probably because English was less of a novelty for them, were beginning to drift away.

"There were only three students today," Rosemary said, coming in after class one afternoon and slumping down on the bed.

"Rosemary, this is Xiao Wang." A Chinese woman whom I had met recently had just arrived.

Rosemary looked up. "Oh I'm sorry," she beamed, making up for her unintended affront with characteristic warmth. "I'm glad you've come. Catriona has told me a lot about you."

"Yes, we are good friends," Xiao Wang said. "Although we have only known each other for a short time."

I had met her in the main Chinese department store a few weeks previously. I knew she wanted to use me to practise her English, she admitted as much. But she was shopping with an old Tibetan woman, a close friend of hers. I was intrigued, and instinctively warmed to her.

Xiao Wang genuinely liked Tibet, although like most people she had tried to avoid coming. In 1980, she married, in Chongqing, a technician on three months' leave from Lhasa. His family thought that their marriage would help him to get back to inland China. But it was

Opposite: Yerpa Valley with the prayer, *Om Mani Padme Hum*, embossed

not easy to get out of the minority regions before your time. Although both families used their *guanxi*, the authorities refused to transfer him. She could transfer to Tibet, however; she would be praised for that. Now that they were both in Lhasa, it was unlikely they would ever get back to Chongqing.

She seemed to have developed a remarkably controversial view of Tibet. Over the last few weeks I had been relaying our conversations to Rosemary – how Xiao Wang thought that living conditions hadn't improved for the Tibetans since the arrival of the Chinese; how much more difficult it was for Tibetans to find jobs, either because they didn't speak Chinese or because local Chinese leaders inevitably favoured their own people. When I suggested that unemployment was a problem all over China she pointed out that it was different in Tibet. Here, there was an ethnic bias. With more Chinese coming unofficially to Lhasa and using the backdoor to get into state work-units, it was likely to get worse.

Rosemary had been wanting to meet her. As she got up to add hot water to our mugs of tea, I noticed her studying my visitor. Xiao Wang was unusually tall, with an expression that seemed permanently serene. But she was not beautiful, about that she was adamant. Her face was not almond-shaped and her eyes were not dark enough to be considered attractive. "Maybe foreigners think I'm beautiful, but to Chinese I am ugly," she told me once.

Xiao Wang was growing uncomfortable under Rosemary's stare and asked her what was wrong with her class.

"Well, most of the students have stopped coming. I had a long talk with the three who came today and they said that all the students like my lessons but they are too busy." Rosemary looked at me doubtfully and then looked at Xiao Wang.

"They should come – they are privileged to have a foreign teacher," Xiao Wang said, sounding for a moment like a Youth League leader admonishing its members. She picked up her mug of tea and blew the leaves across the surface.

"They should come but . . ." She stopped and took a sip from the edge of her mug before the leaves floated back.

"But, you know, apathy is a great problem. Not amongst everyone, of course, but among young people who only come to Tibet for a few years."

Rosemary nodded, encouraging her to continue. I listened, amazed again by her candour.

"But you can't really blame them, can you?" Xiao Wang said.

"They feel low-spirited in Tibet and they miss their families and, often, they feel ill. It isn't easy for us to live here." She stared out of the window. On the next roof, the wind was snapping at the prayer flags which were trying to break loose from their willow branches. "We are not used to the climate," she continued. "For foreigners it is different. You are strong. You can adapt."

We smiled at this Herculean view that many Chinese held of westerners. "Not all foreigners are strong, you know."

In Wuhan it had brought us twice as many classes as the Chinese teachers; our food was better than theirs, we were told. It surprised us then; we were not used to calculating strength in terms of food. But in China, where the diet is generally low in energy, personal strength is directly (and officially) related to food consumption. As I listened to Xiao Wang I recalled our Wuhan colleagues' envy of the P.E. teachers who were stronger than they were because their ration of rice was thirty-eight *jing* a month instead of the usual thirty. I thought of the discussions among my students over how many *liang*, or ounces, of meat and vegetables they would need to give them extra energy during the exams. I am sure it affected their ability to adapt to the altitude too. Sui said that it took him six months to feel well again after he returned from Central China.

Xiao Wang turned to me. "Three of my colleagues became ill recently. They developed a bad heart condition and so they were allowed to go home."

"How long had they been here?"

"Oh, I don't know, quite a long time. For a while they were all right but that often happens, you know." She stopped and then added somewhat wistfully: "Everyone was rather envious."

"Would you like to leave Lhasa too?" Rosemary asked as she got up to close the door which the wind had just hurled open, blasting the room with dust. Xiao Wang laughed. "At this time of year I think everyone wants to leave, everything gets so dirty. You go out for ten minutes and you have to wash your clothes again." She flicked a few grains of dust from the sleeve of her jacket.

Rosemary caught my eye and crossed her arms over her lap to hide the stains on her jeans, trying to divert Xiao Wang's attention by fixing her with a look of concentration.

"No I don't want to leave now. I have my husband here, and I like Tibet. I think Tibetan people are very kind." She stopped. "But I miss my child."

"Your child?"

Xiao Wang took a handful of sunflower seeds and started cracking them abstractedly between her teeth. She'd never told me that she had a child. Suddenly her whole bearing had changed. The poise which, a moment before, had been so striking, seemed to have evaporated, and her forehead was fretted with lines.

"He is only two. It would be too dangerous to bring him to Lhasa," The words came out mechanically. How often had she tried to convince herself of this argument, I wondered. For the next half an hour, her longing for her child was poured out in a minutely detailed account of his life. He was very beautiful and very fat; she described each mannerism, each new development, lingering over the words, oblivious of us almost. It was as though she was losing herself in a dream that she had summoned before to alleviate the sadness of separation. He was being looked after by her mother in Chongqing and she hadn't seen him since she returned to Lhasa eighteen months before, after her year's maternity leave.

"He won't know me now," her voice trailed off. We sat in silence. I couldn't help thinking of the emotional price that China was paying when mothers sometimes had to wait to be grandmothers before they experienced the joys of motherhood. Xiao Wang would bring her son to Tibet eventually, but many couples left their children to be brought up entirely by their grandparents.

Later, after she had gone and Rosemary was teaching her night class, I felt suddenly depressed. I thought of the number of separated families I knew who crossed off the days on their calendars before their next three-month home leave, and then searched for any excuse to prolong it. And the bitterness of Tibetans who felt discriminated against because they only got ten weeks' maternity leave and their annual holiday was limited to a few days at New Year.

When Lhamo came in later I was still brooding. But she scoffed at me.

"Tibet's not good enough for their precious single children."

"But it's not their fault."

She laughed. "I was only joking. I went to a Ji Hua Shang Yu meeting this week and three of the Chinese women had letters from relatives in China saying that their children were ill. They'll make up any excuse to get home."

"How did you go to a meeting? I thought that you had to be a member of a work-unit and be married."

Lhamo looked at me and grinned. "I went with a friend called Mima who wants to have a baby. I am interested in these things. In fact, it

was quite boring. The Party leader read out a list of the people who got
married this year, how old they were, the date of their wedding, and
gave registration forms to the three people who could have babies.
Some people were crying. Once, Mima said, there was a Chinese
woman who pretended that her child was mad so that she would get
permission to have a second one. She had a doctor friend who wrote
her a report."

"Don't the Chinese get jealous that Tibetan women can have two
children?"

"Maybe," Lhamo said dismissively, continuing – as she often did
when excited by something – hardly listening to me at all. Her friend
Mima was annoyed because, like all Tibetans who didn't belong to the
state work-units, she would have been able to have three children, if
she hadn't married a Government employee. Now she would only be
allowed two, and she would have to wait four years before her second.

Lhamo laughed. "After the meeting we were plotting ways of
getting Mima through the back-door. She has a friend at the Ji Hua
Sheng Yu who got her sister a registration form for a new baby, a year
after her first one. Yesterday we took some cigarettes round to his
house, in fact. But his wife said that he'd been sent to Beijing."

Then suddenly, remembering my question, Lhamo rounded on
me. "Anyway, why should they resent us? We've got much more
reason to be resentful. The leaders say that Tibetan state workers are
allowed two children. But if you have more than one, they make you
lose out on all sorts of benefits. Without a 'one-child certificate', you
don't get a bonus every month. Also, when new houses are allocated,
and when the leaders decide who should get a rise in salary, you have
a much better chance of being chosen if you have a one-child card."
She stopped. "Do you think the Chinese should envy us?" she stood
up defiantly.

"Where are you going?"

"I'm off."

"Why? What did you come for?"

"To teach you real things about Tibet!" She laughed, going out on
to the balcony. "And to tell you that I've still got to wait for my
passport. I'm going back to Kongpo for a few months." She vanished
down the steps.

Chapter 17

TSERING

"Tourism must be the central work in developing Tibet's economy." The Tannoy from the unit next door crashes into the evening air. I have come on to the balcony to watch the sunset and write my diary.

"We must unify our thinking and understanding and try in every possible way to grasp Tibet's tourism work in a down-to-earth manner and when this is done well we can foment other economic work."

It is my favourite moment.

"It is Comrade Wu Jinghua," the presenter says.

On the surrounding mountain tops the day is still bright, but shadows are creeping up their slopes. Slowly, like a drowning ship, the valley sinks from the light.

It was the end of April and Tibet's top leader was talking at a meeting on tourism in Lhasa. I gave up and listened. My neighbours, sitting at the other end of the balcony had interrupted their game of mahjong and were listening too. It was an important announcement. Spring had brought with it a flood of foreigners – more already than in the whole of the previous year – and most people had been taken by surprise. All over Lhasa construction sites had broken out in an unsightly rash as new hotels, shops, offices, forced themselves between the houses of the old quarter. All day and half the night the town was filled with sounds of building: the unison chime of workers chipping blocks from vast boulders of stone, the tread of women stamping out concrete floors in rhythmic dances, their melodious songs extemporised above the drone of work.

One day I arrived at the Banak Shol and found my classroom turned into a dormitory. A group of altitude-sick Italians were visibly wilting under the enthusiastic: "Hello, I'm Dawa, what's your name?" welcomes of my students. For us, the chief delight of the tourist season was that the Banak Shol and the hotel next door built showers. The ration was a bucketful of water, heated and poured from the floor above. We showered once with a Khampa, or rather, we showered in adjacent showers. Afterwards sitting outside in the sun, he bent his head between his knees, and his hair, released from months of plaits, fell to the floor in shining tresses. We stared, imagining he wouldn't be able to see us through his hair. Suddenly he parted his locks and grinned.

Older Tibetans were concerned that foreigners would bring in drugs. On the Barkhor a black-market began brisk trade in tourist money for the local *renminbi*. Holiday Inn had arrived. But more serious, as far as Tibetans were concerned, was the swelling of Lhasa's Chinese population. With the promise of a tourist book, sleek, leather-jacketed businessmen, and peasants from the countryside of Central China, were arriving in increasing numbers. They were not volunteers sent by the Government to help with the modernisation of Tibet, they had come to make their fortunes. They were here illegally – they didn't have Lhasa *hukou* – and in many ways their presence added fuel to the racial conflict. While the Tibetan encampments along the river below us were frequently visited by the police, and all those without *hukou* trucked back to their villages, the police turned a blind eye to the Chinese settlers. Tibetans believed that they were being encouraged to stay, and complained that these Chinese got jobs or business licences through the back door. There were 70,000 Chinese altogether in the T.A.R., we were told by officials. These were skilled workers who were being moved out as Tibetans took over. It was another statistic which left us at sea. Chinese leaders dismissed as nonsense the Dalai Lama's claim that the Chinese were in Tibet in their millions and that Tibetans were becoming a minority in their own land. It was hard to know just how extensive immigration was elsewhere in Tibet, but in Lhasa, with its streets brimming with Chinese soldiers and traders, and some of its schools over half-filled with their children, it was hard for us to dismiss the Tibetans' fears.

More and more of the stalls on the Barkhor had been taken over by Chinese. The pavements of the main streets were now an exclusively Chinese domain. Locksmiths, tailors, cycle repairers, dentists with plastic jaws grinning from jars of water, rows of gold teeth and foot-pedalled drills: all jostled with newcomers for space. New restaurants appeared enticing travellers to enjoy a western breakfast at "Dumpling", "The Testy Restaurant" or "The Merry-making Dining Room". One day, with a salvo of fire-crackers and western disco music, a shop opened in Happiness Road flaunting Tibet's first cans of Coke. Thirty thousand more tourists would be coming in the summer, people were saying, and not with unqualified enthusiasm.

Thirty thousand tourists did come that summer, and the following one. Now, three years later, with Lhasa bound under martial law, individual foreigners are no longer trusted. Once more Tibet is only open to the whistle-stop tours.

But Tibet needs tourism. It is one of the poorest regions of China. Despite the new reforms designed to encourage production, it is still almost totally dependent on subsidies from the Central Government. Its native economy has been severely disrupted since the Fifties. The Great Leap Forward which led to severe food shortages everywhere, and later directives to grow wheat in place of indigenous barley, have had far-reaching effects. Today Tibet produces very little itself; almost everything, from food and consumer goods to building materials, travels the thousand costly miles from Central China. The vast state bureaucracy that Tibet supports, and salaries for officials that are as much as three times higher than in Central China, make it administratively expensive too.

The need for the dollars of tourism was great, I realised, listening to the Tannoy again. Wu Jinghua was continuing to present tourism as the panacea for all Tibet's ills. Tannoys in other units had joined in now, and their syncopated promises of "cultural exchanges and scientific contacts with people of all countries in the world if tourism work is done well" filled the evening with voices of paradise.

"Perhaps my son will come and study in England," a woman called down the balcony.

"Maybe," I answered vaguely, my own thoughts occupied with the doubts that must lie beneath this official optimism, with the dangers for the Chinese Government of opening up Tibet. I thought of the Tibetans I had met, monks mostly, for whom this contact with the outside world had great political significance. In monasteries, sometimes on the street even, they befriended westerners with almost fanatical eagerness, spreading stories of Tibet's plight in signs and gestures when verbal communication broke down. I met Tsering like this. He was a monk in a monastery near Lhasa. In 1959 he was involved in the uprising against the Chinese and spent the next fifteen years in prison. Later, when he had served his sentence, he became a "free-worker" and broke rocks at the prison. He was not free, but he earned a small salary, had Sundays off and could visit his family in Lhasa once every year-and-a-half. A few months before I met him, he had been able to return to his monastery.

He walked into my night-class once. The electricity had given up for the evening and in the circle of light that the candles drew around us he emerged like an apparition. The flames caught a draught as he entered, making shadows hover at the edges of his shaved crown. As he sat down on a seat at the back he gestured to me not to interrupt the lesson, but in a subtle way his presence altered the mood of the whole class. The Mao jackets and western anoraks tried hard to make an anachronism of his monastic robes, but in the efforts of the students to win his approbation I sensed the traditional respect that they still inspired.

He wanted to learn English, he told me afterwards; he had to be able to communicate with foreigners. He smiled, but behind his smile he was serious. It was obviously not to broaden his knowledge of the outside world that he wanted to learn English.

He began coming to the class, but it was difficult for him to get permission to leave his monastery at night. A few nights later, however, he came back. We had finished early as the electricity had gone off again, and no one could see the blackboard in the candlelight.

I felt my way down the wooden ladder to the first floor, listening to the confusion of voices and bicycle bells in the street as the students left. He was waiting for me at the bottom, leaning against the railings of the balcony. As I went up to him he put his hands together and bowed his head, uttering the formulaic greeting:

"Genla, kaba terga."

"I'm going home," I answered and bowed too. He looked excited, I thought, as we went out to my bike. His face, drawn tightly over its prominent framework of bones, had a kind of polished smoothness. He laughed as I tied my books to the back with the braid that nomads used to fasten their boots. We talked inconsequentially. He insisted on wheeling my bike, although his robe kept getting in the way, but he seemed preoccupied. For a while we walked in silence and then, suddenly, he said: "Do people in the West really know nothing about Tibet?"

I looked at him wondering what he was leading to. I showed him a letter that I had picked up at the Post Office that afternoon. It was from home, addressed by my mother in her "thoughtfully" large writing: CATRIONA BASS, KONGHA GYATSO, LHASA, TIBET, PEOPLE'S REPUBLIC OF CHINA. It had taken over a month to arrive and, like most of our letters, the People's Republic of China had been crossed out and INDIA via DELHI written over the top in the peremptory hand of the G.P.O.

"This is how much the British Post Office knows of Tibet."

Tsering looked incredulous. "You mean they don't realise that Tibet is now under the Chinese?"

It was hard to believe that what for him was the greatest calamity in history could have passed unnoticed.

I wondered how many letters, if any, had been sent to Tibet since the Raj. Perhaps they thought that letters were still carried to Lhasa by runner over the Himalaya as they were then. Tsering laughed wryly and then broke off. He stopped and turned to me, his face suddenly flushed.

"I sent a letter abroad today with a foreign friend."

"Who to?" I asked, sensing the weight of his words.

He handed me a piece of paper which he had pulled from a bag over his shoulder. It was creased; in one corner there was a round butter stain. "This is a rough copy."

"Who is it to?" I asked again unable to read the curling Tibetan script inside. He leaned towards me, his eyes glittering. "The United Nations – shall I read it to you?"

I looked around us, scared suddenly that someone might have been listening. I was amazed by his boldness. He had just committed what in China is considered a serious counter-revolutionary act. If he were caught he would face ten years' imprisonment. Yet he was discussing it with me, a foreigner, whom he hardly knew, on one of Lhasa's main streets. It was deserted and dark but I still felt uncomfortable. "Let's walk on," I said, taking the bike from him.

He ran his eye down the page, picking out phrases which he read out in a low voice. "The world should know that every Tibetan considered the Dalai Lama to be their leader. . . . Now, the Chinese talk about liberalisation, they say that Tibetans have never had it so good, but Tibetans are still unhappy. We have no real freedom. . . . Many Tibetans are still suffering in prison for their beliefs. . . . They are beaten and tortured and treated worse than the ordinary criminals. . . ."

In China the concept of a prisoner of conscience does not exist. The Government counters any comments or requests made by the outside world by saying that China has no political prisoners. All dissidents are criminals.

Tsering turned to the next page. "The Tibetan people are certain that if western countries knew of the real suffering of Tibetans, they would help them in their struggle."

I watched him fold the letter again, thinking of other Tibetans I had met who clung to this belief that only ignorance prevented the outside world from coming to their aid. Ever since the Fifties, petitions had been smuggled out to the U.N. In the early days people dreamt of an army being sent in – they had heard vaguely of the U.N. forces in Korea. But an army did not come and the "grave concern", which the U.N.'s resolutions of 1959 and the early Sixties expressed, did nothing to ameliorate their lives, or to avert the greater suffering that came with the Cultural Revolution. Yet the petitions continued to be smuggled out. Over the years the U.N. became a symbol on which Tibetans like Tsering desperately pinned their hopes: that it would come to their aid was an article of faith.

Tsering seemed to guess my thoughts, for suddenly he smiled and said, "You think I'm naïve, don't you? Of course, I know that western governments aren't going to suddenly take our side against China. China is more important than we are. It always has been, and now western countries are frightened that if they offend the Chinese Government they'll lose their share of Chinese trade. Is that right?"

But Tsering needed to act. Tibetans like him were not afraid of the Chinese, he said, even though they were powerless against them.

"We *must* talk to tourists, tell the outside world about Tibet, maybe it will change something. Maybe it won't but there is no other way."

I realised then, as we parted at the end of my road, that his letter had been essentially a gesture of defiance. What I had taken for naïve optimism was a kind of elation generated by this desperate act. It was I who felt naïve.

Chapter 18

A VALLEY OF HERMITS

People kept promising to take us to the Yerpa Valley; it seemed enchanted. Clouds of apricot blossom, flowering rhododendrons, giant juniper bushes, slopes of grass growing from a barren landscape. Yerpa had a history of sacredness. King Songtsen Gampo had meditated here, and so had the Indian masters Padmasambhava – or, in Tibetan, Guru Rinpoche – and Atisha, two of the most revered religious figures in Tibet. Over the course of history other ascetics, inspired by their example, spent their entire lives immured in the caves of Yerpa. A chink of sky would be their only light, and the arm of a disciple, passing food through another chink, their only human contact. Summer months brought monks from one of Lhasa's tantric colleges to pass their time in this paradisiacal retreat, studying and collecting medicinal herbs. And lay people would come too, making offerings in the temples and picnicking among the rhododendrons. In the Fifties Deyang's mother's family used to spend a week at Yerpa every June. They had been telling us for months that they would go again with us. But no one could find the *guanxi* to get a work-unit vehicle. Realising eventually that we would never get to Yerpa if we continued to rely on them, we accepted an invitation to go with Stephen Batchelor, an English Buddhist scholar, and his wife Martine. They were writing a guide-book on Tibet and so were visiting places of historical significance in a vehicle hired from the new Lhasa Taxi Company.

It is getting light as we head eastwards out of Lhasa in a heated Landcruiser. There are people walking the Linkhor, lighting juniper fires, turning prayer-wheels, prostrating themselves in the dust. There are pilgrim camps on the pavements, women making tea in long wooden churns, children kicking shuttlecocks. But today it is the comfort of the car, the forgotten sensation of effortless movement, the visions of England that our conversation creates, that seem exciting. The scene outside is normal now, I realise with surprise.

We follow the river for a while and then the road begins to climb, deteriorating as it does until it is little more than a bouldery ledge hacked out of the mountainside. Prayer-flags flutter protectively from sticks wedged between the rocks. *Labtse*, pyramids of stones to which each passer-by adds another in offering to the gods, sprawl underneath.

Stephen sits in front with the driver, talking about Dharamsala, the Dalai Lama's residence in India, where he spent ten years as a monk. After two hours the landscape grows more arid. The Yerpa valley runs somewhere to the north of the road now; we stop to ask the way from a man with a stetson perched on top of his thick plaits. Frightened by the noise of the car, his yak bolts, shedding its sacks of barley in the road. Too polite to go after it, he stands explaining our route in conscientous detail as the yak, slowing to its peculiar mincing trot, disappears further and further up the side of the mountain.

Eventually we find the valley rising steeply northwards into a jagged range of mountains. Houses dot the track ahead of us and here and there, against the muted greys and browns of their walls, an apricot tree spreads a cloud of pink blossom. There is no sign of the shrubs, the juniper bushes of Deyang's mother's stories. But the slopes are dotted with distant sheep and the air is filled with the watery warbling of birds.

Leaving the car in a village at the valley head, we begin looking for a way up the mountain. A solitary child clutching a kitten beneath his chin watches from a doorway, his eyes following us in a wide arc as we pass.

"How do we get to the monastery?" the driver calls out to him. The child stares blankly, hugging his kitten closer, peering at us now through its fur. There is no one else around.

Eventually we come across a goat path and begin the steep climb up the side of the mountain. Above us on a spur, the outline of a monastery stands out against the sky; above that the rock face is pitted with caves. Some of them are black and gaping, others are tiny. But across the mouths of most, crumbling walls remind us of the valley's illustrious past and the great mystics who once sealed themselves inside.

The path forks sharply and suddenly we come upon the monastery. It is a tangle of ruins. Sheep are browsing across the grassy floors of chapels lying jagged and open to the sky.

"It looks as though the whole place has been bombed," I say to

Stephen, as we wander through the similarly desolate ruins of Drak Yerpa monastery further up the mountainside.

He doesn't agree. "It is more likely that it was a gradual process. The interiors were probably smashed up and looted first, and later the wooden pillars and the roof timbers taken away by the villagers for firewood or building. Then over the years the walls have been eroded by the wind and the cold."

I am reminded suddenly of a conversation I had with Deyang not long ago. There was a disastrous shortage of fuel in Lhasa during the Cultural Revolution and the work-units, she told me, began to send their workers out to monasteries on foraging missions. She remembered returning from Ganden once, their truck piled high with altars, pillars, window-frames, books, musical instruments, cauldrons, ladles – anything they could lay their hands or axes on. At the work-unit most of it was distributed as firewood but some things were kept. The elaborately carved covers of religious books were used as washboards, she said. Children made writing slates out of broken-up altars. And the drums and cymbals which had, for centuries, been beaten in offering to Buddhist deities, were used at parades to honour the man who tried to destroy them. Deyang's laughter was bitter as she marched round my room shouting, "*Mao Zhuxi wan sui!*" Long Live Chairman Mao!, punching the air with one hand and rattling an imaginary *dhamru*, a ritual drum, in the other.

Her unit probably came here too, or if not them, some other unit. And after they left the elements completed the process of destruction. The ruins look hundreds of years old, not twenty. Erosion has blurred the brickwork and in places whole buildings are dissolving into the spur-like castles in the sand. As I look down on the monastery from an exposed ledge, I feel the bite of the wind against my cheek, the power of the sun and the cold. Above me the rock is bored with holes, pared to smooth pillars, great boulders poised on top. The elements are all-powerful, they dominate the land, and as I stand there, inspired and numbed, I sense the power that they exert over the human mind. I begin to understand the belief of the followers of Bon, that the forces of nature are gods.

A group of Tibetans appear over the ridge carrying plastic containers of *chang* and bundles of juniper twigs on their backs. They are on their way to make offerings from the summit of Mount Lhari, they say, pointing out a low rounded hill with OM MANI PADME HUM embossed in white stones across its slopes. Stephen asks them if they live in this valley. They are from the village at the bottom, a striking woman with large medicinal plasters stuck to both temples tells us. As she talks, the others watch Stephen with undisguised curiosity, amazed by the fluency of his Tibetan. He explains that he lived in India and they bombard him with questions about the Dalai Lama.

I ask what happened to all the rhododendron and juniper shrubs.

"Cut down for firewood like everything else," an old man in the group says resentfully.

"There's not much left in the caves either," the woman with the plasters adds. "Behind there is Palgyi Dorje's cave." She points to a small chapel which is being rebuilt further up the mountain. "It has been completely defaced inside. Nothing left now. Go and see for yourselves."

She is right, there is nothing left. Once our eyes grow accustomed to the darkness inside, we make out a scattering of precious rubble on the floor and the remains of Jampa, the Future Buddha, half-gouged out of the wall. Further on, the darkness offers up the severed heads of three gods, rescued from the debris and placed, disfigured and sightless, on a raised mound of earth.

I imagine the moment when the temple was destroyed, the emotions of the monks who were meditating here. Did they think then of Palgyi Dorje, the Buddhist monk who, according to legend, protected this cave from a similar fury of destruction? Palgyi Dorje's aggressor was not a group of youths inspired by Communist ideology. It was a ninth-century king, Langdharma, whose aim in wiping out Buddhism in Tibet was to restore the earlier Bon religion.

Buddhist histories describe his reign as a reign of terror in which monasteries were destroyed, monks murdered and the practice of Buddhism banned on pain of death. Stories about Langdharma are still legends in Lhasa. According to the grandfather of a student, he was a demon with horns, which he used to disguise by having a woman plait hair around them. Each time it was redone, the woman would be killed so that she could not reveal his evil secret.

Palgyi Dorje's life became a legend too. He was pious and brave and did not flee Tibet or Langdharma's fury. This cave protected him. One day when he was deep in meditation he had a dream in which he was told how to kill Langdharma, and so free Tibet from the powers of evil.

He left Yerpa for Lhasa, donning a black robe with a white lining and daubing his white steed with charcoal. At the king's palace in Lhasa the New Year festivities were in full swing. As a troop of Black Hat dancers were performing before the King, he watched and then, robed in black, concealed himself amongst them. He waited his moment. Stealthily, he drew his bow from his robe. And fired. The arrow missed Langdharma. He fired a second arrow; he missed again. Now with only one arrow left, he fired again. The king fell, and died instantly. Palgyi Dorje escaped from the palace, jumped on his steed and galloped out of Lhasa. Soon he reached the Lhasa river and there, charging his horse through the deepest part, washed off all the black charcoal. With a flourish he turned his black robe to the inside, so now it was as white as his horse. In vain his pursuers sought a black robed dancer on a black steed while Palgyi Dorje fled to Amdo, where he spent the rest of his life in pious meditation, atoning for his crime.

Climbing higher through the rocks, slowly, as the air is thin, we stop to rest near a small complex of caves. The walls that once closed off the entrances are still intact; a few prayer-flags have been strung across like bunting. After the exertion of the climb, or perhaps inspired by the atmosphere of the place, we are silent for a while. Below us spreads a scene of indescribable beauty, around us a silence that is more powerful than our own: a silence that invades the mind, scatters thought and, like a powerful physical presence, captivates all the senses. Occasionally a goat bleats or a dog barks down in the village. But hardly have their cries reached us before they are drowned in it.

Later other sounds stir, sounds that grow out of nothing so slowly that for a while I wonder whether they are sounds at all. I listen, try to focus my mind. Perhaps after all they are just echoes of silence. But then gradually growing louder they crystallise: I hear the incantatory notes of religious prayer. The silence loses its hold.

"There is someone in retreat up there," Stephen says, looking towards the cave. But the place was deserted, I thought the villagers said. The chant floating out from inside the mountain sounds eerily unreal. Following Rosemary up the last stretch of path, my imagination conjures spirits and demons and mountain gods. We reach the rocky terrace in front of the caves; the sounds of chanting, all around us now, are unmistakably human.

Stephen wants to go inside, but wonders whether he should disturb the monk. Eventually he slips through a gap in the wall to place an offering on his altar. The chanting stops. Rosemary, Martine and I wait by the entrance; sounds of animated conversation are now emerging. After a while Stephen appears again at the entrance and beckons to us.

"*Yarpe*," a voice welcomes brightly as we stoop to avoid the jagged rocks of the roof. It is almost dark. Ahead of us on a makeshift altar, a single wick flickers dully among an assortment of offerings: a heap of wrinkled apricots, an apple, a handful of five-*fen* coins stuck to the rocks with blobs of butter.

"*Suden jia*," sit down, the voice, now filled with merriment calls out. There's hardly space for all of us and, squatting close together on the floor, we block the light from the entrance. Gradually, however, I make out a dimpled face and two sparkling eyes flitting over us. The monk is much younger than his voice suggests, a far cry from the etiolated hermit, with long thick locks matted to a straggling beard which had formed in my imagination as we sat outside. He is full of questions; we are too, and the conversation darts from one thing to the next with Stephen translating for us his thick Khampa accent.

He arrived here only a month ago from a monastery in what is now a Chinese province. "I have brought supplies with me to last a year," he says patting a brightly striped sack of *tsampa* propped up behind him. "If I need to stay longer I'll just start eating more slowly." He laughs. The rest of his provisions are stacked around him: blocks of butter, one opened and already mottled with blue veins, a few bricks of tea, a leg of dried meat. They fill the cramped quarters of his cave almost completely, and he has to clamber over them to place the cakes we have given him on the altar. He arranges the other offerings around them, dusting the already spotless surface and accidentally knocking the apricots off the edge. They rattle across the sloping floor like stones.

"This is Guru Rinpoche's footprint," he says, touching an indentation in the rock above the altar.

"Guru Rinpoche meditated here, that is why I came to this cave."

"Did you have to get permission from the authorities?" I ask.

"No, we are free to make retreats now. The Chinese haven't bothered me at all." He sits down again, settling himself into the rounded mould that his months of immobility have made in the cushion. "Individuals have quite a lot of religious freedom now, at least compared with before. They can put up altars in their homes, visit their monasteries, go on pilgrimages, and for many ordinary people – simple people – this is enough. But it is in the monasteries that we need freedom. In my monastery, we had to get permission to restore even the smallest statue. The Chinese controlled everything." Like Tsering, he says that little religious teaching is permitted. "In my monastery the monks are all old now and will die soon. It is the same everywhere. If they can't pass on their knowledge, Buddhism in Tibet will die with them.''

Now that he feels free to go where he likes, he will visit other sacred places after this retreat, and later he will make the great pilgrimage to Mount Kailash in the far west that he has been dreaming of for years.

He tries to persuade us to have tea with him but he has to fetch his water from the bottom of the valley, and we don't want to deplete his supplies of butter and tea. Leaving him to his meditation, we find a sheltered ledge for our picnic.

Beneath us the rounded summit of Mount Lhari is now spun with whirls of smoke. The villagers emerge and fade again as they toss fresh bundles of juniper on to the fire. Swelling with echoes, their shouts rise towards us, slowly filling up the whole valley.

The monk from Kham thought there were ten other hermits living in the caves. He sees some of them occasionally when he goes down to fetch water, but they have never spoken. Two nuns whom we come across later, however, know everything about Yerpa: which caves are inhabited, what sect each hermit belongs to, how long they have been here. We must visit the fasting Lama before we leave, they say.

The nuns have been here for two years, living together in one cave, if you can call it that. It is little more than shelf of rock sliding beneath an overhanging cliff.

We arrive to find one of them trying to make a fire. The flames, torn by the wind which howls through the entrance, are thin and blue, and the cave is filled with a cold nagging smoke. Sitting close beside it, however, she seems immune to its irritation as she talks to Stephen, continually re-arranging the tiny scaffold of twigs to encourage the flame. I imagine that she looks older than her age, for the wrinkled, weather-beaten darkness of her skin is accentuated by a crown of bristling white hair. She and her sister spent many years doing forced labour on the roads, she tells us – breaking rocks, carrying them on their backs, being burnt by the sun and wind. Even now they have to return to the roads between their periods of retreat because they have no family or monastery to support them.

For this retreat, however, they have begged their alms in the time-honoured tradition. For three months they lived in Lhasa. They recited prayers in the Barkhor, wandered through the tea shops and sometimes knocked at people's doors. Lhasa has always had its population of beggars; in Tibetan society there is no shame in begging, for it helps other people to acquire merit. Now Chinese beggars, rarely seen in Central China, are making the most of this Tibetan tradition.

But one of the nuns looks ill. She hasn't spoken since we arrived and is lying against a heap of sacking at the back of the cave. With a string of prayer-beads in her hand, she seems absorbed in prayer. But ten minutes later she is still on the same bead; her face has a look less of contemplation than of distraction.

"Is she sick?" Stephen asks.

Her sister nods, crumbling a brick of tea into the pot on the fire. "She fell on the mountain yesterday and cut her head."

"Badly?"

"It hurts a lot I think." She turns to her sister but she continues to stare at her prayer-beads and doesn't react. "We went down to the spring to get water and were climbing back up the mountain with the buckets," she says, stopping to balance another twig on the fire. Her voice is sympathetic, yet I sense, as she talks, a kind of serene acceptance: that this is all in the nature of things.

"The path is very slippery and when you are carrying water it is not easy to keep your balance. My sister slid on some loose rock and fell over the edge. But it hurts less today."

I look at the face of her sister bandaged in its red plaid scarf. Around her eyes the fine lines of pain seem to belie this conviction.

We offer to take her back to Lhasa with us and offer them aspirin. But they are confident that she will be cured by their prayers.

The fasting lama, to whom the elder nun takes us, seems to share this serenity. Living on a handful of *tsampa* every two days, he might eventually have visions of Chenresig, like a monk he knew in Amdo who made a similar fasting retreat. He shows the same genial hospitality, the same openness, communicating with us like an ordinary person. Yet he radiates a profound spirituality which his homely exterior only makes more powerful.

Later, on our way down the mountain, I recall how at moments during the day I envied the simplicity of these hermits' lives and the beauty of their surroundings. But now idle thoughts of paradise are dispelled. An evening blizzard blots out everything: the apricot blossom, the glistening peaks that swept across the valley mouth, the echoes of bird-song – the caves themselves.

Chapter 19

A MODERN WEDDING

Mr Li had continued to entertain and infuriate me throughout the spring. I began to be able to predict the timing of his visitations. They were always in the afternoon, and always when Rosemary was teaching. Sometimes, when I couldn't face his banter, I would make my escape down to the river.

We fought about everything: about Tibet, about the West, about African students in China who all raped Chinese women – he knew that for sure. But I had to admit that his clownishness was entertaining. He would go into peels of laughter when I argued with him, and he continued to bejewel his English with contorted idioms. The last time I saw him, like the dénouement of a comedy, he produced his *pièce de résistance*.

He had invited us to a banquet with important friends, the day before. I had refused as we had been invited somewhere else. He insisted – his were important friends. I refused and he insisted and I refused. But, still insisting, he had ridden off.

Thinking, I suppose, that he had had the last word, his important friends prepared the banquet while we, unaware, dined with our friends.

Now his top lip was trembling with anger. I watched the hairs above it, and couldn't help thinking they were like the fronds of an insect-eating plant waiting for its prey. I was a devil, he had known that all along. He wasn't my friend, he had only ever come to practise his English. And now I would regret it because he was never going to enter our house again.

This altercation took place at the crossroads by the post office and a crowd was beginning to gather around us.

"Never again," he swung his leg over his bicycle, turning back to face me. "Never again will I allow you to pick your nose into my business."

★

Summer was approaching, and, with it, the expiry of our contracts and visas. Rosemary decided that she would return to England. She wanted to do a postgraduate teaching certificate. It was to be a stepping stone – a year to allow her to readjust to the West, and to move into a career. The B.B.C. or the British Council or. . . . There was a long list. Plans included being paid to learn languages, coming back to China in some official capacity.

I can't remember now what else was in her future landscape. In this respect we were very different. Rosemary always mapped out everything in great detail. The landscape might change from one day to the next – it frequently did. But it was always crystal clear and sparkling. I too had applied to do a teaching certificate but I was less enthusiastic. I wanted to write. And I didn't want to leave Tibet.

The justification for my decision, which I took a long time to make, was that in six months I felt I had only scratched the surface of Tibetan life. I didn't know, at the time, that the longer you live in a different society the stronger this feeling becomes. You scratch at the surface and there is a more complex surface beneath. Everything that you thought you understood at that beginning becomes increasingly confused.

Where tea shops and their male exclusivity were concerned, we had given up trying to conform. The temptation of relaxing with students after class, or with friends over a glass of milk-tea was irresistible. Anyway, we reasoned, some of the more daring women were beginning to join us.

We went with a group of students to our favourite, the tea shop by the mosque. A padded door-curtain, once white but now marbled with grease, led off the alleyway. Only the bicycles parked on the muddy bank outside suggested that this was not an ordinary house. The curtain opened to a small courtyard where sun filtered through the blossom of a tree on to long tables of Tibetan tea-drinkers. According to the students, the best sweet tea in Lhasa was served here – and the server was rather pretty. Passing between the tables, and returning frequently to ours, filling glasses from a battered kettle, taking a one *mao* note – about 2p – for each glass from a heap we had tossed into the middle.

Tea shops were the tendrils of the grapevine. Most Tibetan men spent at least part of each day there, refilling their glasses with tea and exchanging the latest news. The tea shops were also fertile ground for police informers; people were on their guard.

In every public meeting place and at every gathering there was a network of paid informers who reported back to the police. People talked of a time when police would use threats against relatives of detainees to force them to report on their neighbours. None of us knew, then, that their nightmare descriptions of the past contained a prophecy for the following year. But even now no one could be trusted. There were informers in our classes, we were told; people confided in us things which they said they couldn't tell their own friends. It was clear that the fear which the informer network created made it an effective method of control.

In this tea shop most people knew the informer: he was a pleasant-looking man with a slightly drooping smile who sat by the cauldron of tea. I assumed that, as he was known, his role must be simply to prevent Tibetans from carrying on subversive conversations. Events were to prove me wrong.

Today, and every day for the past three weeks, the tea shop had been filled with gossip about the bank robbery. There were road blocks on all the roads out of Lhasa. No one had been caught yet but daily announcements in the newspapers, on radio and TV, always ended with the same confident threat: *"Bu guan tamen duo jiao hua dou tao tuo bu liao wu chan jie ji zhuan zheng!"* No matter how crafty these criminals are, they can't escape from the proletarian revolutionary dictatorship!

The work-units and street committees called special meetings to urge people to report on suspicious individuals. But things were not going according to plan. The robbers were beginning to acquire the status of heroes with both communities claiming them for their own. According to recent gossip, the *lingdao* of the Gong An Ju thought the thieves must be Chinese.

"There have never been crimes like this in Tibet before," one of the students explained.

"You know why they must be Chinese?" An elderly Khampa leaned across from the next table. "They think Tibetans aren't clever enough to bring it off." He emptied some snuff on to his thumb-nail and jabbed it indignantly into his nose.

The robbers had passed two sets of guards as they entered the building, and had broken the safe without being heard. But for some reason it was the feat of having carried out the whole operation by match-light which had caught people's imagination. The only evidence that they had left behind was a trail of matches stretching from the gate to the safe.

The conversation continued. But with the arrival of Yangzom and

Tsewang, and Sonam who had played Father Christmas at our party, the talk at our end of the table turned to weddings. Yangzom's relative, a vivacious girl called Yudon, was getting married the following week; we had been invited. It was not an arranged marriage, Yangzom explained. She had met her fiancé at work.

"They have been wanting to get married for a long time," Sonam said, moving up the bench to make room for a student who had just arrived. "But she had to get permission from the leaders of her unit, first. Then their families had to save up for the wedding."

"How much do weddings cost?" Rosemary asked.

"It depends on the size."

"People are starting to have big celebrations again now," Yangzom joined in. "This one is going to last for six days."

Draining his glass, Sonam beckoned the server.

"They are planning to spend 3,000 *yuan* on it," he said.

"Three thousand!" Rosemary looked at me in amazement. "That's incredible." Even for a cadre, it was almost a year and a half's salary. "They must have taken ages to save up."

It was not as if there was nothing to spend money on now. Compared with before, the shops were filled with consumer goods; much of it expensive even by western standards.

"It is normal for a wedding of this sort," Sonam passed back our refilled glasses, holding them with both hands, in meticulous observance of etiquette, and scalding his fingers. "Each member of the family usually gives part of his salary."

Later it emerged that Yudon's family was paying for most of the wedding; her fiancé's family would be making the *chang*. As she was an only child and her parents were "small" nobles (Sonam's description), her fiancé would move to their house after they were married. The conversation turned to polyandrous marriages where this was a common practice before 1950. Mr Li used to point to polyandry as an example of the dissolute nature of Tibetan society. But more often than not it was simply an agreement by which a woman would become the wife of several brothers in a family to prevent their estate being divided. The mother of one of our students had lived with two husbands, although he wasn't very forthcoming about it. Like most polyandrous families all the children called the elder husband father and the younger husband uncle, even though he had fathered most of the children. Now, except among nomads in remoter regions, both polygamy and polyandry had died out.

An Amdo woman approached our table to beg for money, followed by a procession of other beggars: a monk, an old man with a withered arm, a group of children. Automatically, as the conversation continued, each was handed a few *mao* from the middle of the table. But it was getting late; the sun had moved out from behind the blossom. The girl students, sitting with their bags on their heads as sun hats, began to complain that they were too hot. The informer watched us leave.

"If his job depends on reporting on us," Rosemary said outside, "he's not going to get very far." Most of our students were too frightened to discuss politics particularly in the tea shops. It was from other people that we learned about Tibet.

The Tenth of the Fourth Tibetan Month of the Fire-Male Tiger Year (22nd May).

Today is Yudon's wedding. The astrologer whom the family consulted to make sure that the elements of their birth dates were in accordance with each other, told them that this was an auspicious day.

It is to be a modern wedding, far removed from the austere Maoist weddings of the 1960s and 1970s but still far removed from the splendour of old Tibetan weddings. In the uncompromising setting of the work-unit there is a certain self-consciousness about the old traditions, many of which have to be explained to Yudon's generation.

We arrive with Yangzom in the afternoon. The metalled road, grumbling beneath a convoy of army lorries, is chalked with the flourishes of religious designs. At the gate, Sonam greets us with the welcoming party of family friends. He tells us proudly that the escort which led Yudon to her fiancé's house at dawn this morning was his responsibility. He couldn't accompany her himself, however, because his aunt died last year and tradition dictates that the bride must only be accompanied by people in whose family there has been no recent death.

We join the queue on the staircase. The families' silk *chubas* make splashes of colour in a drab line of trousers and jackets. Everyone clutches presents – ubiquitous Chinese presents: thermos flasks, symbols of double happiness, money in red envelopes, cork pictures of Chinese landscapes. Suddenly Rosemary points to the man in front of us.

"What?"

"The box."

We laugh. It is the ultimate present: I received nine of different sizes for my birthday last year. Each enshrined a plate with a glass carbuncle; each glass carbuncle enshrined a fluffily simpering nylon cat.

I ask Yangzom what gifts people gave before. She thinks I mean during the Cultural Revolution and giggles. "Chairman Mao, Chairman Mao statues, Chairman Mao pictures, Chairman Mao badges, copies of Chairman Mao's works." She lowers her eyelids with feigned awe. "After my sister's wedding our room was stacked high with them – all identical. No-one dared give anything else."

A sack of dung and a pail of water, decorated with butter, traditional symbols of fertility, adorn the scrubbed concrete landing outside the flat. The guests who are waiting to greet the family inch down the airless passage past those coming out. Ahead of us, people are preparing their *katags*. We will need six of these scarves, one to present to each parent and one for the bride and groom. They must be folded in such a way that when you offer them they ripple open with a conjurer's flourish. Yangzom is not sure how to fold them, so an elderly man in front is called upon to give us a lesson. "Like this," he says, and with a single movement the *katag* unfurls and floats between his dark knotted hands.

We enter at last the family's room. Swirls of incense soften its uncompromising dimensions and lend an almost spectral solemnity to the ritual. On the carpeted couches that line the walls, silk and gauze *katags* lie in diaphanous drifts. All that can be seen of our hosts, who are sitting crossed-legged beneath, are six demurely bowed brocade hats. Before each, we unfold a *katag* and add it to the heap around their neck. Yudon peeps from under her fur brim as I pass her but, catching my smile, quickly returns her gaze to the floor. The two fathers, sharing the couch opposite the door, chat with close friends; the mothers offer soft syllables of greeting from time to time. But the young couple preserve an awed silence.

Later, however, the formal part of the wedding over, Yudon's natural ebullience returns. She and her husband run through the rooms with the *ngupo*, the silver jug of *chang*, serenading each guest, forcing them to drink its extra potent brew.

With lavish meals, punctuated by toasts and dancing, the wedding is like all other celebrations. But lest anyone should feel inclined to escape early, the welcoming party has turned itself into a band of guards who stand fearsomely barring the exit. Eventually at 2 a.m. after a badinage of protests, we are allowed to leave. At the gate they demand a faithful promise that we will return tomorrow. But tomorrow and on the following days, the celebrations are for closer friends than we are; it is a promise we are expected not to keep.

Chapter 20

NEW BUDDHAS

Like most aspects of Lhasa's street life, fights were a form of entertainment. As the weather grew hotter we came upon them more often. One day I was diverted on my way to the river by a brawl between two Khampa men. The crowd which gathered watched to the end, joining the argument, laughing and clapping when one man got the better of the other. Eventually, with their red silk hair tassels lying coiled in the dust, their punches gave way to a tug-of-war with each other's plaits.

One of the more pathetic groups that appeared was a family of nomads. I came across them near Ramoche Temple, surrounded by a large crowd. The father was beating a distracted rhythm on an old tin while his two children, whose mud-stiffened ringlets stuck out from their heads, hopped from one foot to the other with expressions of fearful diligence. Their mother also lacked the brash confidence of other beggars, I thought, as I watched her shuffle through the crowd collecting alms. They reminded me of a scene from *Crime and Punishment*. They were the Marmaladov family: I saw a distraught, consumptive woman forcing her children to dance through the streets of the town. But the next day they were at the river: the children playing on the rocks with other children and the parents sitting round a fire, drinking. I realised then that they were probably no more miserable than other beggars. It was my imagination which had conferred on them the misfortunes of Dostoevsky's heroes.

On the river bank I chatted for a while with an elderly Tibetan woman. Her *chuba* had slipped off her shoulder, revealing a flap of bosom. I shared her tea and a rock-like cube of cheese which, after three hours, still sat in my cheek, undissolved and hamster-like.

Later, as I was finishing my washing, a Buddha appeared. A huge gilt image of Shakyamuni, gliding down the lane in the back of a truck. Everyone stopped. Slowly, he came towards us. His blue top-knot brushed the leaves of the trees overhead and the dappled light made expressions play across his face.

"Where's it going?" I asked the old woman as it disappeared round the bend in the river path.

"I don't know."

"Gyantse," another woman said. "They are taking it as far as Chusul by river."

No one was sure whether it was one of those removed from Gyantse during the Cultural Revolution which was now being returned, or whether it was a new image sent to replace one which had been destroyed.

The conversation of the people around me turned to the bank-robbers – several suspects had been arrested recently – but I turned to my own thoughts. The appearance of the Buddha had set me thinking again about the issue of the monasteries and religious freedom. I had spent an afternoon at Ramoche temple not long ago. It was slowly being restored and was functioning once again. The slogans, the pictures of Chairman Mao that had emblazoned the walls before, were painted over with religious frescoes. As I walked around the circum-ambulation path, the sound of drums and cymbals seeped through the walls of the main ceremonial hall.

At this time in most of the important monasteries a certain amount of restoration work was being carried out. Each time we went to Ganden or Sera or Drepung, a little more had been restored. Some Tibetans expressed enthusiasm and suggested that after the devasta-tion of the last decades, it was a step in the right direction. The authorities pointed to this work as proof that complete religious freedom had returned to Tibet, although restoration was limited, for the most part, to the tourist areas.

More vociferously than Tibetans, westerners, including myself, complained that tourists defiled Tibet's sacred sites. But it occurred to me that China is not the first to use tourism to defray the costs of preserving a religious and cultural heritage. I thought of the gift shops, the audio-cassette guides, the unremitting tramp and shuffle of tour-ists in English cathedrals and was reminded that not only in Tibet was the spiritual purpose of religious buildings being eroded by their secular promotion. But was it that tourism was needed to restore the monasteries? Or was it, as many westerners believed, that the monasteries were being restored solely to encourage the tourists?

"None of this would have been done," an English woman said to me at Sera, waving her hand round a newly restored hall, "if the Chinese hadn't realised how much money they could make out of us."

She may have been right but she went on to tell me that the Tibetans who were going round the monastery with us were dressed in traditional dress for the tourists too. I laughed, and she was offended.

Obviously, there was a significant connection between tourism and the restoration of the monasteries. But, recalling a conversation that I had had with Tsering not long before, I realised that westerners saw a greater significance in it than Tibetans. Tsering's fears about the reforms were very different. He pointed out to me that, despite its new religious tolerance, the Government hadn't changed its stance and still gave publicity to the traditional Marxist view that religion would die out as society evolved.

More than anything else, the Government feared Tibetan national-ism which, it knew, was inextricably linked with religion. It also knew that the devastation and persecution of the last decades had eroded any support that it might once have had. Consequently, Tibetans like Tsering saw this new promotion of religion and the reconstruction of monasteries less in terms of tourism, than as a tactical move by the Government to gain the support of the people. Tsering was concerned less with whether the monasteries were tourist attractions than with more fundamental considerations like new images not being properly sanctified, and money left as offerings being collected by the Chinese authorities. What the money is sub-sequently used for was unclear, but the practice was a major source of resentment.

Furthermore, despite the Government's much publicised claims to be promoting religious freedom, it was at this time extremely difficult to get permission to rebuild monasteries and harder still to get funds. I met an elderly monk once who had been trying to rebuild his monastery for two years. At first, permission was refused because he wanted to change the site. The original monastery was perched among the mountain peaks, a steep climb from the nearest spring, but as the monks were old now, they wanted to rebuild in the valley. However, consideration could not be given to his project unless the monastery was rebuilt on the original site. Having agreed to this condition, a year passed and the monk still did not receive permission. He made the journey to Lhasa again and returned to the Religious Affairs Office. This time he was told to write a report on why he wanted to rebuild the monastery. Now, another year later, the authorities had finally agreed. But after my return to England, I would learn that the funds that they promised had never materialised. This may have been bureaucratic inefficiency. The Government blamed "leftist" or hard-line attitudes among local officials. But, to Tibetans like this monk, it was simply proof that the Government was not genuine in its claims to be allowing religious freedom.

Chapter 21

THE OGRESS AND THE MONKEY

———

Sakadawa Festival was held at full moon in June. For one day, crowds of Tibetans circumambulated the town to celebrate the birth, the enlightenment and the death of Shakyamuni, the historical Buddha. By mid-morning a cloud of juniper smoke had settled over the roofs and the sun was a pallid disc pasted on to the sky. With *tsampa* and butter and *chang* and juniper, we fed the fires which circled the town. Some of the students abstained from eating meat, observing for a day the Buddhist Law, which Tibet's harsh climate has traditionally forced them to break.

June saw the abrupt end of visits to the tea shop with one of our classes. We had become so used to ending the lesson with a few glasses of milk-tea that when the students pedalled off one day, before I had collected up my books, I was taken aback. They had a meeting, they said, but they looked embarrassed. From then on, every class ended in an awkward pause. "No tea shop, teacher, too busy." One day there were no more classes. "Too busy, teacher." Yet they had been the most enthusiastic of our students; we couldn't understand it. Someone suggested that the recently launched "Rectification of the Party Campaign" had made people afraid of losing their jobs.

It was going to be a long time before we discovered the real reason.

Having convinced myself that I was meant to stay in Tibet, it was then a matter not of convincing our *lingdao* – they had been urging us to stay for months – it was, as always, a matter of convincing the Gong An Ju. But I was hopeful. By this time we had become inured to the gloom that surrounded dealings with the police, and to eternal rumours of Peking clamping down.

The term ended in the middle of June. We calculated that if our visas were not renewed we would have three weeks left, and optimistically planned a journey through the closed region of Kham to Kunming in south China. But our *lingdao* had plans too. Acting as though we were about to leave, they rewarded us with an official visit to the Yarlung

Valley – the cradle of Tibetan civilisation – over the mountain range to the south of Lhasa.

We had our doubts about the party which, from our own experiences of trying to bring Chinese and Tibetans together, we were convinced would be formal and awkward. We were wrong. The only moment of tension occurred when one of the Chinese women remarked on how undernourished the monks looked. She seemed genuinely concerned, but a Tibetan in the party retorted aggressively that, thanks to the offerings of pilgrims, they were better off in the monasteries than they would have been in their homes, and he was probably right.

The Number One Guest House in Tsedang, the main town in the Yarlung Valley, was not clean enough, the leaders decided. It looked to us as though it would offer more comfortable a night than many we had passed in China; but the town's newly-built tourist hotel was thought more suitable. An elderly European adjusted his glasses as we crossed the hall; a group of burly Tibetans, two English girls, pounds of fast melting butter, a tea churn and two Chinese.

Over the next few days, the Chinese gave us the statistics of agricultural production, population and literacy in the area; the Tibetans told us the history of the monasteries. The Chinese took photographs of themselves in front of every Government building; the Tibetans in front of each temple. And we, to the surprise of all of them, took photos of mountains and monasteries and people but none of ourselves at all. We climbed the mountain behind Tsedang on the second day from where the Yarlung River, an adolescent Brahmaputra, drifted idly southwards. The valley plaited knife-edged dunes between its strands and the atmosphere was so sharp that the river was still turquoise and glittering when it dropped over the horizon, miles in the distance.

I had with me a book written by the Dalai Lama's elder brother Thupten Jigme Norbu, which told how, in this mountain, the Ogress took the Monkey as husband at the birth of the Tibetan nation.

"We think Tibet is the most fortunate of lands. . . ."

I read while we stopped to rest. "Into this country Chenresig, Lord of Mercy . . . and Dolma his consort, sent their incarnations. Chenresig's incarnation took the form of a monkey, Trehu Changchub Sempa. The monkey incarnation was under vows of celibacy and lived alone in quiet meditation. Dolma's incarnation however was an Ogress and a cannibal called Tag-Senmo. Senmo, the Ogress, became very lonely, having nobody to live with her. She cried and sang and cried. Trehu, the monkey incarnation, heard the crying and singing and hurried to where Senmo was and asked her what was wrong, being filled with pity. She told him of her loneliness and begged him to stay with her and be her husband. At first Trehu refused, saying that this was not why he had come into the world, that he had come to fulfil his vows. But Senmo was so distraught that the monkey incarnation was overcome with compassion, and using his supernatural powers went straight to the great Potala, abode of Chenresig, to ask for advice. Chenresig told Trehu that the time had come for Tibet to have children of its own, and that he was to return and take Senmo as his wife. The monkey and the ogress married and they had six children which some people say were drawn from six kinds of creatures that fill the world: gods, demi-gods, human beings, ghosts, animals and fiends. Others say that the six children represent the six kinds of people found in different regions of Tibet today. In any event, the monkey father left the six children to fend for themselves. On returning a number of years later to see how they were faring, he found that they had multiplied with children and grandchildren. All these offspring were real people, human beings, the first Tibetans.''

At the cave where the monkey had taken the ogress as his wife, a group of pilgrims pressed *chang* upon us and lumps of pig-fat spread with chilli, and took our genuine distaste for politeness. Mr Wang, a shy man from Peking, had accompanied us while the rest of the group was attending a meeting. He was better than either of us at feigning enjoyment, and we giggled about it together on the way down the mountain to "the playground of the monkeys" as the pilgrims told us Tsedang meant.

At Mindroling, the most important monastery of the Nyingma sect, I gave a letter with a hundred *yuan* from Deyang's mother to the senior monk. She wanted him to say prayers for a friend who had recently died. Having honoured us with tea in his room, the monk then showed us around the monastery himself. In the assembly hall, mud flaked from a gash in the wall where a Buddha had been wrenched out; the faces in the murals had deep lacerations where their eyes had been. Foolishly, I took a photograph. The Chinese said nothing but one of the Tibetan leaders was annoyed with me; I realised guiltily that they would be held responsible for our misdemeanours.

We crossed the river to Samye in a rainstorm. Huddled for two hours with a group of monks on top of a stack of willow branches, I envied the horse which had its own compartment at the other end of the punt. We slid through the water like Noah's Ark, running aground

Above: Yerpa. Heads of
Buddhas rescued from
the rubble and placed
on a mound of earth

Right: A nomad with
her child

Above: A picnic tent

Left: The author and Rosemary preparing for a picnic

Below: A school bus near Samye

on sand banks occasionally, brewing up tea on a shoal midstream while the driver repaired the tractor-engine motor. On the opposite bank, a three-wheeled cultivator with a trailer on the back stood waiting. For a further hour we splashed through soggy dunes and puddles to the monastery. A line of stupas appeared on a ridge above us, smooth and white in a wilderness of rock. It was here that Padmasabhava was greeted by King Tritson Detsen when he first came to Tibet in the eighth century to spread the Buddhist faith. And it was under his direction that the king built Samye, Tibet's first Buddhist monastery, designed to represent the universe. Most of what was once a large monastic town, we found in ruins. In the main temple, however, a monk showed us with pride, the statue that had repelled the axes of the Red Guards. He swung his arms about him demonstrating their attacks; the Buddha had remained without a blemish. And in terror at this obvious manifestation of divine power, the Red Guards had fled.

Mud dripped on to our beds as water seeped through the earth roofs of the house in which we were staying. In the narrow alleys we sank up to our knees. Pigs snuffled round us, sheep and donkeys barged past flattening us against the wall. Old women, bent double, peering at their feet beneath the mud, teetered like novices on a skating rink. The rain continued into the next day, but as we crossed the river again towards dusk, the sun re-appeared. A flock of ducks flew up from the water at the sound of our engine, the underside of their wings making a brilliant arc of white against the dark bank of clouds.

Lhasa was chattering over the bank robbery on our return. Two Tibetans had been sentenced. For a week, cadres from the Public Security Bureau appeared on television to praise the Shigatse police, who had arrested them, and to turn the whole affair into a cautionary tale.

They thought they'd be crafty, these robbers. They hid their loot in sacks of yak dung. And then, piling the sacks on to the back of a donkey-cart, they sauntered out of Lhasa. No one noticed as they set off for the Nepalese border. But, unfortunately for them, so the television reported in both Tibetan and Chinese, they saw an ornate Tibetan saddle in the Shigatse market and were overcome with greed. Their bundles of money aroused the suspicions of the trader who, being a good citizen, informed the police. Thus far, the tale retained its adventure's charm. People were proud that the robbers had turned out to be Tibetan.

But then there were rumours of Chinese prison guards beating Tibetan suspects to extract confessions, and Tibetan guards using similar tactics on Chinese suspects. It ceased to be an escapade. A few days later, on television, the men were shown confessing their crime with heads bowed in submission. Their faces were swollen and disfigured with bruises. Their crime had been established by interrogation. This was, in effect, their trial. There was no defence or appeal.

On a Sunday morning, a few days later, Rosemary was teaching at the Banak Shol and I was writing letters at the back of the class. Suddenly the street was filled with the wail of sirens. The students looked at Rosemary in a moment of deference, and then rushed to the windows. It was a while before I understood what was happening. A procession of motor-bikes flanked by police outriders moved slowly up Beijing Road towards the Potala. Tannoys were blaring from the roof of a jeep. I couldn't understand what was being said but in the sidecar of each motor-bike sat a man with his head bowed.

"Who are they?" I asked one of the students.

"Prisoners," he replied somewhat awkwardly, knowing that, as foreigners, Rosemary and I shouldn't be witnessing the scene.

The next day the whole of Lhasa was made to attend the mass sentencing rally in the city stadium. On the following day, posters appeared in work-units and public places, scored with a red tick. The men had been publicly executed at a site near Sera monastery.

"No matter how crafty these criminals are they can't escape from the proletarian dictatorship."

The slogan reeked of its chilling success.

Chapter 22

EAST TO CHINA

While we were in Yarlung three Lhasa work-units took on English teachers, disproving the theory of a clamp-down, at least temporarily. Our passports were returned bearing new six-month visas. This act of generosity inspired us, for one mad evening, to reroute Rosemary's future: a four-month pilgrimage to Mount Kailash, through the mountains of western Tibet; some students had persuaded us to go with them. But Rosemary woke up sensible the next morning. I had committed myself to teaching.

With a month before Rosemary's departure and a tea shop encounter with a long-distance truck-driver, we fixed our plans to head out of Tibet through the legendary region of Kham.

Eve of Departure. Cycling home down Beijing Road, pavements filled with people, handlebars dangling provisions, mind with thoughts of our journey . . . the road to central China is forbidden to westerners but a few have crept in that way . . . I remember, outside the night-class, the glint of daring the journey inspired in them . . . swapping derelict bridges and roads subsiding . . . someone knew someone who had broken his back when a truck overturned. . . .

I pedal on, thinking of these adventurers' tales . . . the pavements are bristling . . . will we have stories like these to tell?

A blast of water. . . .

Another. . . .

And another. . . .

What's happening? Only now I notice that the pavements are bristling not just with people, but with buckets and jugs and enamel bowls. I look back, wanting to retreat, but behind me they have rearmed. I put my head down and paddle through the deluge. . . .

An explosion of water at point-blank range knocks me off through our gate.

"Lhamo!"

She is convulsed with laughter.

"I thought you were in Kongpo." We were planning to stop in her village on the way to Kham. She stares at my wringing-wet clothes; the gateman looks concerned.

Rosemary, on one foot, is pouring water from her shoe. "What's going on?" She flaps her arms helplessly.

"No idea."

Lhamo picks up my bike. "Rain ritual! We're trying to bring rain."

As we rolled out of Lhasa in Tensing's truck the following morning, the sky was its eternal blue. The gods were giving little sign that they had been moved to respond to the rain ritual.

Tensing was a large man by any standards. When he laughed his shirt buttons strained at their moorings, revealing ovals of stomach. He had agreed to take us as far as Ba Yi, the town with the Agricultural University in whose direction the Ministry of Education had tried to send us last October. It was a day-and-a-half by road from Lhasa. Tensing knew all the truckers running the route to Chengdu in Central China, so he would help us get a lift from there. But we didn't want to go as far as Chengdu. Where the road forked in Chamdo, the capital of Kham, we hoped to find something travelling south to Kunming in the Yunnan Province of China. Tensing shook his head and laughed. "No one goes down that road." He couldn't understand why we wanted to leave Lhasa at all. But in the books of early travellers, this region was one of the most spectacular in the world, inspiring titles like "Land of the Blue Poppy", "Mystery Rivers of Tibet". And how could it not be spectacular when the road wandered between the great rivers of the Mekong and Salween?

A family of nomads, with two painted altars they had bought in the market, clambered into the back of the truck while we were waiting at the state diesel dispensary. Tensing made a nice profit, selling the truck's petrol coupons, on the quiet, to Lhasa's new motor-bike-owning community. So this was why all trucks and buses free-wheeled the perilous mountain passes. He chuckled.

Climbing out of the Lhasa valley at Medrogongkar, the landscape began changing by the hour. Fluted mountains, draped from their peaks in drifts of sand, gave way to grasslands and a mesh of streams. Then gradually these dissolved into the desert again. Towards afternoon, crouched in isolated hollows like birds with outstretched wings, black nomad tents appeared. But it wasn't until much later that our passengers banged on the roof of the truck. Tensing shouted out of the window, losing his words in the wind.

"*Lo loss.*" He drew his head inside as he stopped the truck in a cloud of dust.

"Why are they getting out?"

"They live here." Tensing gave me a withering look and swung out of the cab.

It was a desolate, lonely spot. All around us, puckered grassland rolled to the horizon; there was not a bird, not an animal in sight, and no sign of human habitation. An hour later, looking back from the top of the pass, I saw the laden silhouettes of our passengers winding their way towards a still invisible destination.

Watching their figures dissolve into this dramatic wilderness, I found it hard to believe that even they were not beyond state control. Since the Fifties, the Government had been attempting to settle the nomads. In some areas, permanent winter lodgings were built to encourage them, but few had voluntarily given up their nomadic existence. Control became much tighter in the Sixties when nomadic groups were organised into production teams and communes. All livestock became state property, and in return each individual received a ration of food and goods. A Communist hierarchy was imposed on the old social order, with Political study meetings held in the tent of the appointed production leader. At this time, however, with the new Responsibility System nomads had a greater measure of freedom. The household had become the production unit. Families could sell their surplus produce on the open markets and, until 1990, they were exempt from paying taxes. But they still needed ration cards for basic goods, such as *tsampa* and tea. And resident cards prevented them from living outside their prefecture; even to travel, they had to get permission from the authorities.

Rain began to fall as we descended through the pines of Kongpo, rain that probably wouldn't make it over the mountains to Lhasa. The last passenger squeezed into the cab. With Rosemary half on Tensing's lap and me wedged against the newcomer, Tensing's chuckling threatened to burst the button-holes on his shirt completely. He listened to our enthusiasm about the landscape with an indulgent smile. His landmarks were more important: *tsampa* and tea by a stream with a driver travelling in the opposite direction, more tea at a road-workers' camp where he revelled in his role of messenger. And hours spent after dark in a solitary shack which filtered needles of light and female laughter. It was past two when we finally turned into a transport yard off the edge of the road.

With sleepy nonchalance, the caretaker took our three *yuan*, unlocked a wooden door at the end of the row and walked away. Tensing disappeared. Heaps of tumbled linen were strewn across the beds: even by candlelight they were dirty.

But our exhaustion was an antidote to squeamishness. We fell asleep indifferent to smells and scuttling.

Dawn, I think, or just after. The town's electricity line cuts a curve across the window. Idly from my bed, I watch drips of rain racing down its length, chasing each other, converging, colliding then staggering on, plump and shiny, until they drop off below the window with a bounce. I should get up, but the rain is mesmerising.

There is a knock on the window. It is Tensing. *"Nga Ba Yi drug yin."* I am off to Ba Yi. A sleeve rubs a hole in the grime. "And I am going now."

"Can you wait one minute?" Rosemary shouts, suddenly wide awake. We struggle into our trousers and run into the fury of revving engines.

Ba Yi, when we arrived later the same day, was as unprepossessing as its name. "Eight One" – 1st August – it celebrated the day on which the People's Liberation Army was founded in 1927. Its inhabitants, according to Tensing, were 95 per cent Chinese. Army trucks rumbled down the street, taking troops south to the border, where fighting had recently broken out with India over the McMahon Line drawn up by the British at the beginning of the century. In the previous weeks there had been troop movements in Lhasa too. The nights were filled with the drumming of trucks on the corrugations of our lane as soldiers were moved out of the army-unit next door. And for the first time in ten months we saw an aeroplane fly overhead. No one really knew what was happening. There were rumours that, in some quarters of Lhasa, residents were being registered and prepared to be called up. But although sporadic fighting continued until the time I left, the call-up never materialised.

This was as far as Tensing was going. With a smile and a cheery wave he vanished into a work-unit.

For two hours we waited in the muddy road, watched by an incredulous crowd. As we were on the point of succumbing to the lure of the tea shop, however, Rosemary noticed a bus disgorging people at the other end of the road. The Lhasa to Chamdo bus, an old woman said – the bus which we had been told left Lhasa four days ago, and on which foreigners weren't allowed. Gingerly, we approached the driver. *"Qing wen?"* Excuse me?

He was talking to a young woman selling eggs and ignored us. *"Qing wen?"*

He had finished talking now, but he continued to ignore us. *"Qing wen ni dao Chamdo qu ma?"*

He looked up, deadpan. *"Waiguo ren. Yi bai yuan."* Foreigners, a hundred *yuan*.

In his eagerness to get us to pay twice the normal price, he was obviously prepared to overlook the fact that we shouldn't have been there. And we, before fear should change his mind, got on. Later, with the other passengers reassembled, he clambered over the luggage in the aisle to demand his hundred *yuan*. It was too expensive. . . . But we were foreigners. . . . Yes, but we were teachers in China. . . . But we were foreigners. . . . Yes, but we had a Chinese salary. The verbal scuffle continued for half an hour, and then his blustering wrath subsided. Smiling, he took a hundred *yuan* for the two of us as if that was all he had ever asked for.

The bus was almost full. My neighbour was a heavy-jowled Khampa. For the next four days he would utter hardly a word to anyone. Occasionally he would offer a monosyllabic response to his friend by the window on the opposite side, who spent his time cleaning his ears with the eye of a needle. But otherwise, if he was not staring testily at the seat in front of him or nudging me into the aisle, he would unwrap a long, loose-leafed book from a piece of cloth slung round his neck and intone prayers in a soulful mumble. From time to time, when the volume of his chanting increased, he would thrust an arm out of the window and begin drumming on the metal panelling of the bus with his fist. Only then would his scowl disappear.

The seat next to Rosemary was taken by a Chinese cadre, so the extra pockets on his jacket announced. As she sat down he smiled, proffering his bag of sunflower seeds. His face was smooth and, except where his glasses made deep wells in the flesh, strangely uncontoured. He was witty and interesting, Rosemary said later. I never saw more than the movement of his arm from lap to mouth, adding to the tide of sunflower husks, peanut husks, soya husks, and sweet wrappings rising round the luggage in the aisle.

It was not long before the bus had divided into cliques: the coterie of monks and older men in the front rows, and the rest of us behind. One of them, a dark-skinned man in whose face age and hardship had worn grooves, was sitting cross-legged on the engine cover. Over the next few days his running travelogue broke only when he grew short of breath. Reflections on the landscape flowed into anecdotes, and as we passed the ruins of a fort or a monastery, on into angry diatribes. Even I, for whom the occasional phrase, the modulations of his voice and my own imagination could only approximate the subjects of his discourse, was captivated.

The bus climbed for most of the day, dragging us slower than we could walk, teetering on the edge while oncoming trucks rode crab-like round the inside. For a while during the afternoon we left the valleys. We moved on through a landscape of rocks and damp tussocks where streams with beetling banks trickled through the mist. I struck up a conversation, over a handful of dried soya beans, with the man behind me. He worked in Lhasa and was returning on leave to his family home. His father was a Christian, who had learnt English from American missionaries; his English was good too. No, he didn't teach it; his face coloured with diffident pleasure at my suggestion. But he was interested in our teaching, particularly in the class of school-children I would be taking when we returned to Lhasa. He knew Yi Zhong, Number One Middle School where most of the children would be from. He wanted his son to go there: it was Lhasa's model school – but he didn't have good *guanxi*. His son had gone to Number Three, the school which Chinese and Lhasa people despised: children from the countryside were sent there.

Guanxi. He spat out the word and then fell silent. When he began again there was a harsher note of cynicism in his voice.

"You know how Number One Middle School got its own electricity supply?"

"What?"

"It used to get electricity three or four days a week like all the other units. Only the army, the hospitals and other important units have a special electricity line. But you see, Number One Middle School is the best school in Lhasa." The man smiled knowingly. "They simply refused to take the power-station leaders' children until they were given a direct line." He jabbed his cigarette-end into the seat in front. His train of thought seemed to be leaping by angry association. I was finding it hard to follow.

He went on. Before the Cultural Revolution, all the Chinese teachers in Tibet spoke Tibetan and taught in Tibetan. Now the only Chinese teacher he knew, who had studied Tibetan, was teaching Chinese. More and more unqualified teachers were arriving in the Lhasa schools. Most of them were either trainees sent to replace

Chinese on home leave who then stayed on, or women who came unofficially to Lhasa to join their husbands and, despite their lack of qualifications, got teaching jobs to legitimise their position.

"You know what they call Number One, don't you?" He laughed. *"Jiashu Xuexiao."* The Housewives' School.

The afternoon is punctuated by the crunch of brakes and shriek of the horn as the dust reveals an occasional yak or a stray goat, standing somnolently, yet stubbornly possessive of the road. Near dusk we crawl towards the top of a pass. Most people are dozing; I stare out of the window, my thoughts carried beyond the noise to the mist-filled valleys below.

There is a strange sense of limbo as the road creeps past and yet keeps the summit always beyond our reach. The grinding roar of the engine is constant now and creates a new order of silence. Normal voices are whisperings, yells, the vehicle of ordinary conversation. Only occasionally, the sight of a fleeing marmot reminds us of our Bedlam.

We have reached the top of the pass. We round a corner in an explosion of shouts. *"Lha ge lo!"* The gods are victorious! Children stand up on the seats; straining to see the *labtse* – the cairn that marks the summit. Even the Chinese driver is infected by the exuberance and stops the bus without being asked. Everyone tumbles out.

Silence.

Around me people are reaching up the *labtse*, placing their stones in offering to the heavens, sewing prayer-flags on to the skeletons of others. For hours every gesture, every glance almost, has been jolted into aggression. Now they have a poignant grace.

It is dark by the time we turn off the road at a collection of huts in the fir trees. The men climb on to the roof of the bus and start unlashing pots and bundles. Others stand below gesticulating and shouting at the wavering beams of torchlight above their heads. And others wander off through drizzling firs to discover where the sound of the stream is coming from.

Fires hiss into the damp night. The old man who sat on the engine telling stories draws us to his fire where a kettle is already boiling on its cairn of stones. With a genie's skill two men whisk butter into the tea, rubbing a handful of chopsticks between their palms. Everyone kneads balls of *tsampa* for each other, adding sugar to the ground barley and tea, or perhaps a few grains of dried cheese. One of the tea-whiskers is a monk, it transpires. He asks me what I think of

Lhasa, how it compares with my own country. Have I visited the Potala, the Jokhang, Ganden? His face glows with excitement in the firelight.

It is the first time he has been to Lhasa. *Lersa* – the word sounds softer in Tibetan, and he pronounces it with such reverence that I half expect him to prostrate himself. He and his friend have made the traditional once-in-a-lifetime pilgrimage to Lhasa from their village 900 miles away in Kham.

"How long did it take you?" Rosemary asks.

"Three years."

Rosemary and I look at each other, realising what this means.

"Did you prostrate yourselves all the way?"

He nods, replacing the lid on his basket of butter and knotting it in a scarf. Rosemary smiles. It was as if she had asked whether he had gone by bus or train.

Chapter 23

THROUGH KONGPO AND KHAM

The following morning dawned deep in a gothic ravine. Clouds curled pale and spent round the peaks above our heads. The rain had cleared, leaving tendrils of mist between the dark branches of the pines. As we set off, sounds of mantras drifted round us, swelling with the rising sun, dissolving finally in the munch of breakfast. After Pome, where the teacher left, we travelled through a region filled with flowers: slopes of rhododendrons, azaleas, clouds of yellow berberis and, as we got higher, irises, gentians and anemones.

From time to time, however, amid this extravagant luxuriance, slopes would emerge that were completely bald. We had passed them the previous day too. Whole mountains flayed by the axes of the state lumber units. It was a dismal scene. I recalled a conversation I had had once with a Tibetan from a forestry unit in Kongpo. He had complained about laws being ineffectual, and local leaders, in their rush to make money, simply ignoring directives to replant. It looked as though he was right. Around us there were barren slopes with a crazing of shattered stumps and discarded trees – and truck after truck groaning eastwards under its glut of logs.

But from what I knew, China's policy on forestry was impressive. In 1979 the Government described it as "one of the weakest links in the national economy". A law was passed banning clearing for agriculture, and promoting reforesting and careful tending of trees. In contrast to the Maoist years, people were urged to plan for the future. The whole country was to be mobilised to restore China's forests.

More than anything, the idea of the Zhi Shu Jie impressed me. This was the tree planting festival held on the 12th of March each year, in which everyone had to participate. We, the Lhasa City Government Teachers Department, planted 2,000 trees on a sand island in the Lhasa River. But I soon realised that the idea was more impressive than its execution. It was an excuse for a picnic and, although our leader tried to make people take the work seriously, for most it was a question of getting the planting over with and enjoying the rest of the day. As seemed to be the case in so many areas, by the time the policy had filtered down to those who were supposed to implement it, the rationale behind it had been lost. We planted 2,000 trees, that was the quota for a unit of our size. The holes were shallow; I saw a couple of children planting them upside down, but no one seemed to care. The directive had been to *plant* trees and it was taken literally. No one was responsible for nurturing, and when Rosemary and I went back a few months later, the trees planted by most of the units had died. Ours had fared better, because our leader was personally concerned about deforestation and, although it wasn't his responsibility, he had arranged for someone to tend them.

People complained about the futility of the exercise. Tibetans were particularly aware of environmental problems, which they blamed entirely on the Chinese. "Every year we have to come out here to plant these trees," one woman I was planting with said, "and yet we can't even get enough wood for a fire." Like all families who didn't belong to a work-unit, her family had had to send one member to the Zhi Shu Jie. She was especially resentful because, unlike state employees who were paid automatically, she had lost a day's earnings.

Deforestation began in Tibet before the arrival of the Chinese, but the population was tiny then. There were no roads and no trucks to facilitate the massive lumber traffic of today.

"Xiang qian kan!" Look to the future! This was the slogan of the Eighties. As far as forestry was concerned, it seemed to have gone disastrously wrong. *"Xiang qian kan!"* The Tibetan from Kongpo had said, and smiled at its *double-entendre*. Look for money, the phrase also means.

Some time later my thoughts were interrupted by a *Khammo* – a woman from Kham – on the other side of the aisle. She was pointing to a group of vultures, floundering round a carcass in the distance. Offering me some cheese from her necklace rock-like cubes, she told the man next to her – her father perhaps – that we had become friends. Throughout the journey I had found my gaze returning to the back of her head. It was shaved like a nun – although she wasn't a nun, she said – and its perfect contours curved into a fragile nape. It occurred to me, as I looked from her to the several monks around me, that shaved heads gave a new dimension to beauty. The shape of the head was all important. I began wondering idly who, if shaved, would fall from the ranks of the beautiful. The delicate bone structure of this girl gave her head a sculpturesque purity.

"*Aja*," the girl called again. I turned towards her, still mentally shaving heads. A blast of water hit me in the face.

"Hey!" My words fell out in English. The girl was staring out of the window, her shoulders convulsed with laughter.

Another rain ritual? Boredom? Whichever, I realised from the faces around me that it required revenge. War was declared. The whole bus joined in, except for the driver and my neighbour. He went on muttering his prayers without a flicker of distraction crossing his face, nor did he react later when the girl changed out of her sodden shirt and – careless of the old man's efforts to shield her – revealed rosy nipples to other eager eyes.

By the end of the day conventions had dissolved. People dozed in one another's laps; food was shared as far as it would reach. The two old women in front of Rosemary had cures for everything. Not recognising their elixirs nor understanding the ailments from which we were supposed to be suffering, we swallowed the pellets of dough, seeds, and coloured powders which a gnarled hand would pass through the seats.

For most of the afternoon Rosemary had been deep in conversation with the Chinese cadre. It was very important, she had whispered back to me at one point, but I'd have to wait until we got off the bus. It was no use trying to listen: the Khampa was in percussive mood.

When we finally stopped for the night the cadre followed us into the truck-stop canteen. He wanted to help, and urged us to buy, for one *yuan*, rice congealed into bowl-shaped lumps and a watery soup. We were grateful, but left him spooning chilli sauce from a jar in the middle of the table, and went outside.

In the road, groups of Chinese men were gathered around pool tables, bent over in concentration; others slouched against the wall, chatting and smoking. Further on, a Tibetan woman massaged her baby with mustard oil in the last rays of the sun.

We leaned against a fence. "So, what was this important conversation you had?"

"I was talking to the Chinese cadre about the class that was stopped."

"How does he know about it?" I asked.

"I've no idea. He said something about us going to the tea shops; and about discussing politics with our students."

"But we never discussed politics in the tea shop."

"No, I know."

So there *was* more to it than their not having time.

"I think that they were genuinely busy but it seems that the class was stopped by the Gong An Ju."

"Is that what the cadre said?"

"He hinted at it."

Suddenly the drooping smile of the tea shop informer came into my mind. "The informer?"

"Maybe." Rosemary smiled sardonically. "I wonder if he got his promotion."

The following day people began getting off: on the crest of a mountain, in the middle of an empty plain, or simply disappearing off the edge of the road. The fir-clad valleys of Kongpo had vanished. Rutted plains drew the eye further and further north until at some imperceptible point they turned into clouds. For hours the only sign of human life was a horseman riding by the road on an ornately saddled horse. His feet dangled near the ground.

Towards the end of the morning, we stopped at the tea shop of a small village. The two women with the medicines were leaving here. A band of spindly legged children rushed to meet them, and hung round the tea shop while we were having tea. They were ragged and barefoot, like many of the children in the villages we had passed through. The hair of several of them had the reddish tinge of malnutrition.

"What must it have been like in the Sixties and Seventies?" Rosemary wondered as the children danced round her, daring each other to touch her coat. It was hard to imagine. Journeys like this made you appreciate the difficulties that the terrain and the huge distances made for the Government. Rosemary reminded me of a man who once travelled with us from Ganden. He had been on his way from Kongpo to Lhasa to get medicine for his father. We asked him what was wrong with his father. He didn't know except that he thought he was dying. But Lhasa itself is well provided with hospitals, and there are a number of "barefoot" doctors working in rural areas, although they are equipped to deal only with minor ailments. The main problem is transport. Even in Lhasa, unless you have *guanxi*, you are likely to be taken to hospital by bicycle or, if you are lucky, by cart.

We left the beautiful Khammo in the middle of the road near the top of a pass, locked in the embrace of a man. A thick cloud of dust shrouded them from the eyes of the bus as we moved off. By the top of the pass the dust had settled. The Khammo and her man were still there in the middle of the road. Inside the bus, heads were still turned watching – and laughing, now.

My neighbour had left too. I was more comfortable than I had been at any time on this journey. But suddenly, I felt homesick. I, too, wanted to get off the bus, to be greeted by a welcoming family and fêted. What were we doing here? The whole expedition was absurd. These people were all travelling home, arriving with goods from the capital for their families. To them, travelling for the sake of it, like going for walks, was incomprehensible. People asked us where we are going. We didn't even know. Chamdo, I said – the bus went that far. On pilgrimage? Yes, I lied.

The journey seemed decadent, now. As people continued to get off, I began to wonder whether we were going to be left on the bus alone. I must have momentarily dropped off to sleep, for the idea grew in my imagination, fantastically. The bus became a kind of limbo, rattling on for ever with us inside, across the wilds of Kham. Occasionally it stopped to show us the reunions of Tibetan families but it always moved on before they noticed.

As the afternoon progressed, doubts increased, I began to question my ideas about living here. I had thought I wanted the freedom that living in an alien culture brought. Freedom of having escaped from the tedious labels of accent, appearance, upbringing. Of course, we were labelled here but the labels didn't yet ring with deathly predictability. I thought that I enjoyed living outside society, immune to its divisions and intolerances. I thought that we had the best of all worlds. We could make friends with whom we liked. We could behave as we pleased; for as foreigners we were not judged by the same criteria. But what was this sense of freedom, I wondered now? Had we not spent the past six months trying to conform: trying to enmesh ourselves in *this* society's conventions?

We should arrive in Chamdo by six, the driver tells us; his spirits are rising. He even smiled this afternoon. Despite the ill-humour that he has shown for most of the journey, he takes the fragile roads, the furious hairpins with unfailing sensitivity. I suppose thirteen hours a day would be a strain on anyone's nerves. As I anticipate our arrival in Chamdo, my spirits rise too. The only picture I have of the town is from descriptions written before the arrival of the Chinese. It is the capital of Kham and stands at the confluence of two tributaries of the Mekong. But it was the centre of Khampa resistance and so few of the old buildings remain, we've been told. Throughout the Fifties and Sixties the Khampas waged a guerrilla war against the Chinese. For a time the C.I.A. became actively involved. It set up a base in the Mustang valley on the western border of Tibet and Nepal. Khampas were flown from India to the States where they were given a training in guerrilla warfare, and then were secretly dropped back into Kham. However, by 1969, with growing China–U.S. détente, the C.I.A. had lost interest. Under pressure from China, the guerrillas were disarmed by the Nepalese government, and their leaders were imprisoned.

The old man whom we assumed to be the Khammo's father, but who obviously isn't, has invited us to stay with him. At least we think he has – we can't understand his dialect very well. As we round a corner he points through the front window of the bus.

Chamdo.

A promontory rises out of the river ahead. The evening shadow masks the buildings, compelling us to marvel for a while at the magnificence of its site. Two rivers sweep moat-like round each side. Crashing together beneath it, they churn their red waters on towards us – the Mekong now. Above the promontory a range of striped mountains fan out, catching the last rays of the sun in bands of blue and red. But as we get closer, buildings begin to slink out of the shadows: long, drab, uniform.

"Number One Primary School . . . guest house . . . hospital. . . ." Rosemary's cadre rattles off the names of the work-units as we pass. He points out an edifice on the crest of the spur with an aerial rising from its roof. I don't catch its name but it commands the view over the town that the monastery once held.

The bus stops on a steep incline outside what looks like a government building. The driver leaps out to push a rock under the back wheel, yelling "Xia che" at us as he does. Get out here? We look at the old man who is gathering up our scattered belongings and knotting them in a cloth of his own.

"This is where you should stay. Chamdo's new hotel."

I catch Rosemary's eye and my dismay is followed almost immediately by the urge to laugh. So much for our ideas of living as the daughters of a Tibetan in Chamdo. The old man is smiling. But what has happened? Did the driver tell him that he wouldn't be allowed to have foreigners to stay? Or did he always mean to bring us here? Perhaps he is proud to be showing us to the sort of accommodation that he thinks we expect.

"This is too expensive for us," I say hopefully as he insists on carrying our bags into the shiny stone hallway.

"Foreign guest," he says unnecessarily to the phalanx of curved backs of cleaners trailing mops across the floor. "We must look after them well."

I am surprised at his ability to speak Chinese – it is rare for a Tibetan of his age and social background – but the backs don't react. Spilling water about them in a phlegmatic arc, they advance across the floor, forcing us, eventually, to retreat with our bags to the steps outside.

"We can't stay here, it is too good." Rosemary tries again, but the old man is not to be dissuaded. He finds another door and we make our way, in front of the cleaners now, across a patina of water to the reception desk.

"Twenty-five *yuan* a night; foreigners aren't allowed." The receptionist turns the page of her comic. The old man hasn't even opened his mouth.

"They are foreign teachers in Lhasa," he ventures, but timidly now. Her attitude – or perhaps the view of the top of her head and the severe angle of her pigtails – have weakened his confidence.

"It doesn't matter." Rosemary puts her hand on his arm. "We'll find somewhere else."

We are both anxious to avoid a scene which could attract the attention of the Gong An Ju. This woman obviously knows that we should not be in Chamdo and she might suddenly forget her indifference. The old man takes another line. It is twenty-five times the price of last night's bed. The receptionist is finding it hard to concentrate on her book.

"We prefer rooms like last night's," Rosemary pleads. We pick up our bags, realising that it is probably the only way to get out of this situation.

The man looks crestfallen as we part on the hill. The receptionist watches us from the steps of the hotel.

Chapter 24

CHAMDO

There was something peculiarly soulless about Chamdo. It was not just the modern buildings. Even the remnants of the Tibetan town were depressing. Perhaps my expectations had been too high. Over the months, the legendary fieriness of Khampa men and women, the awe they inspired in other Tibetans, the flamboyance of their clothes, above all, the magnificence of Chamdo's position, had led me to expect something of Lhasa's drama. But the old town with its buildings heaped randomly against the slope of the hill was mean and squalid. The houses had neither the charm of the long-eaved huts in Kongpo nor the grandeur of Lhasa homes. They were made of unadorned mud.

Having found beds in a small Chinese hostel, we climbed up through the old town to the monastery.

The darkness offered little: walls, gaping roofs, untidy wood-piles. It looked as though the monastery was being used as a saw-mill. The few monks, gathered in the courtyard, walked away at our approach. A Chinese child, who attached herself to us on the way up, accosted one of them and told him to show us around. Her voice was imperious and she sniggered pointedly when he ignored her.

"Let's come back tomorrow." Rosemary said. In the darkness, the atmosphere of antipathy was almost tangible.

Next morning, we found ourselves brushing our teeth over the drain in the hotel yard with a young monk from India. There was something fastidious about the way he rattled his toothbrush in his mug and leaned far over the drain to spit, holding his skirts back with his hand. Seeing us, his face lit up. He picked his way across the hosed concrete.

"How do you cope with all this," he said in English and, obviously seeing in us fellow sufferers, launched immediately into a tirade about basic conditions in Tibet. He was suffering from altitude sickness and food poisoning and sleeplessness. Without drawing breath, he went on to list the trials of his journey from Lhasa, his childhood in India and the *geshe* exams that he had just passed. He was now a Doctor of Divinity, he said proudly.

An hour later we were still standing by the drain, soap and toothpaste in hand – listening. He was a Bon lama it transpired, and had returned with his father to research the present conditions of Bon in Tibet – provided he could put up with the discomfort.

"Don't worry, you'll get used to it." Rosemary picked up her mug briskly and made for our room.

We spent the morning looking for a truck to Kunming. But every yard was an expanse of windswept concrete. All the trucks – their bonnets standing promisingly open – were going to Lhasa.

By lunchtime, deciding that we were too late to get anything, we set off again for the monastery. The Kunming trucks probably all left at dawn, we concluded hopefully.

The monastery was not a saw-mill, as we had thought the night before: it was being rebuilt. In the first courtyard, monks were sawing tree trunks over deep pits, passing planks along a chain of helpers to the first floor. We ambled out through a long cloistered alley and entered another part.

There was an atmosphere of remote calm. From a line of doorways came sounds of monks chanting; we wandered along the flowered balconies outside, carried from voice to voice. In turn they drew us, their notes swelling as we passed, holding us, lingering, fading, relinquishing us to the next.

At the entrance to a temple, a man was on a step-ladder sculpting the top-knot of a clay Buddha.

"*Genla, kaba terga?*" Where are you going? He called down to us. It was the old man who told stories on the bus. He climbed down the ladder with arthritic haste, holding the side with one hand and wiping the clay from the other on his trousers. With pride, he showed us the new statues with their fresh gold paint, the pencil tracings of new murals, new decorations. He was a monk at this monastery once, he told us over tea, and now he was helping to rebuild it.

Our five o'clock rise next morning yielded nothing. The leader of the bus station, a large motherly Chinese woman, consoled us with bread, hot from the steamer, and told us we were wasting our time. We would never find anything going to Kunming. We should have taken the bus, for the five-day journey to Chengdu.

We made our way back to the hostel. A dog slunk round the front of a department store and disappeared into an alley. Further down the hill, as insomniac street vendor was frying feathery sticks of dough.

"*You tiao! You tiao!*" His incantatory wail filled the empty street. But we needed no encouragement. Buying four each, we laughed at how indulgent this made us feel, and returned to our own thoughts as we slid on through the red mud.

The day dawned tentatively. Above the mountains to the east, black clouds were lying in wait for the sun. Its rays touched the slopes on the opposite side as it appeared above a peak. But they faltered and were engulfed by cloud. I kept thinking of our onward journey.

It was absurd to be depressed about having to take the Chengdu road. We knew little about either region and the route to Kunming was not intrinsically more interesting. It was simply, I had to admit, an infantile desire to follow a less-travelled route. But then, as I was trying to convince myself of this, an idea occurred to me. The Bon lama from India might give us a lift. My imagination was already running ahead to thoughts of spending nights in the tents of his nomadic relatives; collecting plants with him on the mountains; visiting unvisited Bon monasteries. Rosemary doubted that the lama's father would agree. He seemed protective towards his son, and suspicious of us.

But the idea was beginning to take hold. Lashing rain sent us into a department store for shelter, where among open containers of luridly coloured face creams and shampoos, we shamelessly plotted our attack.

It would be evening before we met the lama again. He, unsuspecting, asked us to accompany him for supper. Father looked concerned. "Do you think he is worried that we will lead his brilliant son astray?" Rosemary whispered as we made our way to the small eatery below.

Throughout the meal the lama talked, forcing us to be embarrassingly unsubtle with our hints. He had a mission to spread the word of Bon, and interrupted his discourse only to urge us to write about it when we returned to England. The differences between Bon and Buddhism were, he admitted, slight. Not only had Buddhism absorbed many of the gods and practices of the indigenous Bon religion, but the development of Bon had, in turn, been significantly influenced by Buddhism. Bon began as an animist cult whose exorcists and shamans spent their lives appeasing the gods and preventing the dead from returning to harm the living. The lama looked earnest and continued as if he were delivering a lecture.

The gods were the forces of nature; the mountains and lakes and rivers were their abode. But they were not the embodiment of good or evil, he said, when Rosemary tried to draw a parallel with other animist religions. Their power could either help or harm, so they had to be constantly humoured with offerings. Preparing food, piling stones at the top of passes to provide shelter – these and other rituals which people still perform today, crept into Buddhism from Bon. The *tsampa* effigies that we sent back to hell on Losar Eve, invested with the evil of last year, came from Bon traditions too, according to the lama.

Like Buddhist gods, many of the gods of Bon had both a wrathful and peaceful aspect. But the lama insisted that they were fundamentally different, for whereas Buddhist gods were a device to aid meditation, gods of Bon were real. He grew defensive when we talked about Bon's doctrine which only emerged with the written language which Buddhist scholars brought from India. According to Buddhists, many of Bon scriptures were stolen from Buddhist texts; the biography of Shenrab Miboche, for example, bears a great resemblance to that of Sakyamuni Buddha, the historical Buddha. But the two religions were very different, the lama insisted, and not least because they do not recognise each other's central figures.

After supper the lama and his father took us off to a Tibetan dance festival in a grandiose modern building similar to the hotel where we had been expected to stay. Like the hotel and the five bridges which spanned the river, it was out of proportion with the size of the town. We couldn't help feeling that it was there to impress, and that someone had got his priorities wrong. Inside, the theatre was draped in flags of the P.R.C. A portrait of Chairman Mao leaned precariously from the wall behind the stage. The auditorium looked as though it could hold the whole population of Chamdo: a few Tibetans had turned up. The compère spoke in Chinese, the lama complained throughout, and I had to admit to getting bored long before the end. My imagination had set off once more along the road with the lama. To his father's obvious consternation, he had risen to our bait and had promised to ask the driver if we could join them.

"We were not meant to find a truck today," Rosemary whispered half-way through the performance. I smiled: her thoughts were obviously somewhere beyond Chamdo too.

Back at the hotel, we were greeted by the driver. The lama and his father disappeared with him into their room. We stayed up reading, talking, listening: waiting for him to tell us when we would leave in the morning. The lama arrived, eventually, sliding his yellow woollen hat nervously around his scalp.

"You must give me your addresses." He took a Parker pen from his robes and sat down on the bed. "I want to come to England one day and then I will visit you in your homes." And his home? We looked at him expectantly. He left, urging us again to write about Bon when we returned to England.

Three-fifty a.m. Cold drizzle. Another transport yard. I wander down the rows of trucks. Around me, tarpaulins drip into the darkness; the place is deserted. Crouching under the back of a truck to wait, I am wondering why we ever imagined they left so early.

We have decided to split up today; Rosemary is waiting at the other truck yard but even Chengdu trucks seem unwilling to take us now.

It is after six, and the Tannoy comes to life. A beam of torchlight slides across the wet ground towards me, flitting now and then up the sides of the trucks as it approaches. I get up stiffly and go to meet it.

"Ni dao Chengdu qu ma?" Are you going to Chengdu? The torch shines in my face, hiding the face of its owner. I wait for the voice.

"Qu." Yes.

My heart sinks. The suspicious tone is familiar now. His refusal is out almost before I have made my request.

I wait.

Bu xing – always the same "no's" – *bu xing* – the same embarrassed faces – *bu xing* – truck after truck leaving empty without us. Chinese etiquette won't allow them to say that they are forbidden to take foreigners. They are full – if they give an excuse – and drive away empty.

The prospect of staying longer in Chamdo is distinctly gloomy as I collapse back on to my bed in the hostel but, just as I am dropping off to sleep, Rosemary bursts through the door.

"There is a truck going to Kunming. At least that is what the bus station leader says. The drivers are about to come back."

At the entrance to the bus station, we meet the leader. Squatting with her trousers rolled up to the knees, elbows gripping her ample sides, she is knitting a diminutive pair of split-crutched trousers. Her daughter has had a boy.

"They're back." She smiles and waves her knitting needle towards the first floor.

Even before we get to the top of the stairs, the sound of raucous laughter reaches us from under the door.

"Wei!" Our knock provokes a chorus of shouts in Chinese.

Webs of smoke hang in the light of the doorway. In the almost total darkness inside, men are lounging back on the quilt-strewn beds round the wall. Bottles of beer litter the table and lie broken on the floor beneath.

"You ren dao Kunming qu ma?" Rosemary asks.

A man on the bed nearest the door grins.

"Wo . . ." The end of his sentence is drowned by ribald laughter.

"Watch out for Azong!" Another voice chuckles. "They'd be safer with you, wouldn't they Norbu?"

"Want to go to Lhasa?" someone else shouts.

"We've just come from there."

Linzhi? Nagchu? Pome? Suddenly, it seems that we can go anywhere. After days of refusals their enthusiasm is great, whatever its reason. At least there seems a chance that we will get out. The man they called Azong stands up. He looks in his thirties with huge eyes and a wide, gold-toothed grin.

"So you want to go to Kunming?"

"Yes," Rosemary says.

He chuckles. "We're leaving tomorrow. Wake us at seven."

Chapter 25

JOURNEYS BY SKY-BOAT

The drivers were Tibetan, in fact, but their dialect was so far removed from Lhasa Tibetan that we couldn't understand a word. Although their Chinese was worse than ours, communication was aided by grins, giggles and jokes of a very practical nature.

We slid clattering out of the town, back through the red mud which, after three days of rain, was webbed with streams. By mid-morning we were bloated with tea and *tsampa* and apples and sweets. There was no question of waiting for hours in the truck as we had with Bemba; every few miles we were invited in and fêted by Norbu and Azong's friends.

The house of one woman was filled with children. There were six, she smiled: they were all hers. When I asked if she was allowed to have so many she mumbled in embarrassment. But the advantages for peasant families of having more than the three children that the government allows rural families in minority regions, far outweigh the penalties. She probably would have had to pay a fine, and her children would be denied ration-books until they were eighteen. But here the penalties of not being entitled to free health care and schooling were irrelevant.

As, finally, we headed off for Yunnan Province and Kunming, Rosemary let out a whoop of delight. Azong burst out laughing and launched into an exuberantly tuneless rendition of *Ali Baba*. The Mekong flowed in a deep canyon between red sandstone mountains covered in scrub. The rain was behind us now and the afternoon sun sent warm breezes blowing through the cab. No tortuous climbs – we rolled along a sandy road, strung with villages. On spurs and mountain slopes behind, frittered skeletons of monasteries bore witness to the systematic thoroughness of their destruction. In this region it began even before 1959.

Azong wasn't interested. He wanted to know where our husbands were. No husbands? Surely we must have husbands somewhere? In

England? Lhasa? But he wasn't married. He chuckled and wiped his hand on his well-greased trousers.

"This is my girlfriend," he said, taking a photo from behind the rear-view mirror. It showed a girl in the flamboyant dress of one of Yunnan's ethnic minorities. He was going to meet her in Kunming.

We were near the top of a pass in the moments after sunset, when the sun fleetingly invests the earth with its power. The glare of day had run from the sky into the mountains. Colours vibrated, the outline of the peaks acquired a dazzling sharpness. Even the puddles beside the road flashed gold as we passed.

Then we were over, and descending. No engine, just the rush of wind, the rattle of metal and glass. Like a pendulum without its lead, we hurtled across the mountains from bend to bend gathering momentum with each turn until, long after dark, we careered into a yard at the bottom of the pass.

Azong was obviously popular here, for although it was already two in the morning, an old man emerged and cheerfully prepared for us all that remained in the tiny hut canteen.

The detritus of bones and slops under our table created the atmosphere of an abandoned feast. Not quite abandoned, perhaps. As we were slurping our noodles around a stump of candle, the surrounding darkness filled with figures, rubbing their eyes, hitching up the rope round their trousers. The entertainment provided by a visit from Azong and two foreigners was not to be missed in this forgotten settlement. We were observed with uninhibited curiosity. Refreshingly, Azong and Norbu had shown no interest in the fact that we were foreign, and now, more concerned with noodles and sleep than our customs, they replied to the barrage of questions with dismissive grunts.

But the villagers were not to be deterred. Knowing all about foreigners, the cook held forth, partly in the well-worn phrases of Party propaganda and partly by extension to his own imagination. "If you go outside China, you can't speak Chinese, you know." He turned to Azong "Isn't that right?" Azong opened a third bottle of beer. An old Tibetan woman, obviously remembering the days when her language was discouraged, peered sympathetically into Rosemary's face. "Aren't they even allowed to speak Chinese at home?"

The conversation continued with the strange smell that foreigners had. Not bad, just strange. Then as we were leaving, the old woman took my arm. "Tell me, where *is* England? Is it on the road to Lhasa?"

The cook looked at us, raising his eyes to the ceiling in complicit scorn. "On the road to Lhasa! Of course not. It takes weeks by skyboat to get there."

The road in this region must be one of the most spectacular in the world. From the awesome barrenness of the peaks we were plunged into verdant valleys, and then dragged to the summits again. One day we rode along a vast ridge with the gorges of the Mekong hardly visible below us. Up there where the colours had the hardness of rock, where nothing moved but the clouds, we came upon a wave of yellow flowers of poppy-like fragility. Heaven must meet the earth at the summit of these sacred mountains.

We passed Menkhang, the last village in Tibet. We were nearing Derzhin in Yunnan Province, Azong said. And from there it was only forty-eight hours to the metropolis of Kunming.

"Not long now," Azong shouted as we were swooping down in another descent. Rounding a corner, we nearly ran into the back of Norbu. The nose of his truck was half-buried in a wall of rock.

Sa yum. Landslide.

For a hundred yards, the chiselled line of road had vanished. A chute of rock was tumbling into a canyon where the Mekong roared a thousand feet below.

Azong took charge. Before the pass Norbu had picked up a Chinese man, a lama and his two disciples, so we were now a party of eight.

"We will start clearing tonight until it gets dark," Azong said. "And then we'll have to leave it until tomorrow." He walked over to the edge of the landslide and began dislodging the largest rocks, letting them continue their passage down into the Mekong. Above him the gash in the mountain was seeping water like a suppurating sore.

"The rocks on that side are poised to fall at any minute," Rosemary noticed. I don't think that either of us believed they would. Somehow, Norbu and Azong's routine approach had dispelled for the moment our fear.

There was a road gang working at the other end of the landslide. The leader, noticing us clearing the rocks, waved angrily. Climbing nearer he shouted at us to keep off the landslide and warned that it would be at least five days before we could cross.

"Five days! We would take only a day to clear enough to get through." Azong and Norbu headed off across the rubble to strike a deal with the workers. Azong was still shouting and gesticulating when we saw Norbu turn away and start back towards us. His face was working with rage. "We'll just have to start before they return tomorrow. I'm not sitting here for a week."

After our mean fire had succumbed to the drizzle, we all joined the lama under his appliquéed awning strung between the two trucks. Azong and Norbu chuckled over anecdotes which neither we, nor the monks who spoke the Lhasa dialect, could understand. Their suggestiveness was obvious however, and their laughter contagious. The lama sat in the place of honour opposite the entrance smiling at us indulgently as he turned the loose leaves of his religious text.

The lama was from a monastery a day's climb from Lhasa, his disciples said. They were nearing the end of a six-week pilgrimage to Derzhin. They asked us to teach them English and then Lhakpa, the older of the two, said he wanted to know about the West.

"What do you want to know?" Rosemary asked.

Lowering his voice he leaned forward, almost snuffing out the candle flame. "Have you seen the Dalai Lama?"

We smiled but, for them, he was the West. Lhakpa urged us to tell the Dalai Lama that it was not safe to return. Then he frowned, looking at us almost accusingly. "But Buddhism is under threat outside Tibet, too. Everyone knows that, in the West, there is a conspiracy to disgrace the monks. Many monks outside Tibet have got married now," he said. "And you know why?"

"No."

"Foreign leaders sent beautiful women to trap them and make them break their vows."

Thondrup went outside to tighten the awning which was beginning to leak. Lhakpa looked at us curiously. He started unwrapping his religious book from its cloth and then seemed to change his mind. Glancing at the lama and then at the Chinese man, he began talking in a low voice to Rosemary about religious repression.

Azong feigned pique at having lost our attention. He and Norbu were lounging back against the bundles of baggage, revealing soft expanses of midriff and drinking *arak*. Their stories continued and seemed, from the tone of their laughter and their gestures, to grow bawdier. Then Norbu noticed my camera and insisted that I took a photo of the party.

Both the monks covered their faces. Azong and Norbu tried to pull their hands away, laughing at their shyness; I began teasing them as I returned my camera to its bag. The monks were not coy, however. They were afraid.

The only cameras Lhakpa and Thondrup had seen were police cameras used to identify people in crowds. In 1979 they had joined the thousands of people thronging the gardens of the Norbulingka to catch a glimpse of a delegation from the Dalai Lama. "We wore our coats over our heads so that the police couldn't recognise us," Lhakpa said. "But many people were imprisoned at that time."

The mission was one of three which visited Tibet at the invitation of the Chinese Government. It was part of a process by which it hoped to bring about the return of the Dalai Lama and the Tibetan population in exile. They would return as Chinese citizens: for Peking, there was no question about that. The Chinese leaders have never recognised the Dalai Lama's government. They call it the Dalai Clique – and say it is bent on "splitting" the Motherland. "The Dalai's splittists" were behind the pro-independence demonstrations of 1987, according to the Peking Government, and they are responsible for widespread unrest which, three years later, is continuing under martial law.

As I listened to Lhakpa, a kaleidoscope of conversations with Mr Li passed through my mind. . . . Tibetans were Chinese – Mr Li had explained that many times – if any of them thought differently they were deluded. But, more likely, they were just saying they weren't Chinese because they wanted to please me: it was what foreigners liked to hear . . . I should understand: there were Han Chinese and Tibetan Chinese – and they were all Chinese. . . . The unity of the Motherland was important to everyone. . . .

The unity of the Motherland was sacred. Even Sui and Xiao Wang found the idea of an independent Tibet unthinkable. And so do the leaders in Peking. Since the 1979/1980 missions, the Chinese Government has been involved, more or less directly, in negotiations with the Dalai Lama.

"Negotiation", no, that seemed the wrong word. I searched for an analogy. It was like a game of tennis where the players were serving into different courts, or where the Chinese Government continued to serve instead of returning the ball. Peking's negotiations were over the status of the Dalai Lama, should he return. The Dalai Lama's negotiations were over the status of Tibet and the Tibetan people. "Dalai" would be welcomed in China but he would have to live in Peking. The Chinese Government ignored statements from Dharamsala on the question of Tibet's independence.

In 1987, in the U.S. Congress, the Dalai Lama would deliver a five-point plan for the future of Tibet. Also in 1987 the Chinese would make a concession on the issue: if the Dalai Lama returned, he would

not be obliged to live in Peking, he could live in Lhasa. The proposal
which the Dalai Lama would deliver at the European Parliament in
1988 conceded so much that it caused outrage among Tibetans in exile.
Renouncing total independence, he proposed a relationship of "association" between Tibet and China. Tibet would have virtual
autonomy with a democratically elected government to decide on all
matters except defence and foreign policy. These would remain the
responsibility of the Chinese Government. In Peking the proposal was
dismissed as a disguised demand for independence. It could never be
a basis for dialogue. But they would welcome talks with the Dalai
Lama: they were always open to dialogue with him . . .

Falling rocks which grew in size as fear fuelled my imagination made
for a sleepless night. My mind wandered, drawing back self-
indulgently to savour the scene, imagining it already as a memory.
The Mekong, not just the roar of water through the rain as it was now,
regained the mystique of its name.

The confines of the awning made intimate by the threat of landslides
outside, steam rising from smoke-drenched clothing: everything was
disintegrating into smells and images and sounds. Was this how
I would remember it?

By the time we surfaced next morning Norbu had already set off on
foot for a village further down the mountain to borrow shovels. By
seven we were at work on the road. The monks climbed the landslide
and began sending down rocks from above. Rosemary and I were
clearing the slurry with bamboo baskets brought by Norbu. The
Chinese man was given a shovel; and Azong and Norbu began
building a platform from below.

The rain had cleared but a stream was still running across what had
once been the road. It was demoralising work. Every so often, just
when the wall was beginning to look sturdy, a heavy rock dislodged
one underneath. Norbu and Azong would leap aside cursing as the
whole structure tumbled away down the mountain. The jigsaw
process continued.

The road gang would be returning soon; Azong was growing
increasingly impatient. Suddenly, he dropped the rock that I had just
passed him.

"Lesgo," he shouted, mimicking our English and grinning.

Revving up the truck at the edge of the landslide, he moved across
through a flurry of mud and rocks. He reached the other side without
mishap, and, leaping out, danced round the truck to *Ali Baba*.

But the track had now been churned into gullies of mud. Half-way across, the back wheels of the second truck began skidding. A small stone rolled out from the wall.

"Keep moving!" Azong shouted.

We all watched as the truck roared and gradually lost momentum. Lhakpa slid between the truck and the mountain with a basket of small stones and re-emerged sprayed in mud. Suddenly the truck was free and shot across the last few yards.

"Zou la!" Go!

We glided off down the mountain.

Fongshan. Three days later.

We are no more than an hour's ride down the road. The short journey from our landslide camp was punctuated more frequently than ever by stops for tea, a meal, or simply a gossip. Everyone knew Azong. Once, an army jeep flagged us down. We pulled our hats over our eyes and became engrossed in Azong's comics, but the man was just stopping for a chat.

By lunchtime, when we rumbled down a leafy avenue at the edge of the river, we had covered five miles. Azong sounded a blast of his horn and people came running from the two tin-roofed buildings. Someone wheeled their bicycle out for Azong to admire. And he, demonstrating how it should be used, wobbled and fell, enraging a sow that was snoozing in the road.

Azong took the afternoon to satisfy the curiosity of his audience. Then suddenly, he left, announcing as he set off to climb the mountain, that he was going to his family and would be back in two days.

"Xiao Zhao will look after you." He swung a bundle on to his back, smiling at the young Chinese woman with whom he had been having tea.

Xiao Zhao was nervous of us – or perhaps jealous. There was little to do and little to talk about, so Azong dominated our conversations. Over the three days, she and her Tibetan friend Dajon returned to the same questions. Where had we met Azong? How long had we known him? What did we think of him? And he certainly wouldn't be back on Monday – he had a very beautiful wife who was ill. A wife? What about his girlfriend in Kunming whom, he told us, he was marrying in September? The girls revelled in our consternation, mistaking it for jealousy and kept repeating that he was bound not to come back.

Life was dull in Fongshan, they both agreed. They were from Derzhin originally and had been sent here ten years ago at the age of eighteen. They were desperate for husbands but there was only a truck yard, a store and a primary school – and everyone was married. They were almost too old now, anyway. Together they were in charge of the truck yard dormitory. Not a truck passed in the two days that we were there. Their apathy was contagious. We gave up asking questions about their life; we gave up reading; we gave up writing. We just sat like everyone else.

A child fell off the wood pile on the second day and grazed its knee. The sow, having forgotten the injury inflicted on it by Azong, returned to the road. And on the third day, Xiao Zhao and Dajon began embroidering, in white silk, intricate patterns on the soles of shoes.

But Azong did return. Even he was embarrassed by the warmth of our welcome. And he certainly wasn't prepared for the jokes about his wife and his women in Fongshan. He insisted that they were making it up. He wasn't married, he said, taking the photo from behind the mirror again as proof.

He grinned, whistling to himself as we glided down through the sunlit mountains. Rosemary and I looked at each other and found ourselves grinning too. The bare rocks and the dusty wind of Fongshan were behind us now. As the horizon broadened, a lushly forested range appeared to the west. A quilt of snow spread across its peaks and below, tongues of glaciers stretched out, sparkling through the trees.

I felt an overwhelming sense of relief. Yet Rosemary and I kept returning to the stultifying boredom of Fongshan. There was no sense of village life at all; the settlement existed because of the truck stop, and most of the people had been sent from other places to service it. It was like a remote limbo of displaced people, all waiting – most without hope – to be returned home. But there was a positive side to life in Fongshan which struck us both. Despite the low morale of its inhabitants, there was a sense of harmony that we hadn't come across before. Tibetans and Chinese wandered in and out of one another's houses, sat together, ate together, and unusually, Tibetan culture prevailed. Butter tea was drunk by everyone. It was Xiao Zhao – a Chinese – who secretly showed us the protection cord given to her by a lama from Kham.

In Derzhin, Azong announced that he would not be going on to Kunming for a week and marched us off to buy tickets for the express bus running between the two towns. Although we were tempted to wait, the possibility didn't occur to Azong. We left him in a room like the one in which we'd met, lounging back in the gloom with a girl on his knee. We were beginning to cramp his style.

After Derzhin the altitude dropped. Gradually the air acquired the consistency of water and we were enveloped in a languid fog of oxygen saturation. What did it feel like, I wondered as we rolled down a road still remote but suddenly tarred (proof, my Tibetan neighbour complained, that Tibet is a lower priority than the central provinces). Yes, it *was* like being in water, or like being a jelly-fish which was so relaxed it couldn't move.

People and traffic everywhere. The roads were crammed with convoys of logging trucks carrying wood out of Tibet. Every slope had been wrested from the red earth for cultivation, every mountain-side carved into terraces. Bristling wheat fields emerged; we threshed their harvest which lay strewn across the road. Then, as we delved deeper into Yunnan, florescent paddyfields appeared, studded with conical hats and blue trousered bottoms.

The end of our journey. The lure of Kunming luxury was beginning to dispel feelings of anticlimax – a shower, an ice-cream, a western meal perhaps. By the time we reached Xiaguan, the last town before Kunming, we had decided that it would be good to arrive.

For me, Kunming passed in the night and I was on the journey back to Tibet, alone. Rosemary would be going on to Peking to arrange her flight home before returning to Lhasa to pack up. I was taking the Chengdu train from where I would catch the plane to Lhasa – or so I imagined.

Somewhere around the hills of Guilin, in the depths of Southern China, I discovered that I had mistaken the platform and had added a week to my journey. I would have no option but to make a vast loop north and west, and then back to Lhasa across the Changthang plateau thirty-two hours by bus.

Central China stirred feelings of nostalgia that I hadn't anticipated. Everyone was kind and helpful beyond the call of duty. Wuhan friends, telegrammed from the station in Guilin, were waiting on the platform at Wuhan with fruit and eggs. Through the familiar village-like sprawl of this great industrial city, across the Yangtse bridge as far as the old station of Hankow, we exchanged a year of thoughts and emotions, imagining, like the last time we had parted, that we wouldn't see each other again. A feast awaited me in the rose-latticed courtyard of Peking friends. No one asked why I hadn't warned them or why I wasn't staying. While they queued for my onward ticket,

I was made to rest in their bamboo shade. Their fears of Tibet were gently expressed. It was what they had been told, they confessed, and how were they to know?

I arrived back in Lhasa, grateful for the serendipity that had sent me round China, realising how important for my own equanimity it had been to experience again the kindness and generosity of the Chinese people in their home environment.

Chapter 26

THE YOGHURT FESTIVAL

The Lhasa valley was in full summer on my return. As I cycled beyond Drepung monastery one afternoon, streams glittered in meadows draped with sheets. Along their banks, washing parties lazed under the trees. Passing behind the pinnacled mountain that ends the valley, I rode into a medieval portrait of villages harvesting. The fields were dotted with men loading yaks. Long skirted women threshed wheat and barley, filling the air with the dusty sweetness of chaff. Standing in circles singing, they swung their jointed flails to the ground in sequence like campanologists in a belfry. Others tossed clouds of straw to each other through the wind, and sang antiphonally in rhythm with their work. Children played amongst the thermos flasks of tea, the cloth-wrapped bundles of lunch, and an old man, lying back against a stack, stroked the hairs on his chin, taking an occasional slurp from a bowl of *chang*.

"We hoped *gen la* would have a birthday," one of my students said in class one day when I admitted that I was about to be twenty-five. They had seen on films how westerners celebrated. I was aware that birthdays weren't fêted in Tibet but, having just done a lesson on dates, I asked each student when he was born. None of them knew. "Some time in 1957." "Before the Chinese came." "A Saturday – it must have been in summer, because my mother said there was a thunder storm the night before." Pemba knew that he had been born on a Saturday only because that was his name. Looking at all the Dawas in the class (five men and two women), I asked why most Tibetan women gave birth on Mondays, and everyone laughed.

Traditionally, a lama would be asked to give a child its name. But names like Dawa Tsering – "Monday Long Life", Basang Tashi – "Friday Good Luck" or plain Mima and Lhakpa, "Tuesday" and "Wednesday" were most common among the Cultural Revolution children, when lamas could not be consulted and families had to find their own names. Some children born at that time were simply named "second" or "third" child. But names often had a superstitious significance too. Lhamo had a friend whose brother died before she was born. In order to deter the spirits from returning to harm her, the parents had called her Kyigya – Dog shit. Another family I had met recently used their children's names as a form of contraception. Planning not to have any more children after their third, they called her Ga – "Stop". But the method was obviously not very reliable: the next child was called Tsam – "Finish". I suppose they must have given up after that because the fifth and sixth were called Lhamo and Sonam – "Goddess" and "Good Fortune".

Sho dun, the Yoghurt Festival, took place at the beginning of August in the Norbulinka, the Jewel Park. With picnics, drink and jars of yoghurt, the whole of Lhasa repaired to the wilderness of woods and flowering gardens that surrounded the summer residences of the Dalai Lamas. Our picnic would last for three days, in honour of Rosemary's departure. This was short, the students told us apologetically, but the leader couldn't be persuaded to cancel classes for longer. I had already begun the summer school for teenagers.

On the previous afternoon the men went off in search of beer and *chang*. I went to the market with the women and finally learned the art of testing eggs. The egg merchants had always offered me a telescope of paper to test their freshness. At first, like the other egg-gazers amongst the crates of straw, I had pointed it towards the sun, turning an egg slowly on the end as I saw them doing, but the secrets of the egg eluded me and I resorted to my method of shaking them instead. Somewhere, I must have learned that if an egg rattles it is bad, which it usually is, but, as the weather got warmer, I discovered that eggs that didn't rattle could be bad too.

My favourite egg man, a smiling Chinese youth from Sichuan, showed the semi-circle of by-standers who had gathered to watch his Chaplinesque performance how I usually tested the eggs. Then he turned to me. "You just look at the colour. If, when the sun shines through, the egg is pink, then it's okay. If it's black, it's bad."

We passed the rest of the afternoon in our garden among bowls of water and endless cups of tea; washing vegetables, making *momos* – spiced dumplings – and noodles. Rosemary and I wouldn't make anybody a decent wife, Lhamo said, coming into the garden as the dough I had been stretching into a cat's-cradle of noodles broke and swung into the dust. I was proud of my *momos*. I thought I'd mastered the art of rolling the dough into circles, judging the exact quantity of meat and pinching the pastry in delicate patterns around it. But the test lay in the cooking. And all the *momos* that fell apart were ours, the students teased.

By eight the next morning, everyone and a sprawling mountain of picnic paraphernalia had been hoisted into the back of the unit's truck, and we were bumping and hooting along the river road towards the Norbulingka. With gallons of *chang* strapped to their backs, their cycles invisible beneath a tumble of carpets and tiffin carriers, clans of families wended their way along the river towards the park. We mouthed shouts at each other through the roar of the engine and the wind, and collapsed into soundless laughter. The sun was shining and spirits were high.

By the time we arrived at the Norbulingka it had been transformed into a kind of medieval fair. White canopies were looped from tree to tree and, in the chequered shade beneath them, picnickers marked out their territory with fences of coloured cloth. Here and there, aloof from the sprawl, stood appliquéed pavilions, grinning with dragons, wheels of life, eternal knots and twirls and spirals of religious designs. Once Lhasa's rich traders and aristocrats threw five- or six-day picnics for hundreds of guests from tents like these. Now, at 13,000 *yuan* – £2,500 – for the largest, they all belonged to government work-units.

We stretched our awning under a walnut tree near the Eighth Dalai Lama's Palace. Patterned carpets were unrolled on the grass, the low tables piled with baskets of cakes and sunflower seeds, games unpacked and the ghetto-blaster – the proud possession of Dawa Tsering, a rich trader – joined the mêlée of other tape recorders.

We sit back. The tea, the talk, the uninhibited silence, that will fill most of the next few days, begins. Morning drifts into afternoon. Lunch is laid out on the grass. Our noodles and *momos* arrive steaming from the kitchen of one of Dawa Tsering's friends who lives in the Norbulingka. They are placed in the middle of thirty other dishes: curried delicacies of Indian inspiration, Chinese vegetables, breads, plump tangerines, cheese from someone's nomadic cousin and jars of yoghurt. The spread covers the whole enclosure and invites Gargantuan gluttony. But, to our frustration, Tibetan politeness prevails.

The afternoon grows languid. Covered in black charcoal, having lost at mahjong, I sit alone for a while. Rosemary is beating young Mima at *girim*, a board game of Indian origin with *tsampa* dusted counters flicked into pockets at the corners. Mima graciously ignores the fact that Rosemary is being helped by the expert thumb-nail flick of Dawa Tsering whose hand, disowned by his innocent expression, is resting on her knee. Beneath pink nylon sun hats, a group of girl students are playing cards, eyed from time to time by the *sho* players under the tree: howls of mock rage, bawdy rhymes and forfeit glasses of beer accompany the old Tibetan coins which are moved round a circle of cowrie shells on the carpet.

"*Si, Si* – four, four – please four." A dark, broad-faced man, whom I don't know, breathes over the dice, shaking the wooden pot in both hands with ritual obsequiousness.

> *Si, Si, Si, Si.*
> *Tsi gamshia*
> *Mi rewa mindu.*

"Four, four, four, four. He, whose neck is thin, there's no hope for him." He slams the pot down on the leather mat with a shout. Then, looking round at the reddening faces of the other players, slowly, magician-like, he lifts up the corner. Yes, a four! He pounces on Nyima's counter sending it back to the beginning. The girls look up from their game of cards as Nyima, at eighteen the baby of the class and everyone's favourite, is made to down two glasses of *chang*.

Nyima needs a five. The faces are poised to laugh already, in anticipation of the rhyme that goes with five. Grabbing the pot, shaking it with mock ferocity, he rails drunkenly at the dice. "*Ka, ka, ka.*"

> *Ka, Ka, Ka . . .*
> *Kamdru dang tsermo ma tsi,*
> *Litang la bazo gegeri!*

Five, Five, Five . . . Beware of playing with Khampa children. Give them a chance and they'll snatch your balls! As the forfeits increase, the rhymes become cruder. Eventually the game breaks up when the girls come to watch, and the broad-faced man, drunk as he is, considers the rhymes unsuitable for them.

The rest of us need more *chang*, the *sho* players decide. Forfeits are given to anyone who brings a Chinese word into their conversation and we all (particularly Rosemary and I) get drunker. Nyima suggests extending the forfeits to anyone who fails to use the correct honorific

form★ but Dawa Tsering complains. He was brought up during the
Cultural Revolution when honorific Tibetan was banned as being the
language of reactionaries and, like many of his generation, he still can't
speak it properly.

As the girls' protests slowly dissolve into acquiescence, the *chang*
games begin. A glass of *chang* is passed from person to person while
Sonam's son, a precocious ten-year-old, sits blindfolded with his red
young pioneers' scarf, drumming on an enamel bowl with a stick. He
can't see, he swears, but the glass almost invariably stops at either
Rosemary or me.

The afternoon blurs into a somnolent dusk. For a while, as if in
honour of the sunset, the tape-recorders are quiet; in other enclosures,
families, huge extended families, have thrown themselves into the
next meal. Until the last moment, the sunlight glitters through the
leaves, making sharp crystals of light play over the canopies. Then
suddenly, it is gone. But for a few decorative swirls of cloud above the
mountains, the sky is empty.

We sit around, dribbling sunflower husks and chatting. An old man
in a ragged *chuba* and an expression of unwilling sobriety, comes into
the enclosure. He holds his cap out to Sonam who fills it unsteadily
with *chang*. After he leaves, Nyima collapses. Sitting with his knees
tucked under his chin, ash tumbling from his cigarette, he was
concentrating for a long time on the corner of the table. Now he has
given up and is lying sprawled out on the carpet.

The rest of us dance. As the evening continues, the stamped feet and
flowing arms of Tibetan dances slide into the Chinese four step, the
jiggle of disco and then back again into the slow rhythms of Tibet.
Others follow Nyima, and when the girls start dropping too we
decide it is time to give up. With everyone bundled in the back of the
truck, we creep round the alleys of the old town, dropping fuddled
figures at huge wooden doorways, leaving them to rouse their
gatemen.

"Chang né gun dukgé?" Are you *chang* sick?

The next morning began gently as almost all of us were. Dawa
Tsering arrived with another crate of beer and more *chang* strapped to

---

★To use honorific Tibetan, you need to learn a new set of terms. Take the word
"hand" for example. If you are referring to your own hand, you use the word *"lakpa"*
but someone else's hand, unless he is a social inferior, is always *"cha"*. Every Tibetan
word has its equivalent honorific term.

the back of his work-unit's motor-bike, but until late in the afternoon it was a reminder of *chang* sickness and lay ignored under the tree.

The day followed yesterday's indolent pattern; my only exertion was a brief wander round the park and palaces with Dawa and Deyang who had joined our picnic.

In one room of the Fourteenth Dalai Lama's palace, the guide lifted the corner of a *thangka* with conspiratorial glee to show me a Union Jack, painted into the mural behind. Why the secrecy, I wondered as we passed a trilbyed Hugh Richardson in another mural and, in the bathroom, a Shanks bath and wash-basin. These, far from being concealed, were filled with the coins and notes of pilgrims.

In the Eighth Dalai Lama's palace a silvery light filtered through the windows, warming the colours of the brocade hangings. Everything here was woven with legend. The stuffed tiger, who stared with decaying eyes from a shed outside, had been picked up by the tail at the beginning of the century and hurled to the ground by one of the Dalai Lama's Herculean guards. The garden of the Chensek palace is filled with the scent of antique roses: ordered from London by the Thirteenth Dalai Lama. Further on, two Austin Sevens, now abandoned and rusting in the undergrowth, were once carried by yak over the Himalaya. But as we wandered on through the picnics, Dawa weaved ghosts of a more recent past.

He was eight and Deyang not yet born when the Dalai Lama left Tibet from the Norbulingka on 12th March 1959. For four days the family barricaded themselves inside their house. He lay in bed listening to the boom of mortar fire, terrified at how angry the gods must be. Over 100,000 Tibetans had surrounded the Norbulingka to protect the Dalai Lama from what they thought was an attempt to kidnap him. He had been invited to a cultural performance at the Chinese army camp. But he had been told to come without his usual contingent of soldiers. Convinced that this was a trap, the Tibetans refused to allow anyone in or out of the Norbulingka. One Tibetan official, Phakpala Kenchung, whom they considered a collaborator, was stoned to death. On the night of the twelfth, however, the Dalai Lama, disguised as a layman, slipped through the crowds to begin his flight to India. The Norbulingka was shelled after he left, and in the fighting that followed, tens of thousands of people died. Eighty-seven thousand were "wiped out" before October the following year, according to Chinese documents.

Older Tibetans had talked to me about the Lhasa Uprising, and I'd read accounts of it published abroad. For Dawa, it was not a sequence

of events but a few searing fragments from his childhood memory: the
tunnel that they had to dig through their neighbours' houses to reach
the well, white *katags*, hanging from doorways, and tied to people's
buckets when they finally dared go out for water.

"I didn't understand at the time," Dawa said, "but I knew that if
I went out without a *katag* I would be shot.

"Then there were the bodies. One day I had to go to the Norbulingka with my mother and I saw them. Here, where these people are
picnicking: piles and piles of bodies reaching up to the branches of the
trees. Burning." He stopped and looked at me. "P.L.A. men were
pouring petrol over them and setting light to their hair."

"Don't talk about it." Deyang tried to change the subject by
pointing out marquees belonging to the different work-units. But
Dawa went on, lost in nightmares that still recurred.

"The Cultural Revolution was bad too. During the Campaign
Against Four Olds, we had to go round people's houses and seize their
Buddhas, their *thangkas*, their jewellery: anything that was valuable.
I was always too shy. When they told me that they didn't have
anything, I believed them. Everyone else would return to our Red
Guard headquarters with their carts full, and I would be criticised for
having nothing. It was the same when we were sent round the
Barkhor to cut off people's plaits."

"Cut off their plaits?"

"Plaits were reactionary during the Cultural Revolution," Deyang
explained.

"Other Red Guards would take people by the head and just cut their
hair with a knife. I couldn't do it. When they complained, I let them
go."

On the third day of our picnic, the *Sho dun* itself began. For several
weeks, the monks had stayed in their monasteries to avoid treading on
and killing the young insects of summer. *Sho dun* celebrated the end of
this period of retreat. With its origins in the sixteenth century when
the monks would come down to be fêted by the lay people at a banquet
of yoghurt, it was later combined with the summer operas, and the
banquet gave way to Tibetan theatricals.

On our way to the outer grounds of the Norbulingka with Tsewang
and Yangzom, we pass a glade where large tents stand, veiled from
view by their high sides and from the sun by floating canopies. One of
them is filled with the green uniforms of army officials, picnicking
with their families. In the far corner a drinking game is taking place.

Children are hopping through the drinkers trying to keep a shuttle-
cock in the air with their heels. In another tent, the faces ranged
formally around the walls suggest that the cadre, talking from behind
a microphone and a row of lidded mugs, is going on too long. Even
the buttoned figures on the dais beside him look as though they'd
rather be elsewhere.

Amid this officialdom, the *Lhamo*, the operas, are taking place.
They last all day with clashing cymbals, bells and drums; piercing
recitatives punctuating more melodious choruses; hooded villains,
leaping devils, swirling girls with long silk sleeves. In the past dancers
came from all over Tibet, but today there is only the state-run Lhasa
Singing and Dancing Troupe. Holiday Inn's Tibetan-style marquee
has a prime view next to the leaders of the T.A.R. and is charging its
guests for a day at the *Sho dun*. On the other three sides of the open
stage, Tibetan spectators sit cross-legged in the dust, peering through
the legs of a Chinese film crew. Rapt by the continuous flow of scenes,
they cheer and clap the comic interludes. No one I ask has any idea of
the story.

By the time we return to our own picnic, the window ledges of the
Thirteenth Dalai Lama's palace are casting diamonds of shadow across
its white walls. The wind has got up and a sudden squall sends clouds
of dust through the picnics. The awnings balloon upwards, straining
at their ropes, ready to lift the whole park and its picnickers into the
air.

"Chaba pub drok chigi." It's going to rain, people shout at each other
through the wind. Watching the sun sink deep into a quilt of cloud,
Yangzom breaks into rhyme:

> *Didi coo coo*
> *Mama tsasong*
> *Chaba pubgi*
> *Netche dunshia.*

"What does that mean?"

"Can't you hear? The doves are cooing. They are saying that we
must bring in our quilts because it's going to rain."

All I can hear is flapping canvas and voices shouting. Yangzom
laughs. "It's an old saying we have that doves coo to warn us of rain,
but you don't hear them any more." Then the rain arrives. All around
us, the dust erupts in small explosions as the first steely drops hit the
ground. Tsewang and Yangzom make a dash for the shelter of our

canopy. Rosemary and I walk, filling our lungs, savouring the feast of rain smells that are suddenly let loose.

Despite the storms, the picnic lasts late into the night again. A group of us return home along the river with Rosemary wreathed in *katags* and good wishes for her dawn departure. Sharing her nostalgia, we watch the moon rise through mountains of clouds. In the darkness between them hang stars like the last drops of rain.

Chapter 27

DEATH OF A MYSTIC

"Why has everyone sprinkled patterns of *tsampa* across their door-ways?" I asked Deyang one day in autumn as we were making our way from the University to the Jokhang.

"To stop the spirit entering their houses when the body passes."

"Whose body? Has someone died?"

"Bola has died. Didn't you know?"

"But he seemed incredibly healthy when I met him last week."

"He was an old man." She smiled. You are old in Tibet at forty-five.

I had only met him once. Bola, old man, no one called him by his real name. He was a massive, patriarchal figure with a thatch of white hair. He asked who I was and Deyang introduced me as *inji pomo* – the English girl. But for some reason, I was awed by him and couldn't think of anything to say. I remember asking how long he had been in Lhasa and noticing his slender monk-like hands as he used his fingers as an abacus, counting off the joints with the tip of his thumb as he said three years. I didn't know who he was then; only afterwards, Deyang told me that he was one of the few surviving *jomkern*, the bards of the Gesar epic.

I had heard a lot about Gesar, the legendary Tibetan King of Ling. Western writers suggest that his name might be derived from Caesar and that he was probably a historical figure whose actual life has disappeared beneath accretions of miracle and legend. Tibetans talked of him as the defender of the faith, and champion of justice. Many people, Deyang said, recite his songs as a kind of protective talisman and believe the prophecy that Gesar's return will herald a new era, in which Tibet will be a free land with a just ruler.

But there are many different versions of the epic. The Mongolians believe that Gesar was a Mongol, Khampas believe he came from Kham, and people in Xinjiang believe that he was from there. Although some of the songs have been written down, the epic has always been transmitted orally and it can take weeks to relate in full. According to Deyang, Bola didn't know the whole history. He had nevertheless, a huge repertoire of songs celebrating the exploits of this legendary warrior-king who was sent into the world by Padmasambhava to rid Ling of the powers of evil. From the time Gesar is born out of his mother's head, not as a baby but as an articulate child, he is invested with supernatural powers. Moments after his birth, giant birds with metal beaks swoop down out of the sky and die beneath his tiny arrow. The king's steward is determined to kill him and has employed the magic powers of Ratna the hermit. But Ratna is no match for Gesar. In a battle of magic, Ratna is entombed in his cave by a *torma*, a piece of offering cake, which turns into a boulder as the child throws it at the magician. All attempts on his life fail, and so Gesar is banished from the realm. But eventually, after years in exile, his luck turns. He falls in love with a beautiful girl and becomes King of Ling by winning a horse race on his magic horse. Padmasambhava allows him a few years to rule in Ling and then begin countless crusades in which Gesar, equipped with Padmasambhava's own magic quiver, hat and whip, goes into battle with the forces of evil.

The tales are filled with fantasy but there is no question of them being fiction. As Deyang talked about Bola, I remembered a horseman I had met in Kongpo who showed me a stone column on which was marked Gesar's height. The child was taller than a man. Was this tall by foreign standards, the horseman wanted to know. For him, there was no doubt that Gesar was real.

But the miracles extended beyond the epic. I had been reading Alexandra David-Neel, a Buddhist traveller in Tibet in the Twenties. She wrote somewhat sceptically of the *jomkern* and how they often claimed to be inspired directly by Gesar. As I sat under the trees and listened to Deyang, I watched Bola talking with colleagues about cadres in the University. He looked serious and academic. Deyang was telling me how, after falling into a death-like trance at the age of nine, Bola began to sing the Gesar songs. He was found after a week, on the side of a mountain, and the lama who was called told his parents that they had a special child, of whom they should take great care. Despite this, however, the villagers thought he was a fraud and it wasn't until an itinerant *jomkern* arrived years later, singing songs that were almost identical to Bola's, that he was recognised as being a real *jomkern*.

Bola seemed at ease with life in Lhasa, but it was hard to tell. He had come from Kongpo in 1983 when liberalisation brought the official fostering of Tibetan culture. He was described as a "national treasure".

A Tibetologist had been sent to his village to carry out research and return with him to the University. But he was there for weeks before Bola would admit to being a *jomkern* and longer before he could be convinced that he wouldn't be punished if he related the stories. He pretended, at first, that he couldn't remember anything. He was afraid of being tricked into revealing his knowledge and then being punished as he had during the Cultural Revolution.

Bola refused to come to Lhasa. He told his family that he was about to die and didn't want to leave his village. The researcher remained for a while, making recordings of the epic, and then Bola unexpectedly changed his mind. He had had a dream in which Gesar told him that he should go as there were many people in Lhasa who wished to hear the history.

"But why did he die so suddenly?" I asked Deyang as we crossed the Jokhang square. We were on our way to wash in the river. It was the week of *Karma Derba* when the stars invested the waters of the Tsangbo with powers to purify the spirit and the body.

"He wasn't ill, was he?"

"Not at all. Before he died, he had been singing: songs more beautiful than his daughter had ever heard before. All morning he sang. Then he said he would rest for a while, and as he lay down he died."

Outside the Jokhang, Bola's relatives were distributing tea and *tsampa* to beggars. Most of it had been taken to the family by neighbours with offerings of *katags*, and money to help pay for the funeral. Like other acts of piety this would help Bola's soul through *bardo* – the period between death and rebirth. It would also prevent the soul from returning to harm the family.

"Did he die on an auspicious day?" I asked, remembering that when the man over the wall from us had died, not only his family but many of the neighbours gave food to the beggars and visited monasteries to protect themselves. It was a Saturday and the 29th of the month which made it doubly inauspicious.

"I don't know. But when his daughter went to the astrologer to find an auspicious day for the funeral, something very interesting happened." Deyang seemed excited. "He said that her father had died three years ago."

I looked at her, not understanding.

"Don't you remember?" she said, searching my blank expression impatiently.

"Remember what?"

"Bola had said that he was about to die before he came to Lhasa. Three years ago!"

We crossed on to *Kuma Lingka*, the Robber island, with the bridge bouncing and swaying beneath our feet. The sun struck low over the valley, catching the festoons of prayer-flags strung across the river, and casting a luminous halo around the cows on an island down-stream. For a week the shallows of the Tsangbo had been fringed with naked figures. Even Lhasa girls, unexpectedly abandoning inhibition, wavered in groups along the bank, occasionally submitting to its sanctified waters. But this was the last night of Karma Derba. Tomorrow the river, as cold and sparkling as it had been today, would no longer have the power to cure sickness or cleanse the soul. We sat down to wait for the stars.

Lhamo appeared.

"Gen Catriona la! Gen Deyang la!" she shouted, coming towards us across the sand. She had been looking for us everywhere.

"I'm leaving tomorrow!"

"Leaving?" Deyang looked up in surprise.

Lhamo lowered her voice.

"I've got a lift to the border."

"You got your passport?"

"No." She looked defiant. "But I'm going anyway."

She had known that the process of getting a passport would take a long time, but she had thought that she'd get it eventually. She could prove that she was visiting relatives abroad and she had her family in Kongpo to guarantee her return. Furthermore, the friends with whom she had planned to travel, had got their passports. They had already left, to visit relatives and to make a pilgrimage to the Dalai Lama in Dharamsala.

"No, it looks as though I won't get it now." She glared at the river.

"Will you stay in India?" I asked.

"I'm not returning to work for the Chinese, that's for certain."

She began to talk loudly, defiantly, as if she wanted people to hear her anger. A couple of soldiers idled past and stopped just beyond us. One of them drew a cigarette from his trouser pocket and then a box of matches. His fingers felt for the end and slowly, indolently, he lit up. He was watching a group of people undressing further down the bank.

"Look at them!" Lhamo said loudly in Tibetan. Deyang seemed embarrassed but, as the soldiers continued to stare, Lhamo was ready to confront them. Then the bathers noticed that they were being watched, and a man, standing up out of the water, started shaking his fist. The soldiers laughed and sauntered on.

"Tomorrow I'm leaving," she repeated, staring hard at the backs of the departing soldiers. "Even without a passport." It was as if she was seeking confirmation in us of her own resolve.

"Was it because of your friend that they refused your application?" I asked, remembering her fears of a few weeks before. We had been drinking tea in my room one evening when she said that she had something very important to tell me, something that she had been considering telling me for a long time. A close friend of hers was in prison, she said. Late into the night, she talked about this man who had been caught pasting a pro-independence poster on a wall outside the Jokhang. He was detained and subsequently sentenced to five years' imprisonment. Lhamo said then that she thought it might affect her chances of getting a passport.

"It could have something to do with him. They don't give you a reason." Her voice sounded strained and I wondered whether I should have spoken in front of Deyang. But then she continued – Deyang knew about him already.

"Did I tell you that his family was allowed to visit him this week? It's the first time they've seen him since he was arrested."

"His father must be pleased." Suddenly, the man's face came before my mind's eyes. I had only met his father once – during a ceremony at Drepung monastery. He was alone and so Lhamo invited him to share our picnic. Between them, there was a joke which Rosemary and I didn't understand, and throughout the meal he kept breaking into loud rumbling laughter. Afterwards I was on the point of asking him to explain the ceremony when, quite suddenly, he got up and fled. He had noticed, standing behind us, the man who had arrested his son. The family was under surveillance. He had been seen talking to foreigners, he told Lhamo later, and was terrified.

Deyang seemed to have lost her good-humour since Lhamo's arrival. She had hardly joined in the conversation and was laying out the picnic with unnecessary concentration. I suspected that she was worried about Lhamo. I remembered her telling me, once before, that she didn't think Lhamo was aware of the difficulties involved in getting out without a passport. Security along the border was relatively lax at this time; increasing numbers were crossing the mountains

into Nepal. But Deyang had heard stories of people losing their way in
the dark and walking round in a circle, and of others being caught by
the border controls.

"I think we should wash," she said, catching me shivering, and
trying, very obviously, to change the subject. "Catriona la will be cold
soon – and the stars are almost out."

However beneficial and sacred the water may be, I had to admit that
I was beginning to think I might prefer to remain impure. A gritty
autumnal wind had risen, whipping the prayer-flags against the iron
cords of the bridge; many of the other bathers, I noticed, had washed
without the stars and gone home.

"It was much colder today," Deyang agreed, turning to Lhamo;
I sensed that she was weakening.

But Lhamo was already half-undressed.

"Come on, the water is warmer when it is cold outside." She took
her bar of soap and disappeared down the bank.

After a while, we followed her down. Weakly, Deyang and
I decided that washing our feet and faces would be beneficial enough.
Lhamo kept up a constant banter from the water.

"You won't pacify the water spirits that way!" She scoffed as
Deyang threw the remains of our picnic into the river.

Catching her irreverence, I suggested that we might be feeding an
ancestor of hers. Deyang had been telling me earlier how expensive it
was to have the "sky burial" – as the Chinese described the traditional
ritual of feeding the corpse to the eagles – and how poor people often
buried their dead in the river.

"Well it's better than burying your ancestors under the ground as
you do." She grimaced, splashing out of the river. "Ugh, I'd hate that.
It's so dirty. Slowly, slowly, your body goes bad. And just think of all
those other lives you waste."

"What do you mean? What lives?"

"All those worms who eat your body – well, when they've finished
you, what happens? They starve!" She giggled and looked at Deyang.
"No, I'd rather be fed to the birds; at least there's nothing left. It's
clean."

I didn't think I could develop non-attachment enough to be able to
watch my relative's body being cut up. But Deyang pointed out that
the relatives didn't usually take the body to the burial rock.

"Anyway, they don't go to watch, they go to give tea to the *dopden*
who cut up the bodies. It is important to treat the *dopden* well, so that
they cut the body cleanly and make sure that every piece is eaten by the

birds." The ritual feeding of the body to the eagles was, in a way, the ultimate offering.

Bola was not taken to the rock beyond Sera where the corpses are cut up at dawn. With the respect usually only accorded to lamas, his body was cremated.

"Friends took the body to Pabonka monastery," Deyang explained, as we made our way home. "I met them at a tea shop where they had stopped for a while to ensure that the spirit didn't follow them home. They won't go back to the family today lest the spirit return there. But for the next seven weeks – the period that the body remains in *Bardo* – they will eat and drink with his family on the day of the week that he died."

As we walked back along the white river path through the sharp star-made shadows, Deyang added the finale to Bola's life. Before he died, Bola had told his daughter that his skull and little finger should not be burned, but kept in their house. She couldn't bear to keep his finger but the skull was important. It was the ultimate proof of his genuineness, for the skull of a real *jomkern* bears the imprint of Gesar's horse's hoof.

As I listened to Deyang, I felt, for the first time, that I was being confronted by her world. Before, the mysteries of Bola's life had rested comfortably in the past. But Deyang's friends had seen his skull with the imprint of the hoof. She, my mentor in so many things, was certain about it. To doubt her conviction seemed arrogant, ignorant even. It was perhaps best to think no further but explain it as the world is explained in the Buddhist text the *Prajna Paramita*.

> As forms created by a mirage or by clouds
> in the sky, as images seen in a dream, thus
> must all things be regarded.

Chapter 28

A LAST MONASTERY

Lhamo's departure heralded a spate of departures. Unable to prolong his leave in Lhasa any longer, Deyang's brother, Dawa, returned to Ngari. Our leader had been sent off to Central China and without him, my contract wasn't renewed.

Autumn passed in a fleeting blaze of gold. For a while the last leaves clung to the trees like drowning men, buffeted by waves of wind. Then the high dry winter days returned the Lhasa valley to its stark beauty, and cold.

With only a few days before my departure, I made promises to myself and my students that I would return in time for Losar next year. I was certain I would, but inside me something sneered, something warned me that I had been certain before. Deyang's mother prayed for my journey and told me to leave my room as if I had just gone out for a moment: the floor unswept and the door ajar. The week before, when a pair of shoes I had taken to be mended fell out of my bag, she assured me that I *would* come back. A lost pair of shoes, she said, had been a sign of their owner's return, since the eighth century when Padmasambhava left his, after the great debate at Samye between Indian and Chinese Buddhism.

I found myself retaining images and sounds and smells, and even the voices of friends, in a kind of self-indulgent anticipation of nostalgia. Experiences regained the sharpness that they had had when I arrived. Now it was not novelty but imminent loss which made them vivid. In class, I timed written exercises to coincide with the sun's appearance above Bumphari, and watched its light burning slowly down the pinnacles of the Jokhang.

The last morning arrived. Students and friends woke me before dawn with *katags* of farewell and a last extravagant picnic on the tarmac of the bus station. Crouching in the darkness we ate with the other parties waving relatives off on pilgrimage to India.

And then the bus left. I was alone. The people around me were full of excitement; they were setting out on a journey.

I was returning home.

I was leaving a home. A home which had vanished as I walked out of the door, which had vanished again as I left my friends. My mind refused to go. For five days I travelled to London through Kathmandu and Karachi. My mind travelled backwards, and forwards. It would return as far as the eve of my departure – and then stop.

The sun fills the shadows with the colours of dawn as Tsering and I cross the Tsangpo with our bicycles in the yak-skin coracle. On the opposite bank, a group of men sit brewing tea among sacks of dung and juniper twigs. They are on their way to the market in Lhasa, having walked all night from their village.

"You'll have difficulty with those," one of them says eyeing our bicycles.

He is right. The track strikes out across the flat valley floor and then curls round the base of the mountain range. Since I was last here the winds of autumn have hidden long stretches of it beneath drifts of sand. We abandon our bicycles eventually and, turning east, begin to climb into the mountains.

Tsering is in a cheerful mood. We chat about his monastery. A statue has been recovered from China by the Religious Affairs Office and he is involved in reciting prayers to sanctify it. Only momentarily, when he tells me about some *thangkas* that have been taken for an exhibition in Peking, does anger break through.

"They have no idea how to take care of them." He stops on the path and glares at me. "Several of them were returned broken last time."

But he seems not to want to dwell on gloomy thoughts. The valley rises steeply into the mountains which have been quilted with snow overnight. Further up the track, houses cling round the base of a rocky pyramid. The ruined monastery rises into a cradle of peaks.

We stop to rest at the village. Removing the layers of clothing which protected us from the frozen dawn, we squat in silence. Across the road, a young woman kneads heaps of straw and yak dung, shaping it into round patties and pressing them on to the white wall behind her with decorative thumb-patterns. From where we crouch, the syllables of her mantra *Om mani padme hum* are blurred to a soft drone.

Tsering asks if we could leave my bags while we go up to the monastery and she invites us into her house. I notice with surprise the elaborate dressers and the large tape-recorder standing on top.

"Yes, life is good now," she smiles. "We get a good profit selling our things in Lhasa." Pouring a cauldron of tea into the long wooden churn, she works the plunger making a soft frothing sound.

"Did you meet my husband?" She turns to Tsering.

"Where?"

"On the road to Lhasa; he left last night."

"The men on the bank of the river?" I suggest.

"Was he selling dung?"

"That was him."

Her husband acts as an agent for the whole village. Only he, and the other men with him, have the much sought-after permits to trade in the free market. They are paid a commission by the other villagers to sell their agricultural surplus. After two cups of tea I am happy to go on talking, but Tsering wants to get to the monastery.

"There is a monk there now," the woman says, retying her tasselled plaits around her head. "He's from Drepung but we asked him to come and help us."

After another two hours we reach the monastery.

"Is the lama here?" Tsering asks two men standing by the path.

"He's in there," one of them says. "We'll take you if you like." They lead us through a jagged doorway.

The monastery was deserted when I came once before. Now there are men working among the ruins. We find the lama in a temple that has been redecorated. Tsering offers him a *katag*, prostrating himself three times at his feet. One of the men, Gyanseng, bustles around preparing food for us. When he addresses the lama he sucks back his breath, his tongue half-extended in the traditional gesture of respect. Ngodrup, the other man, is more relaxed and sits talking with us. It was he who had initiated the rebuilding of the monastery and asked the lama to come here.

"It was a famous monastery before," he says. "Monks from Lhasa used to come for the summer."

I sit listening, watching the faces around me, waiting for the next episode, willing him not to tell us. Today, selfishly, I want to ward off the past. My imminent departure has provoked a flood of confidences. Conversations last late into the night, leaving me feeling guilty, exhausted and desperately powerless to help. Even in the most humorous moments, bitterness and grief are not far below the surface. Parties, meals with friends, conversations even, so often return to the same sadness. But the progression is inevitable. Without emotion, he describes the destruction of the monastery, blowing occasionally on his tea and taking a sip beneath the butter. It was attacked in 1963, long before the Cultural Revolution.

"A Chinese leader came up from Chusul with a truck full of Tibetans and Chinese. They told us that the gods were only made of clay and the monks were cheating us. After a while, some of the people in our village believed them, and began attacking the monastery too."

As Ngodrup talks, I am reminded of friends in Lhasa who blame the peasants for destroying the monasteries. His voice carries their self-righteous indignation and from time to time he looks meaningfully at Gyanseng who trails behind us as we are taken to admire the restoration work, trying forlornly to be useful, to contribute to the conversation. He repeats Ngodrup's hopes that other monks will come here soon and tells me that the rebuilding has been entirely paid for by the villagers.

"I give all my money to the monastery," he says, his eyes searching Ngodrup's face for approval.

But Ngodrup is dismissive. "Most of the villagers do." And always have done, I remark to Tsering, realising, that in this sense, life in the villages has changed very little.

Eventually, when Gyanseng asks if I have a picture of the Dalai Lama, Ngodrup's irritation breaks through.

"He's not a Buddhist," he says, although Gyanseng takes the picture eagerly and places it on his head in reverence.

Tsering turns to me and smiles. "They are the people you see making continuous *korwa* of the Jokhang, turning their prayer-wheels, prostrating themselves desperately, trying to acquire merit to make up for their sins."

We come out of the monastery. Around us, the peaks are caught in the luminous moment of sunset. On a mound of straw beneath us, a small boy is lying on his back, staring up at the sky. There is silence. As he notices the lama, his eyes crease in a smile.

"We've got rice tonight, Gusho la," he calls. "Are you coming?"

EPILOGUE

"Write about us." When I left Tibet the friends who had suggested I wrote had added, "Write about the culture, don't drop into politics."

For months I hesitated on the brink of Chapter One, fearful of engaging in something that could endanger people. It was impossible not to be political. Simply to describe them as Tibetans and Chinese instead of Tibetans and Hans was subversive. I knew I would have to disguise the identities of some people to prevent their being investigated by the Public Security. I discarded incidents, jumbled characters. I waged a running battle with the censor inside my head.

In the autumn of 1987 I began writing about our arrival in Tibet: the night with the traders on the border, the Potala, our walks through the back streets of the old town. I was buried in Tibet's romantic image.

But on 1st October, the world was hit by another image of Tibet. I opened the newspaper and found in its pages screaming faces, wounded bodies, monks with fists raised in defiance. This was an image of Tibet the world hadn't seen before.

I read every newspaper; all of them carried the same pictures. There was the face of a monk whom I recognised from the Jokhang. There was a view of burning jeeps with two boy monks and a woman, her plaits dangling loose down her back, hurling rocks at the police station. There was a man carrying a wounded child. All the reports seemed confused.

Only later, when friends of mine returned to England, did it become clearer to me. In September 1987 the Dalai Lama had proposed in Washington that Tibet should be turned into a Zone of Peace. The authorities in Lhasa responded by mounting a publicity campaign against him. On 27th September a group of monks from Drepung monastery walked up to the Tibetan Government offices in Lhasa, in protest. They chanted "Tibet wants independence!" and waved the banned Snow Lion flag. When they drew level with the Potala they were arrested *en masse*.

The demonstration that followed on 1st October was partly in

protest at the arrest of these monks. It began with a circumambulation
of the Jokhang by a group of lay people and monks from Sera who
were immediately arrested. It ended with crowds setting fire to the
police station where the protesters were being held, the police firing at
them with automatic weapons.

I wanted to find out what had happened to our friends, but I didn't
dare write to Tibet. In the last three years I have only had news of two
people:

Tsering's name appeared on a list of detainees which reached
Amnesty in 1988. According to a friend of his who wrote to me from
India, he had been arrested for demonstrating outside the Jokhang. He
had been released by that time, but he hadn't been able to return to his
monastery. Guards in the prison had broken both his legs.

I heard from someone else that Lhamo had returned to Tibet from
India. She had wanted to join the demonstrations. In the summer of
1989 I saw her name on a list of detainees.

Over the last three years protest has spread upwards through
Tibetan society and outwards across Tibet. During this time I was
writing about experiences of a more relaxed era, when the oppression
now visible to the world was hidden beneath a quilt of normality. On
the surface, the lives of those around us were unremarkable: we
worked, we went for picnics, we visited monasteries. When people
talked about experiences of imprisonment and torture, they made
them seem distant. They got on with their lives, and that, for the most
part, is what we saw.

But while I was writing, reports of widespread police brutality in
Tibet began to emerge. Knitting and novels were no longer pastimes
of Political Study as they had often been when we were in Lhasa.
People were being arrested in meetings for refusing to declare their
belief in the unity of the Motherland. Soldiers armed with automatic
weapons were patrolling in front of monastery gates.

I began writing about Monlam, the ceremonies in the Jokhang, the
crowds massed in prayer before the temple. But the I.T.N. news one
evening showed a police video of the 1988 Monlam which had been
leaked from Lhasa. Five soldiers were beating a man on the ground in
turn with long clubs. The man escaped, and the soldiers grabbed him
again. Inside the Jokhang a monk was being pushed off the balcony;
other monks were attacking a soldier. At the end the monks were herded
out to army trucks, covered in blood. There were soldiers looking on,
smiling.

As I was describing how police controlled crowds with the *dian ban*, the electric baton, Amnesty International was getting reports of a different use of the instrument: prison guards were putting them into the mouths and genitals of detainees to force confessions.

In March 1989 people were saying that the protesters themselves were more aggressive. I began to fear for Chinese friends in Lhasa. Until this time reports had underlined the peaceful nature of the demonstrations. Most began with a group of monks or nuns, chanting slogans and making a circumambulation of the Jokhang. They threw stones at heavily armed security police and overturned a few police vehicles. But in March 1989 pictures appeared of protesters stoning a Chinese cyclist, and Chinese shops burning beyond the Banak Shol Hotel. China's Minister of Public Security imposed martial law.

There seemed to be a relentless parallel between the progress of my book and the events that were unfolding in Tibet. By the time I was writing about the summer classes for Yi Zhong, six pupils from the school had been arrested. They were caught making Tibetan flags and pasting up independence posters. One had been sent to a detention centre for re-education through labour. The others are still awaiting trial, as is a teacher from the cement factory school who wrote reactionary songs on the blackboard.

"Things have calmed down in Tibet, haven't they?" someone said to me recently. I had just been reading new reports of detentions without trial and summary executions. Not calmed down but clamped down: it made me realise how similar the two could appear, even to people who go to Lhasa.

Now the civil administration is again welcoming Westerners. But, restricted to groups of no fewer than three, and shepherded by guides, people are even more in danger of seeing the Tibet that the authorities want them to see. In October last year a delegation of British politicians spent three days in Lhasa; they said that the atmosphere in the town was "relaxed". Only hours before there had been a demonstration, "a protest march of a thousand separatists" as the *Tibet Daily* reported, which won a medal for the artillery officer who broke it up.

All too often we find what we go to find, a minority thriving under the patronage of China, a land of beggarly Tibetans and opulent Chinese . . . all too often we only find ourselves. Since the first climbers pitted their strength against Everest, Tibet has been a remote playground for the Western imagination. Even now, with people in Lhasa living under martial law, the west can still dream up adventures for Tibet. A few Englishmen recently flew to Lhasa and dined with Tibet's Communist Party leaders. They were proposing a motor rally in Paris–Dakar style. Lhasa to Ngari, round the sacred mountain of Kailash.

Tibet has been exposed to the world in the last two years, but with a disproportionate amount of coverage given to the minimal mishaps and daring of Westerners, the picture of Tibet we see now is still that of a Westerners' Tibet. The demonstrations of 1987 are referred to as the first demonstrations, and are often described as being inspired by contact with tourists. It is true that they were the largest to have taken place for several years. But to Tibetans they were not extraordinary. They fall into a pattern of resistance that has existed in Tibet since the arrival of the Chinese. The Sixties saw the armed resistance of the C.I.A.-trained Khampa guerrillas, and the independence struggles rumbling beneath the Cultural Revolution. By the beginning of the Eighties people were rebuilding monasteries and celebrating religious festivals illegally. People shouted independence slogans in crowds massed in welcome for the Dalai Lama's brother. A man planted a home-made bomb outside the new Telecommunications building in 1985, to mark the twentieth anniversary of the Tibetan Autonomous Region. If the latest series of demonstrations were a first, it was not that they were inspired by the west: it was the first time that the west had witnessed them.

Tibet is still the victim of myths created by the outside world. It has taken thirty years for the Dalai Lama's role to be recognised in the West, but in December 1989 the Nobel Committee awarded him their Peace Prize, describing him as the "political and religous leader of the Tibetan people". It was a watershed. Although some governments still keep their eyes fixed on China, the Dalai Lama is now being honoured by the new democrats of Europe.

But it is not from the sphere of international politics that change will come. It is from within the Great Wall of China, and, there too, Tibet is still, for the moment, the victim of prejudice. The spectre of Han chauvinism cannot disappear overnight. But the Chinese Communist Party's credibility has been crushed on Tiananmen Square. And the myth of the barbarian inhabitants of Tibet, reinforced for so long by the Party, is showing signs that it too may be overtaken by reality.

INDEX